STRANGER IN THE MIRROR

Stranger in the Mirror

THE SCIENTIFIC SEARCH

FOR THE SELF

ROBERT V. LEVINE

Princeton University Press
Princeton and Oxford

Published by Princeton University Press,
41 William Street, Princeton, New Jersey 08540
In the United Kingdom: Princeton University Press,
6 Oxford Street, Woodstock, Oxfordshire OX20 1TR

press.princeton.edu

Jacket art: Saul Steinberg, *Untitled*, 1948. Ink on paper, 14 1/4 x 11 1/4 in. Beinecke Rare Book
and Manuscript Library, Yale University. © The Saul Steinberg Foundation/Artists Rights Society
(ARS), New York

Library of Congress Cataloging-in-Publication Data

Names: Levine, Robert, 1945- author.
Title: Stranger in the mirror : the scientific search for the self / Robert V. Levine.
Description: Princeton : Princeton University Press, 2016. | Includes bibliographical references
and index.
Identifiers: LCCN 2015039794 | ISBN 9780691167916 (hardback)
Subjects: LCSH: Self. | Personality. | Identity (Psychology) | BISAC: PSYCHOLOGY /
Cognitive Psychology. | PSYCHOLOGY / Neuropsychology. | PSYCHOLOGY / General. |
PSYCHOLOGY / Personality.
Classification: LCC BF697 .L41255 2016 | DDC 155.2—dc23 LC record available at http://lccn
.loc.gov/2015039794

British Library Cataloging-in-Publication Data is available

This book has been composed in Adobe Caslon Pro and Futura Std

Printed on acid-free paper. ∞

Printed in the United States of America

10 9 8 7 6 5 4 3 2 1

For Trudi, Andy, and Zach

Contents

Acknowledgments

This has been a long and circuitous project that has taken me to corners I didn't know existed. I have many people to thank for guiding, teaching, prodding, encouraging, and opening my eyes along the way.

I begin with my colleagues at California State University, Fresno where I have had the good fortune to work in an unusually energizing academic subculture inhabited by a group of bright, curious, and enthusiastic scholars who not only talk to each other (Imagine that!) but take an active interest in each other's ideas and work. I am particularly grateful in this regard for the input of my intellectual buddies Tom Breen, Connie Jones, Spee Kosloff, Lorin Lachs, Hong Ni, Karl Oswald, Aroldo Rodrigues, Martin Shapiro, and Criss Wilhite. I have also been fortunate to have received research assistance and inspiration from a number of impressive students, including Arantes Armendariz, Anne Marie Clayton, Michelle Fabros, Gary Hagy, Deanna Halliday, Emily Hentschke, and Ruthie Lichtenstein.

I am indebted to the scholars who patiently sat through interviews and/or instructed me in their areas of expertise, notably: Paul Crosbie and Shirley Kovacs on the subject of parasites; Jason Bush on epigenetics; Kalmon Post on the brain; Buzz Hays from SONY on the art of video animation; Paula Durette on computer animation; Charles Fernyhough on hearing voices; Joyce Kamanitz on the double experience; Nancy Segal on twins; Jerry Coyne about *his* parasite; Annan Paterson on the social psychology of acting; Chris Sorensen and Maxine Olsen on the artist's way of seeing; Jack McDermott on reading and cognition; Richard Bertken on all things scientific; Neil Altman and Larry Siegel for our perpetual discussions about what it's all about; and my colleagues who gathered data in their respective countries for the cross-cultural studies scattered throughout the book: Suguru Sato of Doshisha University in Kyoto, Jyoti Verma at Patna University in India, Virginia O'Leary at Tribhuvan University in Kathmandu, Dasho Karma Ura and Karma Wangdi of the Centre for Bhutan Studies in Bhutan, Fabio Iglesias at

Universidade Federal de Brasilia in Brazil, Vladiney Gouveia at Universidade Federal de Paraíba in Brazil, Luiz Menna-Barreto of the Universidade de São Paulo in Brazil, Xing Zhanjun at Shangdong University in China and, closer to home, Becky Slaton at California State University, Fresno. To the staff of *Radiolab* (with a special shoutout to to producer extraordinaire Tim Howard) for their many provocative leads, most notably the Jerry Coyne and Karen Keegan stories. A special thanks to Mike McGarvin, not only for taking the time to recount his path to Poverello House but for all he does for so many otherwise forgotten souls in the Fresno community. My appreciation goes also to Mirko Zardini and the Canadian Centre for Architecture and to Veronica Strang and the Institute of Advanced Study at Durham University in the United Kingdom for providing me with extended fellowship/residencies that were rich with resources, interpersonal stimulation, and time to focus at early stages of this project; and to the many people at California State University, Fresno who have done so much for me throughout.

A big "thanks, again" to Kris Dahl, my agent at ICM. My great appreciation to Barbara Price and Connie Jones for their spot-on comments on an earlier draft; and to copy editor Beth Gianfagna, whose corrections and suggestions enhanced the final product on many levels. To my editor at Princeton University Press, Meagan Levinson, you turned these chapters into a book, for which I am more than grateful. You are terrific. My enormous thanks to Zach Levine, my unofficial editor every step of the way—and who, I'm also proud to say, is not only an upcoming star in social anthropology but my son.

STRANGER IN THE MIRROR

1
Introduction
Theseus's Paradox

I used to subscribe to *People*.
Then I switched to *Us*.
Now I just read *Self*.
—My friend Lenny

I love hearing people talk about their "*real*" selves. I still remember my first girlfriend, the seemingly perfect Natalie Duberman,[1] spooking me with the warning: "Be careful. You don't know the real me." Was she a werewolf? Could she be in the witness protection program? No, Natalie explained, "It's just that I'm not this nice with guys I like." She went on to detail how insecure, jealous, and passive-aggressive she had been with her first two boyfriends. I wondered what it would take for this new version of Natalie, the one I knew, to assume the mantle of "the real Natalie"? What if we were together for a year and, during that time, she never once became insecure, jealous, or passive-aggressive toward me? What if it stayed that way for ten years? How would she decide when the new Natalie qualified as the real one?[2]

Then there is my friend Lenny, who utilizes an infuriating twist on Natalie's warning. When Lenny acts badly—which, incidentally, is more or less constantly—he explains it away by saying, "Forgive me. I'm just not myself today." Really? Who are you, then? Because I'd like to know the name of the guy I'm thinking about punching in the nose right now. And when do you expect your real self to return? I'd like to lodge a complaint with him.

And then there is the issue of myself. How will I be remembered when I die? Will there be an iconic Bob Levine—the guy who looked the way I did at some flattering moment when I was twenty-one, or when I was forty-one—who somehow stood out in peoples' memories? Or will it be some kind of average me, as if all the people I've been were thrown into a blender? One thing I know for sure is that when my loved ones are asked what Bob Levine was truly like, no two accounts will be the same. For one thing, each person will have known me at different times in different situations. None of them, certainly, are going to lay out the only accurate description, which would be to detail every version of me that existed over my lifetime. No one would stick around to listen. I know I wouldn't.

We tell ourselves that we—our "selves"—are coherent entities. We imagine a thing that we can neatly label and point to as if it were a sculpture sitting on a shelf. But it is just a story we write—or, more precisely, are constantly rewriting. The image we have of the person we are is, in fact, a never-ending narrative in which we do our best to connect all the iterations of ourselves—bodies, minds, and personae—to who we feel like at the particular moment. We filter, distort, and weave the images together as best we can. When the story works, it enables us to think of ourselves as one person. It creates a sense of unity and continuity.

But good storytelling should not be confused with accurate reporting. The self is not a thing. We are, in fact, ultimately indescribable. Always. This holds true for every aspect of our self, from the nuts and bolts of our microbiology to the highest intellect of our minds. One moment my cells and organs work fine. A few hours of a stressful day later, I look and feel like Father Time. Twenty-five years after that I've turned into Father Time's father. The social and psychological transformations are no less incessant. There is the me-as-professor doling out advice to a student. The next moment I've become me-as-father getting angry at my son. Next thing you know I'm acting sweet and ingratiating toward an old friend. I sometimes feel as if I'm watching a movie, wondering which version of myself is going to appear on screen.

Here is another thought to consider: If you live long enough, almost every particle in your body will be replaced by a new one. The average life span of most human cells is estimated to be less than ten years. As old cells die, new ones are created.[3] We go through some types like used

Kleenex. The cells lining our stomach last five days. Red blood cells wear out about every 120 days. The entire human liver gets replaced every three hundred to five hundred days. Our skeleton is replaced about every ten years. It was once assumed that neurons were the single exemption to the replacement pattern, but we now know even this isn't always the case. For example, neurons in the hippocampus, where our memories of faces and places are recorded, die out after an average of twenty to thirty years; it is estimated that we grow 1,400 or so new hippocampal neurons each day. All told, about 98 percent of the atoms in the body are replaced annually. Only the DNA gets passed on.[4]

This turnover recalls the ancient paradox of Theseus's ship. According to the Greek legend, Theseus owned a ship that sailed for many years. The planks in the ship decayed over time and, as they did, each was meticulously replaced. Eventually, not a single original plank remained. The question: Did the Athenians still have the same ship that once belonged to Theseus? Later philosophers, notably Thomas Hobbes, added to the puzzle: What if you refurbished the old planks and used them to build a new ship? Which, if either, of the two ships—the old one with the new boards or the new one with the old boards—is the original vessel?[5]

Our bodies are a lot like the old Greek ship. Imagine that scientists found a way to transplant the cells of preserved bodies to living people. In order to prevent rejection, it would need to be a gradual procedure: 1 percent of your cells would be replaced each week for one hundred weeks. Let's say I got to acquire the cells from my childhood hero Jackie Robinson. What would the transformation look like? After the first few transplants I would no doubt still be Bob Levine. After one hundred weeks, however, my cells would be totally Jackie Robinson. But what about the time in the middle? At week fifty would you say I was half Bob Levine and half Jackie Robinson? And what in the world would that mean? That I would now be half as good a base runner as the former Brooklyn Dodger?

And isn't this what happens as we simply grow older? The body we have today and the one in our baby pictures have hardly a molecule in common. Is there a point where I would shift from one identity to the other? Because if there is, it means that one cell makes the difference between being me and not-me, which is absurd. Isn't it?[6]

***

This book is a travelogue of a sort. The chapters that follow take us on an excursion through the landscape that defines the very fabric of our lives: the slippery, quirky, brilliantly creative and often downright ridiculous entity that we call our self. My own field of specialty is social psychology, a discipline that casts a wide net. We focus on both the individual and his or her social surroundings and, most tellingly, on the give and take between the two—what our founding father Kurt Lewin called the "life space." It is a broad and dynamic approach that, I believe, provides a well-suited lens for our excursion. The pursuit of a better understanding of the self led me to work from an array of sciences, and the insights from these different perspectives turned out to be related to each other in ways I had not expected.

Prepare to cover a lot of ground. We will explore cutting-edge research, along with case studies and other insights, from experts across these many disciplines—from the so-called hard sciences like neurology and genetics to soft sciences like social psychology. We will also hear from artists and writers who target many of the same questions from a less systematic but often more provocative perspective. Some of the stops delve into facets of experience that are familiar to all of us. Others describe experiences that few of us will ever face. The latter are not intended as mere curiosities, although curious they certainly are. I believe these extremes offer perspectives we all can learn from. Pathologies enable description. Description enables possibilities.

Be warned up front that our journey never reaches a destination. It is, in this way, like trying to penetrate the essence of any complex geographic place. Think about a trip to, say, Paris. If you are a diligent tourist, you might walk the neighborhoods, ride the metro, visit a few museums, sit around some cafés, and the like. If you're lucky, you get to chat with some Parisians and perhaps some Algerian immigrants. Maybe you even get invited to stay with a friend for a few nights to experience "the real Paris." You explore as many facets of the city as you can, and the more you do, the more you learn. But you will not find a nugget at the center— just more facets. And if you visit a year later, everything has changed. Even the boundaries might have shifted. The real Paris? It might as well be the sign at the airport that reads "Bienvenue à Paris." Then again, the airport is twenty-five kilometers outside the city.

So it will be with our exploration of the self. We will travel inside and outside, from the micro to the macro, from seemingly tangible physical organs to the invisible forces of collective behavior, with plenty of stops in between. But don't expect a singular, take home photo (dare I say selfie?) waiting at the end of the road. Our very identity, the conduit for everything we experience, turns out to be more like a city or a country than a thing. There must, we are convinced, be a there there. After all, every person is different from every other, just as "there is no place like Paris." But capturing the totality of the person you call yourself, all at once, head on, is not to be. It is like trying to capture light or time. You can see reflections. But the whole is simply a story we weave to convince ourselves that the parts fit together. "Trying to define yourself is like trying to bite your own teeth," the philosopher Alan Watts once observed. To me, this doesn't diminish the pursuit but is what makes it such a compelling journey. It is, in fact, my intention to not only demonstrate that our prey is beyond capture but to do this from as many perspectives as I can.

Much of what follows may at first seem to be anecdotal and idiosyncratic. But I hope to show that, taken together, the research and observations to be covered point to four overarching themes. First, the boundaries of the self are vague and arbitrary. Looking outward, there is not so much a line between ourselves and the outside as there is an ever-changing gray zone. Looking inward, we are, literally, part us, part other.

Second, we are more like a republic than an individual, a collection of the many, diverse, and sometimes adversarial. "I am large, I contain multitudes," Walt Whitman famously wrote.[7] The great poet was right on more levels than he probably imagined. In the chapters that follow we see that the entities we call "my body," "my brain" and "my mind" are, in fact, conglomerates. We consist of the many from the bottom up—from the biology of our chromosomes and cells to the underpinnings of our thoughts and our actions. And, we will see, our various selves often seem to have minds of their own. They can be self-centered, pigheaded, and poor listeners. Sometimes, in fact, they go to battle. One role subverts

5

another role. The present self makes life unnecessarily difficult for its future self.

Third, we are malleable to the core. Everything about us, from our bodies to our neural circuitry to our personalities, is in perpetual flux. Change is our resting state. I hope to demonstrate how marvelously elastic we humans are, inside and outside, from situation to situation and, most curiously, from one time frame to another. It's not a question of whether we are able to change. We are nothing but change. You've heard the old Taoist saying, "The only thing that is constant is change itself." That is us.

To say that we lack a true self has a hollow ring to it. But the stories in this book are not meant to belittle. Rather, I hope to show, they reveal tremendous possibilities. This leads to a fourth theme: The very features of the self that can be so problematic—its arbitrary boundaries, multiplicity, and malleability—creates possibilities for change.

***

The questions we explore in the following chapters address fundamental human nature: Who are we? What does it mean to have a "self"? Where is the line between ourselves and everything else? Can we control the person we become? The questions are clear, but the answers are anything but.

Scientific knowledge has accumulated so rapidly in recent years that some contemporary scholars envision a time not so far away when science as we know it will have reached the end of its mission. Astronomers, for example, can now peer so far back in time that they can almost see—literally see—what the universe looked like at the moment of the big bang. Physicists are closing in on the tiniest particles that constitute matter. Biologists have mapped the entire human genome and are now well on their way to building genomes of life forms from scratch; designer organisms are just around the corner. And neuroscientists are mapping the structure and function of previously unimagined details in the brain so swiftly it's hard to keep up. When it comes to the issues in this book, however, this "end of science" eulogy is just chatter. In fact, it is the mystery of the self that makes it such a compelling subject. Even the questions it raises are ripe with opportunity.

"How can it be that, of all things, one is *this* thing, so that one can say, astonishingly . . . 'here I am'?" the writer Rebecca Goldstein eloquently asked.[8] But who is "*this* thing"? And exactly where is the "here" that I might find him?

***

A note about the progression of the chapters: I've tried to arrange to move from the perspectives of the harder sciences to those of the softer ones—from neurology and biology to the social sciences, from our bodily selves to the self of personal experience. With that, let us begin, at the beginning, with the machine that runs the operation.

2
The Brain

I used to think that the brain was the most wonderful
organ in my body. Then I realized who was telling me this.

—Emo Philips, comedian

I was staring at a live brain. The occasion was a neurosurgery where I had
been invited to observe the removal of a large tumor pressing on a patient's right frontal lobe. Over the past two hours I had watched the
surgeon make an incision into the man's scalp, carefully fold over a patch
of outer muscle, cut through an section of the skull, followed by the protective dura mater and bits and pieces of the other protective membranes.
Finally, there it was: a moist, throbbing, living brain.

The opportunity grew out of a conversation with my colleague Tom
Breen, who has been a professor of physiological psychology for more
than forty years. I had told Tom that I was beginning a book on the psychology of the self. "If you're going to study what it feels like to be a
person," he advised me, "you need to start at the beginning. You need to
meet the organ that drives the whole routine in the flesh." And in the
flesh this certainly was. I've taken more than my share of biology courses,
but this was something else entirely. Never in my life had I been so intimate with anything so vital—so much, in fact, that it felt almost voy-
euristic. Could anything be more naked? I was leering at the inside of a
psyche.

The object in front of me looked, technically, much like the pictures in
my anatomy books. This live version, however, was more vibrant and
more interesting, even beautiful. Kalmon Post, who is chairman emeritus
of the department of neurosurgery at Mt. Sinai Hospital in New York

City and the surgeon I was observing in action, is not a man prone to hyperbole. You wouldn't know it, however, by how he describes a living brain. "It's incredible," he says. "When you look at the brain, especially when you're operating with a microscope, it's a spectacularly beautiful thing to see. When you're outside of the brain, looking at the blood vessels and the nerves, when you see the complexity and think about what it is doing, it's awesome. You know how in some scary, sci-fi movies they like to show the brain dramatically pulsating. That's really how it is. It's pulsating in your operating room. It really is awesome."

At first, the magnitude of what I was seeing felt enormously exciting. This was the home of an entire human consciousness. Then the questions arose. Could this three-pound piece of meat really be what drives an entire human being? This was someone's innermost mental engine? I kept moving around and squinting inside the crevices, trying to find something, anything, I could relate to as human about the object. Other than the throbbing arteries, it looked to me like a slimy arts and crafts project, maybe a clay sculpture waiting to go into the kiln. This nebulous object was at the center of life itself? I've heard people compare the brain to a cauliflower, but, sorry, I couldn't picture it in any produce section I've been to. This was a piece of meat; if it was in any store, it should be a butcher shop. But a human mind? It was hard to make sense of.

I thought of the people whom I've loved and the ones I've hated, or feared, or stood in awe of. I think of my wife and children, my mother and father, my first girlfriend whom I wanted so badly to love me, my first coach whose every word I clung to. Has all this sound and fury been about nothing more than brain matter wrapped in skin? We speak to their faces, the outer wrapping, trusting with all our might that a real person is hidden inside. But any neurologist will tell you there is nothing behind those faces except amorphous tissue. Francis Crick, the co-discoverer of the structure of DNA, calls it the "the astonishing hypothesis," the realization that "'You,' your joys and your sorrows, your memories and your ambitions, your sense of personal identity and free will, are in fact no more than the behavior of a vast assembly of nerve cells and their associated molecules. As Lewis Carroll's Alice might have phrased it: 'You're nothing but a pack of neurons.'"[1]

I haven't looked at a human being the same way since that day. If I talk to a person long enough, there comes a disorienting moment when I begin questioning what I'm talking to. I don't mean exactly who I'm talking to. I know there's a person in front of me. My problem is figuring out where, specifically, I should be looking to find that person. I know I'm supposed to focus on the eyes. But I also know it makes as much sense to believe there is a personality in a cornea as to think there is a personality in the sweat on his skin or the makeup on her nose. Milan Kundera put it nicely in his novel *Immortality*. The human face "reflects neither character nor soul, nor what we call the self. The face is only the serial number of a specimen."[2]

But where else should I look? How does a social being carry on without clinging to some belief, no matter how claptrap, that the face we see reflects the mind within? We talk about the eyes being the windows to the soul or the mirrors of the soul or whatever rigmarole we can conjure to connect what we see on the outside people with what we imagine to be the habitat of their selves. It is hard to say exactly what we think we are seeing through those windows or in those mirrors. When you look at the smile on your friend's face, are you imagining there is an actual smile inside his skull? It is unlikely you're envisioning endorphins or neural circuitry. So what are you picturing on the inside? Precisely what it is seems less important than believing it just is. Kundera again puts it well: "Without the faith that our face expresses our self, without that basic illusion, that arch-illusion, we cannot live or at least we cannot take life seriously."

One thing is clear: If you were to pull off a person's face or open his or her skull to look inside, the only significant object you would find is that very brain. Is that the mind I'm talking to? When I picture that person's brain, however, it makes me want to giggle. Am I trying to communicate with a slippery heap of tissue? "When we see the brain, we realize that we are, at one level, no more than meat: and, on another, no more than fiction," the British neuropsychologist Paul Broks observes.[3] Meat and fiction?

When railroad trains first appeared in the American West, many native "Indians" were mystified about what made them run. After considering the possibilities, they concluded there must be horses in the engines. Imagine their surprise when they looked into the engine and discovered nothing but slabs of metal and pools of oil. I felt the same way when I looked at that human brain. Surely there is something more than this to who we are. So, like all the mind-body dualists before me, I resolve my confusion by conjuring the existence of something called a mind that must be mysteriously hidden in the machine. But I have no more evidence for this than the Indians did for their engine-horses. The British philosopher Gilbert Ryle called this way of thinking "the dogma of the Ghost in the Machine."[4] Ghosts, horses, selves. Whatever.

***

In December 2008, a woman—call her Patient T—who had been horribly disfigured underwent the first near-total face transplant in the United States. Completely altering one's appearance obviously has a radical impact on one's self-image. But would anyone question that T remained, deep down, the same person afterward? T knew she was still T, and all who met her, after their initial shock, no doubt continued to think of her as basically the same old T, just in different packaging. If the accident did change T profoundly—perhaps she became chronically melancholy or fatalistic—people might say something like, "T isn't the same person." But what they really meant was that T had changed, not that she was no longer T.

What would you say, however, if T had undergone a brain transplant? It's an odd question, I know, but I'm not the first one to consider it. In an unusual survey conducted by the Kaiser Permanente Medical Center, people were asked if they would be "willing to have [their] brain removed and replaced with another one if [they] had terminal brain cancer and transplant surgery was possible." Forty percent of those questioned said yes, they would opt for the transplant.[5] This is, of course, a hypothetical question for the time being. But it may not be for long. Partially successful transplants of the sort have already been performed on monkeys. In fact, Robert White, a professor of neurosurgery at Case Western Reserve University School of Medicine, has successfully transplanted the entire head of a monkey onto another monkey's body. The recipient monkey not only survived for some time after the operation but was able to smell, taste, hear, and see the world around it.[6] What if T had that transplant? Would she seamlessly shift into the identity of the donor? Would there be remnants of her old self? Would T's old self remain in command? Defy common sense and take possession of the new brain? Is there a ghost in the machine?

The philosopher Derek Parfit has asked an even stranger question.[7] Imagine that you and your two brothers, identical triplets, are in a terrible car accident. Your body is destroyed but, miraculously, your brain remains intact. Your brothers suffer the opposite fate: Their bodies are fine but their brains are destroyed. Let's also imagine that the two hemispheres of your brain happen to be functional duplicates. A brilliant neurosurgeon is able to remove your brain and successfully transplant one hemisphere to each of your brothers. (It is, in fact, possible to survive with a single brain hemisphere, as we will see in the next chapter.) Have you survived? If so, are there two you's? And does this mean there were two you's all along? Or, are there now two half-you's? Say one of your brothers dies during surgery. Would that mean only half of you has survived? What is a half self?

Okay, enough of the Frankenstein shtick. Let's try a more manageable thought experiment. What if we could cut and paste elements to a brain? Consider memory. If you lost your entire memory, as in severe Alzheimer's disease, would you still be you? Certainly, we can agree, you wouldn't know you were you. But what if it happened piecemeal—one memory at a time? Doing this, I might add, may soon be very possible. Recent research indicates that the control of specific memories are not as far off as you might think. A team of scientists at the SUNY Downstate Medical Center in Brooklyn recently discovered that it is possible to permanently erase individual memories in monkeys by interfering with a specific molecule (PKMzeta) in the brain. All it took was a single dose of an experimental chemical (ZIP) to "areas of the brain critical for holding specific types of memory, like emotional associations, spatial knowledge or motor skills." The injection of a single chemical and, pfft, a memory is gone.[8]

Imagine, then, that we could add or remove chemicals controlling particular types of memories. Perhaps, say, you had an accident that required all your motor memories to be replaced? If the donor's memories transferred properly, you would now find yourself able to make movements you never could before. Maybe you would be able to ride a bike for the first time in your life or could break eighty on the golf course. Of course, you also would lose some skills. Perhaps you could no longer swim or even hammer a nail. It would be strange, to be sure. Your essential identity, however, would no doubt remain intact. But say, now, you also received a transplant for your memories of smells. Afterward, when you think back to being a child in your mother's arms you find yourself imagining the scent of someone else's mother. Then, say, your visual memories get replaced. Then your verbal memories. At what point are you no longer you? Is there such a thing as a half you? A hybrid you? When does the self become other? Or nothing?

***

Let us assume our minds really are nothing more than a property of physical tissue. Exactly where in that tissue, then, should I search? If I close my eyes and try to mentally locate the center of my mind, I imagine it to be somewhere in the top, front of my skull, just behind my eyes. But when I try to hone in more specifically, the epicenter gets fuzzier and fuzzier. If I look too hard, in fact, I lose track of what I was looking for. I feel caught in a surreal offshoot of Heisenberg's uncertainty principle whereby it's said that "If you're doing something you have to concentrate on you can't also be thinking about doing it, and if you're thinking about doing it then you can't actually be doing it."[9] Here's what I do know: My mind is incapable of locating itself.

Perhaps I'm looking in the wrong place altogether. For most of recorded history you would have been laughed at—if you weren't burned or beheaded, that is—to suggest that the brain had much to do with higher human functions. Four thousand years ago, the ancient Egyptians were convinced that the heart, not the brain, was where you found the essence of the human being. When preparing a body for burial, Egyptian priests would snake a hook through the nose of the cadaver and fish out, shred by shred, as much of the brain as they could. The heart, on the other hand, was meticulously preserved in the body. "The ibis-headed god, Thoth, would then ask the heart forty questions about the life of its owner. If the heart proved to be heavy with guilt, the deceased would be fed to the Devourer. If the heart was free of sin, the deceased would go to heaven." The brain? It got tossed in the garbage.[10]

Aristotle pretty much agreed. The great philosopher took a more systematic approach than the Egyptians to understanding the mind. After adding up the evidence, however, he came to the same conclusion: The heart had to be the core of the mind. To begin with, it made geographic sense. The heart was close to the center of the body. If the brain was in charge, why would God house it so far on the periphery? Aristotle didn't toss his opinions around frivolously. He conducted an ambitious program of human and animal dissections, leading many to call him the first biologist. When he dissected stillborn babies, the first organ he saw taking shape in the embryo was the heart, which, he was convinced, is precisely what you would expect from the most important organ. It seemed especially logical that the heart was the center of feelings, since you could literally feel it beating. The next time you hear someone say they have a broken heart, or they feel heartsick or disheartened, think Aristotle. Then there was the matter of heat. Aristotle believed that heat was connected to intelligence. The warmer the animal, the smarter it was. And the Greeks believed the heart was the source of a body's heat. The main contribution of the brain was to prevent the heart from overheating. It was, they believed, little more than an elaborate cooling device.

Henry More, an influential philosopher in the 1660s captured history's opinion of the brain: "This lax pith or marrow in man's head shows no more capacity for thought than a cake of suet or a bowl of curds."[11] To be honest, I have no idea what suet is. But I'm pretty sure Mr. More was describing what I was feeling when I peered into a brain in that Mt. Sinai Hospital operating theater. Could anyone really believe, More added, that this "watery, structureless substance" contained our humanity?

Thanks to more sophisticated understanding of the nervous system, we now take it for granted that the brain is the nucleus of the mind. The assumption is so well grounded that "brain dead" has become the usual criterion for distinguishing life from non-life. The brain is the machine that drives our sensations and emotions, our thoughts and memories, and those strange phenomena we call consciousness and awareness. We know that a functioning brain is necessary for these experiences.

But where and how all this happens remains an even greater mystery. In the past two decades, neurobiologists have made enormous advances in mapping the circuitry that underlies the self. But what they have found is no less complicated and confusing than what we envision in our own meditations. If you hook people up to an fMRI and ask them to think about their selves, areas all around the brain are prone to light up, especially in a group called the cortical midline structures, which run all the way from the center of the brain to the frontal lobes near our foreheads. But no particular area, in isolation, can account for the experience of having a self. To further muddy the map, the pattern of brain areas that light up when people think about their selves constantly changes. You will not find consciousness in a single neuron, or even in a complex structure like the spinal cord. If the self does have a physical home, it appears to be in forever changing neural connections. This is one slippery animal.[12]

***

It would be presumptuous to criticize anyone's theory of the mind: what it is, how it works, where it comes from. The only thing I'm sure of is that none of us—scientists, philosophers, religious scholars, shamans, and everyone else who thinks about these matters—have irrefutable answers to the big questions. Is it anything more than an emergent property of our neural circuitry? What is consciousness? What is the self? Does all human experience boil down to the mass of meat inside our skulls? And if not, where else should we be looking? Perhaps someday we will have satisfying answers to these questions. Or maybe we won't. All I know is that, for now, we are all dancing in the dark.

One thing I've learned is you won't get your answers by looking at a brain—at least not with today's scientific toolkit. Any surgeon who has probed behind the mask will tell you that what I saw in the operating room is all that he or she has ever seen. It's tissue, just tissue. Paul Broks, who has been studying these matters for more than twenty-five years, put it well: "Where is the mind in this tangled wood of neurons and nerve fibres? It isn't anywhere. And the self? What did you expect? A genie in a bottle?"[13]

Don't get me wrong. I intend no disrespect for this magnificent organ. The more we learn about the brain, the clearer it becomes that it is a machine without equal, an astonishingly intricate, efficient, and powerful web of elements that communicate within and without at breathtaking speed and with astounding ingenuity. There are estimated to be one hundred billion cells—called neurons and glia—in our brains. Individually, neurons are fairly straightforward biological structures. They typically comprise a cell body, dendrites, and an axon. But each of these cells is mind-bogglingly complicated, containing not only our entire genome but billions of molecules that are themselves woven into intricate patterns.

These are massive power plants. Electrical impulses fire at a rate of up to hundreds of times per second. "If you represented each of these trillions and trillions of pulses in your brain by a single photon of light, the combined output would be blinding," observes neuroscientist David Eagleman.[14] And every time a neuron fires, it influences whether, how, and in which direction its neighbors fire, and so on down the line. Networked together, they emerge as complex communities. Each neuron is linked to roughly ten thousand other neurons, many of which are a good distance away. The possible connections are so enormous that they challenge linguistic description. It has been calculated that, if you add up the potential combinations and permutations within the network, the total exceeds the number of elementary particles in the universe.[15]

This magnificent creation is also a workhorse. Remember the old schoolyard adage that you use only 10 percent of your brain? We now know this is nonsense. Functional brain imaging studies have yet to find any so-called silent areas—nonfunctional sectors that never light up. "You can delete the 10 percent fallacy from your brain and use the room for something else," as neurosurgeon and science writer Katrina Firlik puts it.[16] And it performs so efficiently. It has been estimated that the entire brain consumes on average of about twenty watts of power. That is one-fifth of what it takes to run the incandescent bulb in my reading lamp. Who'd have thought? The brain is even a state-of-the-art energy saver.[17]

We sometimes speak of the brain as a supersophisticated computer, but that is an insult to its—um, how else to put it?—to its intelligence. The brain reacts and accommodates, assimilates and extrapolates, responds to the past and prepares for the future. One of the most exciting new discoveries in neuroscience concerns the plasticity of the brain. We used to think that the brain's structure is fully and permanently formed by the time a person reaches early adulthood. We now know that it is anything but. Study after study has demonstrated that the brain not only reacts to new experiences but that it reconstructs its fundamental physiology to meet these challenges. It creates new neural pathways and synapses, or modifies existing ones, in order to learn new information, create new memories, and prepare for what is to come. It is what scientists now refer to as "neuroplasticity."[18]

Consider what happens when a part gets broken. Say a person suffers damage to a small area of the brain responsible for speech production (namely, Broca's area in the left frontal lobe) or even loses the functioning of an entire half of the brain after a stroke. The brain, given enough time, is capable of remarkable feats of self-repair. It will try to fix the damaged neurons or to generate new replacement neurons in a process called neurogenesis. And if these blue-collar repairs don't succeed, it may reprogram its entire circuitry. Or it might reassign the damaged functions to healthy areas of the brain that had no previous experience with these functions. There are cases of people born with half a brain that wires itself to work as a whole one.[19]

Think about this: The human brain can literally change itself. How can a machine be so labyrinthine and yet so flexible? I challenge you to find a computer that can fix itself when whole parts break down. Try removing half the insides of your laptop and see what happens when you try to turn it on. Dr. Post, the brain surgeon I observed, says this changeability is one of the challenges in his work that people forget about. "The brain isn't holding still for you right then and there. Things are moving all of the time. You're operating on a moving target." When we were back in his office, Dr. Post told me a joke about a heart surgeon who brings his car to a garage to have it repaired. The mechanic, a former patient, fixes the car. When he hands the surgeon the bill, he asks a question: "Why do you get paid so much more for your work than I do for mine?" "I'll tell you what," the surgeon answers. "I'll pay you what they pay me if you fix my car while it's running." This brain is one active machine.

***

But, no matter how remarkable it may be, it is hard to fathom how a brain transmutes into the experience of a self. The brain is a thing. You can touch it. The self is ethereal. We imagine there is a *my*self and a *your*self, a *you* and a *me*, as if they were entities we could buy and sell. But they are apparitions. Try to pin yourself down and you discover a ghost—in fact lots of them. The self is a mental creation, a story we tell ourselves. It is both a work of genius and everlastingly fragile.

"The brain is ultimately just a big lump of atoms strung together in a particular configuration, no different in this sense from a teakettle or a crown of broccoli," science writer Steven Johnson observes.[20] So how is it that we are conscious of our selves but the teakettle and broccoli are not? Forget about the *why* questions—why we, in this world, in this universe exist—that religions are trying to answer. We have barely begun to understand *how* the awareness of a self can possibly happen.

Dr. Post has been studying brains for more than a half century. He is now widely recognized as one of the preeminent neurosurgeons in the world, and it is doubtful that anyone knows more about brain anatomy than he does. I asked Dr. Post what he has learned about the human mind after all these years of work. "I have the same awe now that I had in the beginning, maybe even more," he said. "Sometimes I look at this dead organ in the laboratory and wonder 'How the hell did this function? How did it do all of those mysterious things? How does it know? How does it know?' I have no answers. I don't understand it any more now than I did when I was a first-year medical student in an anatomy lab in 1963."

When I reported back to my colleague Tom Breen, the psychophysiologist who originally suggested I begin my research with the brain, he asked if it had been a waste of my time. "I guess you didn't get the answers you were hoping for," he said. On the contrary, I told him, I couldn't be more satisfied. How boring to think the secrets of the self can be reduced to organic brain tissue. I, for one, would find it claustrophobic. I prefer to believe that who we are has as much to do with our relationship to the world around us as with the anatomical tissue inside our skull. Because if it does, our lives take on so many more possibilities. To me, it is this malleability of the self—its multiplicity and plasticity—that makes existence so astonishing.

3
Two Brains, One Person

Let not thy left hand know
What thy right hand doest.

—Matthew 6:3

I spent many years as a wannabe artist. No matter how much I accomplished in the university world, my sixties-hippie heart of hearts nagged me to do something *truly* creative. And it wouldn't be enough to just splash around abstract patterns like any old shoot-from-the-hip, self-ordained artist. I wanted—and I know this sounds lame in the art world—to draw realistically. But, alas, no matter whether it was in black and white or color, two- or three-dimensions, whether I used a pencil, a brush or a palette knife, everything I tried looked like a Gumby cartoon. To be honest, I couldn't draw Gumby, either.

More than anything I wanted to draw people, particularly faces. But as it is for most failed art wannabes, these seemed to be the hardest of all. I really tried. I studied anatomy. I bought books on how to draw a head. ("Begin with a ball. Drop a line from mid-forehead to the chin. 'Slice off' a circle at the side of the head, and from the front of this circle, curve a line down to the chin. Complete the plane of the face with a line on the other side. Now add the jawline," one directed.) I memorized ideal proportions—the eyes are usually midway between the top and bottom of the head, the nose is one-third up from the bottom, the outside edge of the nostrils is almost directly below the inside edge of the eyes, and so on. I diligently practiced drawing noses, lips, hair, and eyes. But it hardly mattered. When I tried a portrait of a real person, it still came out like an etch-a-sketch on a police blotter—which looked like Gumby.

On my thirty-sixth birthday, I signed up for a drawing course with Maxine Olsen, an artist I admired who at the time was painting larger-than-life, superrealist oil portraits. I was attracted by the startling nuances in her paintings. They were like painterly photographs that looked too realistic to be photographs. I told her I wanted to be a real artist and asked if she could please teach me how to draw people. "I don't know what to tell you about the artist bit," I recall her words. "I'm not even sure what that means. But learning to accurately draw people, or anything else that's in front of you, is a lot easier than you think."

The worst thing I could do, she explained, was to try to draw "*a* nose" or "*a* face" or "*a* whatever." Drawing is about seeing. You need to concentrate on every minute nook, cranny, twist, and turn, observing millimeter by millimeter. It doesn't matter whether it's a nose or a tree or a car. The trick, if you can call it that, is to notice every speck of every line, every subtle change in shape, brightness, and color. The skill of drawing isn't lodged in your hands. It doesn't matter if you can't draw a straight line. In his classic book, *The Natural Way to Draw*, the art teacher Kimon Nicolaides writes that drawing "has nothing to do with artifice or technique. It has nothing to do with aesthetics or conception. It has only to do with the act of correct observation."[1]

It helps to not think about names and labels, Olsen taught me. Otherwise, you get caught up in what something is supposed to look like instead of seeing what it actually looks like. If you try to make it look like a nose, you'll end up drawing a symbol of a nose instead of the real thing. Labels lead to stereotypes and stereotypes create expectations. That rang a bell with me. It is a principle I also teach in my social psychology courses. "Seeing is forgetting the name of the thing one sees," to quote the title of Lawrence Wechsler's biography of the influential artist Robert Irwin.[2] Try to conjure up an image of a "typical" face. There's no such thing. We can only visualize individual faces—because there only are individual faces.

You have to turn off thinking when you draw. It's a lot like meditation. Quiet your mind. No preconceptions. No expectations. Learn to be fully present. Practice focused concentration. Olsen recalled one of her own teachers who had made the students in her class mark out a one-inch square area of dirt and to then draw everything in it for an entire hour. Most were bored after a few minutes, but the instructor ordered them to keep at it for the rest of the hour. The longer they stared, the more they saw. "By the end of the hour I'd completely forgotten I was looking at dirt," Olsen said. "And I knew I hadn't finished my drawing. That's what I mean by really seeing."

My particular problem, she explained, was an unfortunate by-product of what I did well. "You're a cerebral kind of guy," she said. "You're good with words and logic." These were exactly the skills I needed to be a good professor, but they were terrible for drawing. As another artist friend, the gifted sculptor Chris Sorensen, elegantly put it, "Your theories can't see for shit." But my cerebral self didn't want to accept this. It was arrogant. It couldn't get through its brilliant skull that it was an idiot when it came to drawing. "The smart way to draw is to think like a moron," Sorensen told me. I hereby pronounce this "The Chris Sorensen Theory of Creativity": Sometimes the smartest thing you can do is make yourself stupid.

***

I had my diagnosis. Now for the treatment. For this, I—the psychology professor—was offered a lesson in applied brain anatomy.

"You have to learn to fool your brain," Olsen said. She referred to a book called *Drawing on the Right Side of the Brain: A Course in Enhancing Creativity and Artistic Confidence*, by art professor Betty Edwards.[3] The title appealed to me, starting with the scientific hook and ending with that last euphemism about "enhancing . . . artistic confidence." This, I thought, was a book for overeducated intellectuals who are artistic fiascos. In other words, for people like me. Humans, Edwards explained, have two different and sometimes conflicting modes of knowing, different modes of information processing. We have an "L-mode," which is verbal, rational, symbolic, and analytic. And we have an "R-mode," which is nonverbal, intuitive, concrete, and time-oblivious. The two modes, she said, are housed in different hemispheres of the brain: The L is associated with the left hemisphere and the R with the right hemisphere—a physiological distinction we will get to soon. The student who lacks artistic confidence needs to shift from L-mode to R-mode. Edwards had designed a number of exercises to force that shift.

The first one I tried was an upside-down drawing. Our task was to copy a remarkable line drawing of Igor Stravinsky by Picasso. The portrait is composed of dozens of unique, intricately curving lines that intersect in complicated patterns. Taken together, they somehow add up to a dynamic, unmistakable likeness of the great composer. When I looked at the portrait right-side up, the assignment appeared well beyond my capabilities.

Edwards's instructions were to turn the drawing upside down and then copy it as it appeared. My drawing of Stravinsky, in other words, would also be upside down. We were to work on our drawings for at least thirty consecutive minutes. It was important, Edwards instructed, not to turn our drawings right side up until we were finished. Before beginning, we were to remove or cover any watches or other timepieces and to set an alarm for the duration of the drawing. Doing this would help us forget about "keeping time," which is a decidedly L-mode activity.

The reasoning behind the exercise was that, seen upside down, nothing in the portrait would be easily recognizable. Turn any photo or drawing of a face upside down and you will see this is true. Even previously familiar faces now look unfamiliar. You are forced to "forget the name of the thing you see" because everything now looks like abstract lines and shapes. As Edwards explains it, the left hemisphere is now forced to surrender and it relinquishes the task to its "dumb partner," the right hemisphere. Chris Sorensen got it right. Out with the L-mode, in with the R.

I set my alarm, flipped Picasso's portrait upside down, and went at it. It was confusing for a few moments but, sure enough, the "switch" kicked in quickly. I found myself simply looking at a lot of lines, shapes, and angles. It was easy to take them in one at a time and to track how they fit together. I started following how the lines connected, where one ended and the next one started, their relation to the edges of the paper, and their angles on the paper and in relation to each other. Taken one at a time, the individual lines were easy to copy.

It was a hypnotic experience, like getting lost in a seductive puzzle. I'd copy a line, connect it to the next line, and the next, getting lost in how everything fit nimbly together. Then I'd check to make sure the lines were properly positioned in relation to each other and to the edges of the paper. I forgot I was working on a drawing and was surprised when my alarm went off. I sat back and looked at the two upside-down drawings. A few of my lines were obviously out of position, so I kept at it a while longer. When I was reasonably satisfied, I flipped both drawings right side up. To my astonishment—and I say this with no hyperbole—it was by far the best drawing I had ever done.

There were several other exercises. One, known as "pure" contour drawing, was a lesson in raw observation. We were told to move our eyes along the edge (that is, contour) of an object as slowly ("millimeter by millimeter") and precisely as possible, while simultaneously recording every nook and cranny we observed in an uninterrupted line on a piece of paper. The key, however, was to never once look down at your drawing while it was in progress. One's eyes were to remain fixed on the object's contour throughout. As a result, I was seeing nameless curves and wiggles. I chose to draw my left hand—an awfully challenging shape, I thought—and this one, too, turned out ridiculously better than anything I had done before.

In another exercise, a "negative space" drawing, I drew the spaces surrounding an object rather than the object itself. Instead of drawing the shape of a body standing in a doorway, for example, I drew the spaces between the rectangle of the doorway and the edges of the body. We can't put names or labels on these nebulous forms, so, once again, there was the switch into R-mode. Chalk up another triumph.

***

Artwise, my lessons were an unqualified success. They taught me what's referred to in art-speak as "the artist's way of seeing." Over time I've learned to use this skill to create my own visual creations. I can't vouch for the quality of my work, but I do know this creative outlet has become a very important part of my life. But there was something more remarkable here than learning how to draw. It was the process I used. I'd achieved my goal by pitting one side of my brain against the other. I couldn't will myself to draw. But I could trick my brain into letting me draw. Crazier yet, the side of me that planned the strategy—the so-called L-mode thinker—represented the same side of the brain that I wanted to subdue.

There is a biological caveat here. Much as it felt as if I was pitting one brain hemisphere against the other, the physiology of the process is considerably more complicated. True, the human brain is divided into two distinct hemispheres. Also true, each hemisphere has its own specialized functions, which scientists have known for more than a century. The left hemisphere is almost always (except in the case of a few left-handed people) the seat of language, logic, and interpretation. It is also the side that marks time and sequences, thinks in labels and symbols, and is good at arithmetic. The right hemisphere is the seat of spatial skills, visual pattern recognition, and intuition. It thinks concretely and is better at tasks like geometry, perception of depth and movement, and auditory discrimination.

But here is the caveat. In a healthy brain—like mine, I like to think— the hemispheres don't work independently. They are connected by the corpus callosum, a huge network of fibers consisting of more than a million connections. As a result, any activity that occurs in one hemisphere is quickly communicated to the other hemisphere. The corpus callosum sees to it that neither hemisphere is ever completely out of the loop. In other words, my drawing exercises decreased the activity in my left hemisphere, but there is no reason to believe it completely shut it down. This, however, raises an intriguing question: If I felt such a profound disconnect between the two ways of thinking with a functioning corpus callosum, what might it be like to operate without one? What if a person lost the connections between the hemispheres? In a series of ground-breaking studies conducted in the 1960s, Roger Sperry and his students, most notably Michael Gazzaniga, tested this very question.

Their sample consisted of a small group of patients who had undergone a radical surgical procedure to alleviate their suffering from epileptic seizures. The procedure, known as a "commissurotomy," involved neurologically isolating the two hemispheres by cutting the corpus callosum. By doing this, it was hoped, seizures that initiated in one hemisphere would be prevented from spreading to the other. The operation was a remarkable success. Not only did it eliminate the spread of the seizures but, unexplainably, it dramatically curtailed them from occurring at all.

But Sperry wasn't so much interested in the surgery's effects on seizures as in other ways the so-called split-brain patients were changed. Earlier studies of people whose corpus callosum had been severed had reported surprisingly few detectable behavior problems. Patients appeared to carry out conversations, complete assigned tasks, and perform other actions pretty much as they had before the surgery. They appeared to be so normal that the famous psychologist Karl Lashley once quipped that the only function of the corpus callosum seemed be to keep the two hemispheres from floating apart.

At first glance, Sperry's patients also seemed to be normal. "From the beginning one of the most striking observations," Gazzaniga says, "was that the operation produced no noticeable change in the patient's temperament, personality or general intelligence."[4] But, to paraphrase an old saying, there was more here than met the eyeball. Sperry devised a series of ingenious tests, for which he was awarded the Nobel Prize in Physiology or Medicine in 1981, that revealed just how much this was so. In one test, for example, patients sat in a chair with their hands out of sight under the surface of a table. A pencil was then placed in one of their hands. Recall that the right hand sends signals to the left (verbal) hemisphere of the brain and the left hand sends signals to the right (nonverbal) hemisphere. This means that information coming from the right hand should be accessible to verbal description, but information from the left hand should not. This is exactly what happened. When the pencil was placed in patients' right hands, they quickly described it as "a pencil." But when they held the same pencil in their left hand, they couldn't for the life of them say what they were holding.

Sperry then changed the problem. With the pencil still in the left hand, which was still out of sight under the table, the patients were shown a group of objects—a key, a book, and a pencil, for example—and asked to point to the object they were holding. This was a visual task, which is what the right hemisphere does well. Sure enough, with the pencil in their left hand the patients immediately pointed to the pencil. When asked the name of the object they were pointing at—an object they were looking at with both eyes—the patients easily identified it as a pencil. But when once again asked what they were holding in their hand, they still didn't have a clue. It did not matter how many times the sequence was repeated. When asked to point to the picture of the object that was in their hand, they correctly pointed to the picture of the pencil. When asked the name of the object they were pointing at, they correctly said it was a pencil. But when asked to name the object in their hand, they hadn't the faintest idea.

In another experiment, the researchers used a device called a tachistoscope to flash words and pictures separately to each hemisphere. They did this by having patients fix their eyes on a point in the middle of a screen and then flashing an image to one side of the point. The visual system is structured so the left side of each eye sends messages to the right hemisphere of the brain; the right side of each eye sends messages to the left hemisphere. Because of this, any information appearing to the right of the point goes exclusively to the left hemisphere; any information appearing to the left of the point goes only to the right hemisphere.

In this particular test, the letters HE were flashed to the left side of the eye at the same time the letters ART were seen by the right side of the eye. In normal people, the two hemispheres share each other's information, so we process the word HEART. But when the split-brain patients were asked what they had seen, they all said "ART." These were their left hemispheres talking. When they were now shown two cards, one printed with the word HE and the other with the word ART, and asked to point with their left hand to the word they had seen, the hand always pointed to "HE."

The patients were as confused by their behaviors as we are when we hear about them. In another test, they were shown a string of pictures of ordinary objects during which a brief image of a nude woman was suddenly flashed to either their right or left hemisphere (that is, to the left or right side of their eyes). The patients were clearly amused no matter which hemisphere received the picture. They were asked what they found so funny. Those who had seen the picture with their left hemisphere said it was because the woman didn't have any clothes on. But those who had it with their right hemispheres were at a loss for an explanation. One woman initially said she'd seen nothing. "But almost immediately a sly smile spread over her face and she began to chuckle," Gazzaniga says. When he asked why she was laughing, the woman said, "I don't know . . . oh, that funny machine."[5]

It as if these patients were experiencing two distinct, simultaneous realities, as if they were two strangers sharing the same body.[6] Yet should you meet them on the street, they would probably appear perfectly normal. It is only under particular circumstances that the unusualness becomes noticeable. Then again, couldn't the same be said about all of us?

***

The story gets more curious yet. In some cases the two hemispheres aren't simply strangers. They go into battle. One of my all-time favorite movies is Stanley Kubrick's 1964 Cold War classic, *Dr. Strangelove*, in which Peter Sellers plays the title character, the neurologically impaired ex-Nazi turned U.S. Air Force general. Dr. Strangelove is a high-level adviser to the president with an embarrassing habit: Every time he starts to give military advice, his leather-gloved right hand snaps into a Nazi salute, which he has to force down again and again with his other hand. Now and then the hand goes for his own throat, looking as if it's going to strangle him.

Kubrick probably didn't know it, but what he was describing is an actual medical condition, a rare symptom of split-brain syndrome now officially labeled "alien hand syndrome" (AHS). The first case was reported in 1908 by the renowned German neurologist and psychiatrist Kurt Goldstein, who had been visited by a fifty-seven-year-old woman with a highly unusual complaint. Her left hand, she told Goldstein, had developed "a will of its own" and was bent on carrying out a sinister agenda. The hand, she said, "is a law unto itself, an organ without will. When once it has got hold of something, it refuses to let go. . . . If I'm having a drink and it gets hold of the glass, it won't let go and spills [the drink] out. Then I hit it and say: 'Behave yourself, hand.' I suppose there must be an evil spirit in it." Lately, she told Goldstein, it had turned violent. With no warning, the hand would wrap its fingers around her neck and try with all its might to throttle her. The only way she could stop the attacker was to pull it off by force.[7]

Goldstein's patient, like all cases of alien hand syndrome with organic underpinnings, had suffered damage to her corpus callosum. It is almost always the left hand that feels alien in AHS, presumably because it is operating under instructions from the nonverbal right hemisphere. The helpless left hemisphere has no control over the rogue hand, merely the words to think, "What is going on with my hand?" Fifty or so cases of AHS have been diagnosed in the century since Goldstein's first case, although it is speculated that others have either gone unreported or were given another diagnosis.

There appear to be no limits to the chaos. Reported cases include:

- A fifty-four-year-old right-handed man who had to stop driving when his left arm grabbed the steering wheel and started whipping it around like a deranged driver.[8]

- A patient whose rogue hand would crush the cups on her hospital tray. She would then plead with the hospital aides for new cups. When they came, the hand crushed those, too.[9]

- A patient who was constantly putting on his glasses with his right hand and pulling them off with his left.

- A woman whose left hand developed an embarrassing habit of tugging on her shirt and sneakily unbuttoning her gown.[10]

- Another patient could not even get dressed without outside help because every time his right hand tried to button up his shirt, his left hand "was coming along right behind it undoing the buttons."[11]

- One patient's hands duked it out over exactly what to wear. On one occasion, for instance, her right hand pulled a pair of red shoes out of the closet. Her left hand immediately yanked the shoes away, tossed them back in the closet and picked out a pair of blue shoes. The right hand again tried to pick up the red shoes, but this time the left hand slammed the closet door on the right hand.[12]

- "When asked to write with his left hand," a patient's right hand "took the sheet of paper and dropped it to the floor," his neurologist reported. When asked why he would do such a thing, the patient denied it was *he* who had done it.[13]

- One frustrated woman wanted to smoke cigarettes, but every time she tried to light up, her right hand would snatch the cigarette from her lips and put it out. "He" didn't want her to smoke just then, the woman would say.[14]

- Every time another woman tried to eat, her left hand would grab the fork from her right hand and throw it down. After dinner, it was more of the same. "If my hand doesn't want to do the dishes it shuts the water off," she said. "If I try to open [a drawer] it will shut it. If I try to shut it, it will open it."[15]

The unpredictability of the alien hand requires sufferers to be constantly on guard. One woman said her left hand would periodically crash into her right one. It was like she had a drunk driver attached to her shoulder. She said it felt as if "someone from the Moon" had hijacked control of her left hand.[16]

The alien may turn violent. One AHS patient had to wrestle his left arm to keep it from beating up his wife. Another thought he was being mugged on a bus but, to his embarrassment, ended up defending himself from what turned out to be his own right hand. Other alien hands have tried to punch their owners in the face. A few, like Feinberg's first patient, tell of fighting off murder—not suicide, but murder—by strangulation. In the middle of an examination by her physician, one terrified patient yelled out, "Look, it's coming. Please help me." Sure enough, when the physician turned to look, he saw the arm flexing and jerking arrhythmically toward the woman's face. "Please stop this monster," she screamed. "It will kill me."[17] Others say they couldn't sleep at night for fear they'd be assaulted if they closed their eyes.[18]

The alien hand isn't always a problem child. There are scattered cases where it has come to the rescue. One patient was rudely awoken by a hand slapping her across her face. When she heard her alarm going off, the woman realized she had overslept and had almost missed an appointment. Then she looked at the hand and saw it was her own. "My left hand slapped me awake," she said. Her left brain had been fast asleep when her right brain decided to step in.[19]

There is no known cure or even a treatment for alien hand syndrome. The best most sufferers can hope for is some form of damage control. The first course of defense is usually to just grab hold of the hand; or to swat at it. Some people get more creative. One man kept it draped in a large oven glove. Another made a point of sitting on the hand. Others treat the hand like a person. They might try to reason with the hand, verbally explaining why it is in both of their best interests for it to stop. Some say they are constantly berating the hand as if the two of them were stuck in a bad marriage. One patient was heard shouting things like, "What are you doing there? Are you crazy?" at his wandering limb.[20] Sufferers sometimes wonder whether to call an ambulance or the police. Chaos rules. It has been suggested that a better name for the condition might be "anarchic hand syndrome." My own preference is "Dr. Strangelove syndrome."

***

Is our brain a single entity? If the question is whether the hemispheres are physically connected, then the answer, for most of us, is yes. But to say they work in unison would be a leap. A normal machine operates as a single unit. My toaster has plenty of parts, but all of them work to make good toast. The two sides of my brain seem to have wills of their own. The conflicts light up when the machine gets damaged, as we see in the cases of split-brain patients and AHS sufferers. But the divided wills are a reality for all of us, even if we are fortunate enough to have two healthy hemispheres and a functioning corpus callosum.

As Roger Sperry and Michael Gazzaniga continued their experiments, they were struck by the extent to which each hemisphere was capable of operating as an independent agent. These two minds "exist as two completely conscious entities, in the same manner as two conjoined twins are two completely separate persons,"[21] Gazzaniga remarks. The patients they observed, he says, convincingly demonstrated that "one hemisphere is sufficient to sustain a personality or mind." If this is true, he concludes, "the individual with two intact hemispheres has the capacity for two distinct minds."[22]

It is a reality that takes some getting used to. But think of the power it offers. We don't simply have two minds but two toolkits to work from. If this sometimes leaves you feeling split from yourself, then so be it.

4
Bodies without Borders
Or, Pardon Me, Is This My Arm or Yours?

He had ... mixed feelings about having a "self" at all,
just as he had mixed feelings about having a "body."

—Allen Shawn, *Wish I Could Be There*
(describing his father, William Shawn,
longtime editor of the *New Yorker*)

Owning one's body is a cornerstone of the sense of self. But what exactly do we mean by "*my* body"? It assumes, to begin with, that we know what our physical self looks like. And that we can tell where it begins and ends. This is my body. That's yours. These arms belong to me. Those belong to you. The boundaries are obvious. Or so we like to think.

***

There is an exercise called "the rubber hand illusion" that I sometimes use to spice up lectures.[1] To experience the effect, you'll need to gather a few simple pieces of equipment: (1) A phony hand. One cheap possibility is an inflated rubber glove. This works with many people but, in my own experience, it is better if the hand looks more realistic. The most effective is a prosthetic hand. Realistic fakes from costume shops or Halloween stores also usually do the trick. (2) Two small brushes. I prefer one-inch wide foam paintbrushes. (3) A large enough barrier for your real arm to hide behind. A piece of cardboard with something to hold it up will do. (4) A friend or other assistant.

Place the fake hand on the table in front of you. You should drape something over where the arm would be so it looks as if the hand is peeking through. If you're using a mannequin arm, cover everything but the hand. Now place your real arm outside and next to the fake one. It is important to line up the two arms—the fake one and your own—so they are parallel and in the same position. Next, place the cardboard barrier between the two arms. Do it in such a way that the barrier blocks your vision of your own real arm. In other words, you should be looking directly at the fake arm and unable to see your real one. When you look down at where your real arm should be, you are instead seeing the fake arm. Finally, have your friend simultaneously tap and stroke the fake hand and your own concealed hand with the brushes. The movements of the brushes should be identical. Stare at the fake hand until you start to believe you're feeling the brush rub against it.[2]

The illusion often takes hold quickly. In one laboratory study, 80 percent of participants became convinced they felt the brush on the fake hand within fifteen seconds. Sometimes it can take a few minutes, though, so be patient. When the effect does kick in, it's eerie. You actually feel the brush on your phony hand, even though you know the sensation is being created by the brush stroking your real hand. When, in one study, the experimenter bent a finger on the virtual hand into a physiologically impossible position, subjects not only said their finger was being bent but their SCR (skin conductance reaction)—a reliable physiological measure of fear and anxiety—also spiked significantly.[3]

Our minds are so easily fooled that you can pull off the trick with *two* phony hands. In one study, two identical prosthetic hands were placed in a parallel position next to each other. The subject placed his real hand underneath the table between and parallel to the two prosthetics. All three hands were then simultaneously stroked for one to two minutes—the two prosthetics with a specially designed double paintbrush and the hidden real hand with a third brush. Sure enough, when the experimenter dramatically stabbed either of the two rubber hands with a needle, subjects said they were frightened and their SCRs spiked. And if you think the spike could have been caused by simply seeing anyone's hand stabbed by a needle, think again. In a control condition in which there was no stroking of the hands beforehand, subjects didn't react at all when the rubber hands were stabbed.[4]

***

Proprioception, sometimes called our sixth sense, refers to the mental maps that allow us to keep track of our own bodies. It is how we know which part is connected to which and how each part connects to the surrounding space. The rubber hand illusion manages to short-circuit the system and, in doing so, underscores the fragility of our sixth sense. How can it be so easy to corrupt our mental maps? The explanation is twofold, and it is a wicked combination: insufficient hardware and vulnerable software.

First, the hardware problem. Our perceptual machinery, incredible as it may be, isn't up to the demands of its task. We are confronted with more inputs than our sensors and brains are capable of processing. Even in simple situations, there are thousands of bits of information competing for our attention at any given moment and, if we attended to each one, the system would break. Engineers refer to this problem as "system overload," a condition that occurs when a structure is faced with more demands than it is capable of handling. When excessive weight is placed on a bridge, for example, it collapses. The same holds true for our senses: If they are flooded with too many inputs, the system breaks down.[5]

This is where the software problem comes in. In order to prevent a breakdown, we learn to simplify. We filter, interpret and distort inputs to create the most intelligible picture we can. Proprioception relies on these shortcuts and, like any shortcut, they are prone to error. Albert Einstein once observed, "Everything should be made as simple as possible, but not simpler." Too often, unfortunately, our shortcut thinking is better described by H. L. Mencken's observation: "For every complex problem, there is a simple solution. And it's always wrong"—perhaps not always, but often enough, which is why our perceptions can become completely out of whack with reality. Our mind's eye and our real eyes may seem to be watching different movies. It even happens in the most straightforward of situations—when we try to recognize our own bodies.

***

First, let us look more closely at the psychology behind the rubber hand illusion. Tricks like these were once just clever party entertainment. Recently, however, neuroscientists have been pushing this psychology in provocative directions. Henrik Ehrsson and Valeria Petkova study body swapping. Not to worry—they are neither criminals nor swingers but, rather, cutting-edge neuroscientists at the Karolinska Institute in Stockholm. Their experiments toy with peoples' perceptions of their bodies by intentionally pitting what people think and feel against what they see. How would you react, for example, if you looked down at one of your limbs and saw someone else's limb there instead? What if you tried to move your limb and the other limb did what you expected your own to do?

Ehrsson and Petkova set up an ingenious experiment to test these questions, and I visited their laboratory to be a subject. Petkova took me into her lab and fitted me with a special pair of goggles. The lenses in the goggles were actually tiny video screens. She put a specially designed helmet on her own head that had two video cameras attached on top. Our devices were wirelessly connected so that images from her helmet-cameras were transmitted to my goggle-receivers. In other words, when I looked "through" my goggles I would actually see what Petkova was looking at.

The power to our camera-receiver devices was turned on. We arranged our arms in parallel positions. We both wore short sleeves. I looked down and, in front of me, I saw Petkova's bare arm precisely where mine should have been.

It was a very strange sight: the wrong arm was in the right place on my body. When the experiment had first been explained to me, I wondered how my mind would deal with the conflict. My guess was it would search in panic-mode for my real arm. I was wrong. There was no panic, nor even an inkling of confusion or conflict. The body swap occurred immediately and seamlessly. The moment I saw Petkova's arm jutting out of my body it felt like mine. It's hard to explain how or even on what level I felt it was mine, but I did. Here's the best I can explain it: Look at your hand right now, just your hand, without tracing its connection to the rest of your body. Visually, it's just another object in space. But you *know* it's connected to your arm, which you know is connected to the rest of you. You don't have to think about it or check that it's connected, right? You just know it. I recognize that doesn't sound very scientific but that's exactly how I felt when I saw my new hand, which I began thinking of as my "Petkova-hand."

That, however, was just the beginning. Petkova then had us stand facing each other. Our arms were again arranged in matching sight lines—each of us were looking at our own arms in the same positions—but this time we reached out and began shaking hands. Our squeezes were guided by the rhythm of a metronome to ensure they were synchronous. In other words, my Petkova-hand appeared precisely where my real hand should have been. And it was shaking that real hand. It was—try to follow my technical jargon here—a really, really weird sight.

This led to a more challenging experimental question: In which hand would I experience tactile sensation? When we usually shake someone's hand, of course, we feel our hand shaking the other hand; the sensation of touch is totally in our own hand. But my mind was convinced the Petkova-hand it saw was my hand. How would I resolve the conflict between what I was seeing and what my fingers were feeling? I expected a formidable battle. For one thing, the touch sensors in the human finger are exquisitely sensitive. Studies have determined that our fingers can detect a bump as infinitesimal as one micron high. That's one–four hundred thousandth of an inch or roughly the diameter of a bacterial cell. Human eyes, on the other hand, even young healthy ones, can't distinguish objects much smaller than one hundred microns.[6] For precision, then, I expected my mind to trust what my hand felt over what my eyes saw. But one should never underestimate the clout of visual perception: The neurons for visual processing number in the hundreds of millions and take up about 30 percent of the cerebral cortex. Those for touch constitute only 8 percent. (Neurons for hearing account for 3 percent). Each of the two optic nerves, which carry signals from the retina to the brain, consists of approximately 1.2 million fibers, which even further dwarfs the number for any other sensory nerve.[7] This heavyweight of a visual system isn't easily bullied.

The battle lines were drawn: Visual illusion versus actual tactile sensation. Brute power versus refined precision. Batten down the hatches, I thought. This could be a wild ride. Hardly. It felt as wild as, well, a handshake. Vision trumped from the get-go. The moment we began shaking hands, it not only looked to me like Petkova's hand was my hand but I also felt—literally felt—the tactile sensation in her hand. The hand I saw was the hand I felt, and I experienced this unequivocally from the first squeeze. At one point, I tried to will myself to feel the sensation in my own hand but couldn't. It was as if Petkova's tactile sensors had been literally transplanted along with her virtual hand. Sight didn't simply trump the tactile sensations from my own hand. It convinced my sense of touch to play along with the visual deception.

My experiences, I learned, mirrored what Ehrsson and Petkova have found in controlled studies. Virtually all of the twenty men and women in their initial experiments succumbed to the hand swap illusion. These were some typical comments:

"Your arm felt like it was my arm, and I was behind it."

"I felt like my real, own body was someone else."

"I was shaking hands with myself."[8]

While I was dwelling on this, Petkova pulled out a knife and moved it just above her (my virtual) wrist as if getting ready to cut her hand. It scared the wits out of me. Then she pulled the knife away and made the same threatening movement toward my real wrist. It wasn't a pretty sight, but didn't feel nearly as frightening. My response to the knife threat was also typical. In fact, Ehrsson and Petkova say the most tangible evidence for the reality of the illusion—the psychological reality, that is—are peoples' physiological responses to the knife threat. In controlled experiments, subjects' SCR (skin conductance reaction) dramatically increased when they saw the knife threaten their virtual hand. Remarkably, their SCRs remained significantly lower when the same knife threatened their own real hand. This was true whether the knife threatened their virtual hand first or their real hand first. In other words, as the experimenters observe, their "emotional systems reacted more strongly when the new body was threatened than when their own body was under threat." This, they add, "is a quite remarkable observation that speaks of the strength of the illusions."[9] They won't get an argument from me.

The oddest feeling of all, however, was how comfortable I felt with my new arm. In fact, I'll admit it: I liked the arm. At one point, truth be known, I made what was probably an inappropriate comment to Petkova: "You know, I love being inside your arm." Maybe it was her skin, which was much smoother than my own. But what made it so strange was it was clearly a woman's arm. How peculiar, I thought, that I was so pleased to have a woman's body part attached to my torso. Petkova told me later that this reaction was also typical of those who experience the illusion. All but one person in their original study, both males and females, said they liked their new arm.

Our susceptibility to virtual body swaps is ripe with possible applications. Consider racial prejudice. To begin with, recent studies have demonstrated that it is surprisingly easy to induce virtual possession of a hand of a different race. Several experiments, using a variety of virtual reality techniques, have found that it is no more difficult to create virtual body swaps across skin colors than it is across genders.[10] Studies have consistently found, in fact, that the willingness of a person to assume virtual ownership of a different colored hand—a dark-skinned hand by a light-skinned participant, in most of these experiments—is unrelated to the person's pre-experimental level of prejudice toward people with the virtual skin color.[11] In other words, even white racists find it difficult to reject a black hand as their own.

More important, studies have found, the virtual experience results in decreased prejudice toward people with the new skin color (black, in these cases) on post-experimental measures. It is not just attitudes toward black hands that improve but toward black people in general. These changes are related to the strength of the experimental effect: The more intensely participants accepted the black-skinned hand, the more their attitudes toward black people improved. Lara Maister and her colleagues, who have conducted some of these studies, have an interesting hypothesis as to why this happens. They point to another finding in their research: Participants rated the virtual hand color as more similar to their own after experiencing the swap. This, they suggest, leads to a blurring of their own self-image with their image of the other racial group. As a result, the out-group merges with the in-group. The studies conducted thus far leave a number of unanswered questions, not the least of which is how long the reduction in prejudice endures. If the results hold up, however, and if Maister's hypothesis turns out to be correct, this approach will offer an innovative and potentially powerful new method for changing even deeply held stereotypes.[12]

***

How far can the swap be pushed? What if the new arm is really ugly? What if it were covered with scars or psoriasis or somehow misshapen? Heroin tracks? How about if it was a gorilla's arm? At what point does the mind draw a line in the sand and declare, no, I refuse to accept this arm? Or, say the illusion did kick in for an ugly or unappealing arm. Could you accept the new limb as your own on one level of awareness but at the same time find it repulsive on another? Is your mind capable of deciding that "this looks like an arm and it's where my arm is supposed to be so it must be my arm" at the same time that you are repelled by the new object?

Perhaps even more consequential is the matter of confronting oneself as an outsider. In my case, I watched myself shaking my own hand. This, in itself, was rather jarring. But what if I'd been looking at the entire me? This wasn't possible when I was hooked up because of the video receiver hiding my face. But technology is on the brink of conquering this glitch, too. Video receivers are now being developed that will fit over one's pupils like contact lenses.

Think of the therapeutic possibilities. What if we added role playing therapy to virtual body swapping? Role playing refers to a commonly used clinical technique in which a patient is told to act the part of a person with whom he or she is experiencing difficulty. It has proven especially useful in couples counseling. Hair-raising as this can be, in role-playing you don't actually see yourself. Now imagine you could be made to feel as if you had really swapped bodies. You would get to watch yourself in the flesh, or so it would seem. And you would get to see that self through your partner's eyes. What a potent lesson in empathy. It might not save your marriage, but it would certainly alter your view of yourself.

***

The body swap experiments demonstrate how swiftly our proprioceptive maps can be transformed. They also expose the quirkiness of the process. And, most important, they are leading to promising applications. Consider, for example, what must be the most unusual medical procedure ever devised: the virtual amputation of a phantom limb. Phantom limb pain has to be one of the cruelest of medical conditions. Following the amputation of a real limb, an estimated 90 to 98 percent of patients are left with the persistent, unambiguous, and eerie feeling that their limb is still there.[13] Silas Weir Mitchell, the American neurologist, poet, and novelist who coined the term "phantom limb" in 1871, spoke of "fractional phantoms" haunting people like "unseen ghosts of the lost part."[14] In the worst of these cases, the phantom limb is chronically painful. It's a wicked double curse: You give up a limb and feel pain in return. One study found that 70 percent of people who experienced phantom limb pain were still suffering pain twenty-five years after losing their limb.[15] The pain can be excruciating. Patients become depressed. Some have committed suicide.

For the past hundred years, it was believed that the pain was either a figment of the patient's imagination or it was emanating from the swollen nerve endings, called neuromas, in the stump. Some surgeons tried killing the pain by cutting away at the stump, over and again in some cases. The stumps got shorter, but the pain never wavered. Next, they sometimes tried severing the nerve endings at their source on the spinal cord. In a few cases surgeons severed the patient's thalamus, the organ at the base of the brain that processes the sensation of pain. None of this had any effect on the pain.

V. S. Ramachandran is a behavioral neurologist and the director of the Center for Brain and Cognition at the University of California, San Diego. Ramachandran had a different theory about what caused phantom limb pain. When reviewing the case sheets of his paralyzed phantom limb patients, he noticed that their problems could all be traced back to actual limb paralysis. They had suffered serious mishaps, perhaps a fall or a motorcycle accident, that severed the peripheral nerve, which is the main nerve supplying impulses to the arm. "So the patient had an actual arm, which is painful, in a sling for a few months, or a year, and then in a misguided attempt to get rid of the pain in the arm, the surgeon amputates the arm," he says. The result was a phantom arm with the same symptoms as before.

Ramachandran noticed that about half of these patients described their pain as an excruciating cramp or spasm. It was as if their old limb wasn't just still there but that it felt frozen. "Doctor, the phantom limb is paralyzed," they would say to Ramachandran. "It's fixed in a clenched spasm and it's excruciatingly painful. If only I could move it, maybe the pain will be relieved."[16]

The patients aren't delusional. They know there is no actual arm. But the pain is no less intense. Unfortunately, their brains refuse to accept this and persist in the doomed effort. The brain says, "Move." But it can see that the arm doesn't move. So the brain tries again. "Move," it commands. The arm still doesn't move. The brain persists in this way, creating an escalating, dysfunctional feedback loop. If this were a functioning arm, the muscles from the hand would tell the brain to take it easy: "This isn't working." But in an amputee there is no feedback, so the brain doesn't know when to stop. The brain concludes that the phantom limb is locked in a spasm, which results in the experience of real pain.

Ramachandran believed if he could figure out a way for patients to unlearn their learned paralysis that the excruciating, clenching spasms would disappear. But how does a neurosurgeon treat illusory paralysis? The answer was an illusory surgery. He would replace the painful phantom by creating an illusory swap with a healthy arm; or, more precisely, with an illusory clone of the patient's good arm. The apparatus consisted of a cardboard box with a twenty-inch square drugstore mirror standing upright in the middle. The box was open at the top and had two holes in front through which patients inserted their arms. The holes were on opposite sides of the mirror. The patients are told to place their real arm through one of the holes and their stump through the other. The side holding the stump is covered so the stump cannot be seen. They look into the top of the box on the side of the mirror that holds their real hand and, in doing so, also see the reflection of the hand in the mirror. They are told to hold both hands in the same clenched posture. They now feel like they are seeing two complete, clenched hands. The whole setup cost three dollars.

Ramachandran's first test was a young man, whom he referred to as Philip, who had paralyzed his arm in a motorcycle accident ten years earlier.[17] The useless arm was kept in a sling for a year before it was amputated. Philip had been living with severe phantom pains ever since. Philip placed his arms through the holes in the mirror-box. Ramachandran then told Philip to wiggle both hands—the real and the phantom—while looking in the mirror. "I want you to move your right and left arm simultaneously," he instructed Philip.

"Oh, I can't do that," Philip said. "I can move my right arm, but my left arm is frozen. Every morning when I get up, I try to move my phantom because it's in this funny position and I feel that moving it might help relieve the pain. But . . . I never have been able to generate a flicker of movement in it."

"Okay, Philip, but try anyway," Ramachandran told him.

Philip tried to move both hands as instructed. "As he gazed into the mirror," Ramachandran recalled, "he gasped and then cried out, 'Oh, my God! Oh, my God, doctor! This is unbelievable. It's mind-boggling.' He was jumping up and down like a kid. 'My left arm is plugged in again. . . . I can move my arm again. I can feel my elbow moving, my wrist moving. It's all moving again.'"

It was the first time in ten years that the patient had felt his phantom limb moving. And, most stunningly, the cramping pain instantly subsided. Instantly. After a while, Ramachandran told Philip to close his eyes. The phantom froze again. "I feel my right hand moving, but there's no movement in the phantom," Philip said.

"Open your eyes," Ramachandran told him.

"Oh, yes. Now it's moving again."

Ramachandran knew Philip couldn't walk around looking at a mirror the rest of his life. He told Philip to take the mirror home and practice with it ten minutes a day. Two weeks later, Philip phoned. "Doctor, you're not going to believe this," he said. "It's gone . . . this phantom I've had for the last 10 years. It's disappeared."

Ramachandran explained it this way: The mirror box had confronted Philip's brain with tremendous sensory conflict. Visually, it's receiving messages saying that the old arm is back. But it isn't getting any muscle feedback from the arm. Does his brain believe what it sees or what it feels? Sound familiar? Vision won out, just as it did in Ehrsson and Petkova's experiments. Philip's brain said, "To hell with it, there is no phantom," Ramachandran recalled. Visual feedback had tricked his brain into thinking his hand was clenching or unclenching, and this had interrupted the escalating, dysfunctional dialogue between his brain and his missing hand: "No." "Move." "No." "Move." "And when the [phantom] arm disappears, the bonus is the pain disappears because you can't have disembodied pain floating out there, in space," he says.

It was, as Ramachandran is fond of saying, "the first example in medical history of a successful amputation of a phantom limb." Ramachandran repeated the intervention with eight other amputees, and, in all but one case, "phantom hands that had been balled into painful fists opened, and phantom arms that had stiffened into agonizing contortions straightened."[18]

***

Phantom limb surgery is just the beginning. Virtual treatments are being explored for many types of pain, and researchers are finding that the virtual manipulations need not be so dramatic. A little exaggeration of reality—*augmented reality*, as it is known in the virtual reality profession—can be enough. Daniel Harvie and his colleagues, for example, have shown how this works for patients suffering from movement-evoked pain resulting from chronic neck problems. In their study, patients with neck pain were fitted with a virtual reality head-mounted display that projected imaginary scenes—a landscape, for example—before their eyes. They were then asked to take in as much of the scene as they could by rotating their heads, both to the left and the right, until they felt pain.

This is where the bogus feedback came in. The virtual scenes were manipulated to change in a way that gave patients the illusion that they had either moved their heads further than they actually had or vice versa. Perception consistently trumped reality. On the negative side, the patients' pain started before their usual pain-free point when they had been manipulated to falsely believe that they had turned beyond that point. More important, on the positive side, they were able to turn their heads beyond their usual pain-free point without pain when they were manipulated to perceive that they hadn't turned beyond that point. In other words, virtual reality increased their range of motion in physical reality. Another victory for virtual orthopedics.[19]

Virtual therapies are being developed for many conditions. They are, for example, being used to treat symptoms of strokes, which typically have a component of learned paralysis. Focal hand dystonia, a neurological condition causing one's fingers to curl up and then bend out uncontrollably, also appears to be virtually treatable. Back at the Karolinska Institute, Henrik Ehrsson and his colleagues are exploring promising therapies to alleviate phantom limb pain through illusory touch.[20] The possibilities of treating problems like these with painless, inexpensive interventions, with no apparent physical side effects, opens an exciting new frontier.

***

Virtual reality isn't the only alternative to flesh-and-blood medical intervention. Engineers are now developing tangible augmentations to biological reality that exploit the fickleness of proprioception. Among the most notable work are procedures that have targeted people in need of real-life body part replacements. Consider, for example, individuals who are missing a limb. Until recently, one's options were pretty much limited to lifeless, flesh-colored plastic or wooden prosthetics. In a remarkable medical breakthrough, however, surgeons have now developed procedures that allow them to transplant a healthy limb from a dying person. Medically speaking, these operations can be quite successful.

The most common limb transplants are hands. As of this writing, a total of seventy hands have been successfully transplanted onto fifty patients around the world since the first successful surgery in 1998.[21] In perhaps the most publicized case, Matthew Scott showed off his new left hand by, albeit awkwardly, throwing out the ceremonial first pitch on opening day for the Philadelphia Phillies.

Surgical transplants have a number of shortcomings, however. Motor control, particularly fine motor movement, is limited. Tactile feeling, even in the most successful transplants, is restricted to the crude detection of sensations like hot versus cold and smooth versus sharp. Recipients can also anticipate chronic medical complications. And they will certainly be taking drugs for the rest of their lives. The biggest disappointments, however, are often psychological. It turns out to be very difficult to take mental ownership of an arm that neither works nor looks like your old one. This is exacerbated when the arm comes from the body of a stranger. Creepier yet, from a stranger who was on the brink of death.

Some recipients have been happy with their surgeries despite the shortcomings. Matthew Scott, for example, recently celebrated the tenth anniversary of his new arm with a press conference during which he emotionally thanked his health team for the "wonderful success" that changed his life for the better. Many other recipients, however, have found their new hand harder to embrace. The first attempt at hand transplant surgery in 1966, for example, was a medical success—the hand was physically accepted—but the recipient found it so repugnant to look at the alien hand that he eventually demanded that it be surgically removed. In a later case, a much publicized pioneering double hand transplant surgery, the recipient told his doctors that it took months for him to stop referring to one of the hands as "it."[22]

These problems with live body transplants are not likely to be solved in the near future. But a more promising alternative is in the works: the transplantation of artificial body parts—prosthetic limbs—rather than real ones. And, oddly enough, the success of these procedures may depend as much on the psychology of virtual body swaps as on traditional medical technology. To begin with, artificial limbs have come a long way from the old lifeless attachments. There are now dazzlingly sophisticated devices on the market. One humanoid prosthetic hand, nicknamed the "Pisa-hand" in tribute to the Italian city where it was created, is a space-age robotic device with five independent fingers driven by six motors. It allows a range of movements that mimics those of a human hand, with joints in all the same places. Designed by artists, it can be customized with a photo-realist flair that makes it look like the recipient's actual hand. Most remarkably, it can be controlled almost like a real hand. The prosthetic is attached with electrodes to the amputee's stump so that electrical impulses from nerve endings in the stump send signals, via a computer, to receptors in the artificial hand. When the recipient thinks "clutch pencil with thumb, index and middle fingers," the robotic fingers clutch the pencil.

Hugh Herr, director of the biomechatronics research group at the MIT Media Lab, is at the forefront of prosthetic designs. Herr lost both his legs from frostbite following a mountain climbing accident when he was seventeen and began designing artificial limbs soon afterward. He says he had two goals. First, he wanted to design limbs that would allow him to start climbing again. Second, he wanted to show his high school classmates "that being a bilateral amputee could be fun."

Herr thinks of the body as a blank canvas on which he can improve upon biology. He usually has eight or so different types of bionic legs in his closet: one for running, a few types for climbing—one with spiked feet that penetrate ice walls, another for balancing "on edges the width of a coin." He also has a pair for swimming which, he says, "can make me into a merman, with giant fins." "We'll soon be rethinking what clothes are," Herr predicts. He envisions skinlike fashions that add support and structure. They'll be smart enough to change depending on the activity. If you go out for a run, for example, the skin he is designing will stiffen to reduce joint stress. In addition, Herr predicts, we'll be attaching robots to our existing body parts. For example, he says, "Let's say you want to go running, and that causes pain in your left knee. You put on this robot that spans your knee. That robot would take the stress away from your biological knee, and you could run without further degradation of your tissue."[23]

Prosthetics like these may be as close to immortality as we can get. "My biological body will degrade in time due to normal, age-related degeneration," Herr says. "But the artificial part of my body improves in time because I can upgrade." He predicts that "when I'm 80 years old, I'll be able to walk with less energy than is required of a person who has biological legs, I'll be more stable, and I'll probably be able to run faster."[24]

A major shortcoming of prosthetic devices has been the absence of sensory feedback. In a prosthetic hand, for example, the fingers may move, but the amputee doesn't feel them move. This is where the body-swap illusions come in. Another Swedish-led research team, this one headed by Birgitta Rosén, has demonstrated that the illusion can be modified to induce amputees to "feel" sensation in their artificial hand. In the most remarkable of these experiments, two amputees were first trained to mentally control the Pisa-hand through impulses from their stumps. The training took all of two hours. They were then instructed to move the robotic fingers into different positions and to watch the fingers as they moved. In addition, they sometimes received the rubber hand treatment: As they were manipulating their fingers, the experimenter synchronously stroked their stump and the robotic hand with a brush. After three minutes, both subjects began feeling the sensation in their robotic hand instead of their stump. This suggests, Rosen and her colleagues observe, "that a patient with a normal mind can be tricked into experiencing an advanced humanoid robotic hand prosthesis as part of their own body."[25]

For now, the illusion only works when the amputee is looking at the prosthesis. But new techniques are being developed. One, for example, would attach stimulators to the robotic device and receptors to the stump. Whenever the robotic device moves, it would send signals to the stump. This, in turn, would trick the brain into feeling tactile sensation in the artificial part. Hugh Herr looks forward to sometime in a decade or so when an amputee will "not only be able to walk across a sandy beach, but [will] actually feel the sand against his prosthetic foot."[26]

Engineers are already creating artificial body parts—hands, arms, legs, and, yes, those other organs—that can do everything and more than our real ones. Designers are making them look like our own. Behavioral scientists will soon make them feel like our own.

***

These examples—virtual body swaps, phantom amputations, and replacement parts that we learn to own—demonstrate the plasticity of our proprioceptive maps and how far these maps can diverge from the physical realities of our actual body. But to see just how detached perception may become from reality, let us turn to one last example of proprioception gone amok—a perplexing medical condition called "asomatognosia," in which patients become convinced that one of their limbs is not their own. As in Dr. Strangelove syndrome, the feeling most commonly centers on a paralyzed left arm or leg following a stroke to the right hemisphere of the brain. The patient may refer to the limb in the third person ("it," "that thing"), give it a derogatory name ("my little monkey," "the dummy"), refer to it as dead (it belongs to the hospital) or even describe it as someone else's ("my [deceased] husband's hand," "it belongs to the nurse," "it's the devil's hand"). Some asomatognosics just ignore the arm, but others are so repulsed by the foreign invader that they attack it or try to throw it out of bed.

There is also an extreme variation of asomatognosia called "body integrity identity disorder" (BIID). It is a rare condition, affecting an estimated several thousand people worldwide, mostly men, whereby people feel so alienated from a body part that they ask to have it amputated. One patient said, "It seems like my body stops mid-thigh of my right leg. The rest is not me."[27] Adding to the strangeness of BIID is that, unlike typical asomatognosia, the problem involves limbs that are physically healthy. In many instances, the desire to be rid of the limb becomes an obsession. If the afflicted can't find a doctor to perform the surgery—which, as you can imagine, can be difficult—they may try to do it themselves. Science writer Anil Ananthaswamy, in his book *Do No Harm: The People Who Amputate Their Perfectly Healthy Limbs, and the Doctors Who Help Them*, describes a number of such cases.

Consider, for example, the case of David, who desperately wanted to cut off his leg for as long as he could remember. He made his first serious attempt just after leaving college, when he locked himself in his room and bound the leg with a tourniquet made from an old sock and strong baling twine. He gave up after two hours, however, when the pain became so excruciating that he feared for his life. Failure seemed to increase David's obsession. Being rid of the leg consumed his thoughts. At home, David started hopping around as if the leg wasn't there. When standing, he'd keep all his weight on his good leg. When sitting, he'd push the bad leg as far to the side as possible. It wasn't enough. David says: "It got to the point where I'd come into my house and just cry. I'd be looking at other people and seeing that they already have their lives going good for them. And I'm stuck here, all miserable. I'm being held back by this strange obsession. The logic going through my head was that I need to take care of this now, because if I wait any longer, there is not much chance of a life for me."[28]

Another sufferer, Patrick, recalls having felt strange about his leg since he was four years old. As with David, the feeling grew into an obsession to remove it from his body. Patrick says he would spend days on end thinking, "How can I get rid of it? What can I do? How can I do it? I don't want to die in the process." When he came across an amputee on the streets, or even a picture of one, he couldn't get the image out of his mind. "It would just drive me nuts. That could last for several days. All I could think about was how I could get rid of my leg."[29]

Patrick took a more methodical approach than had David. A BIID sufferer who had managed a successful amputation of his own limb suggested to Patrick that he practice first. So Patrick went about cutting off a part of his finger before taking on an entire limb. Ananthaswamy describes the surgery: "With a pen and a rubber band, [Patrick] made a tourniquet for one of his fingers and stuck it into a thermal cup full of ice and alcohol. After part of the finger became numb and Patrick was unable to bend it, he took a hammer and chisel and chopped off the bit above the first knuckle. He even smashed the detached digit. 'So [according to Patrick] they couldn't reattach it even if they wanted to.'"

Neither David nor Patrick ever removed his "bad" limb on his own. Eventually, however, each found a surgeon to perform the operation.[30] Both were as happy as they had anticipated with the end results. "I looked down and couldn't believe it," Patrick recalls thinking when he awoke from the anesthesia. "It was finally gone. I was ecstatic." Looking back, both say it was one of the best decisions they ever made. "I wouldn't want my leg back for all the money in the world, that's how happy I am," Patrick says eight years after the surgery. His only regret is he didn't get it done earlier.

This reaction is typical of BIID sufferers who have the operation. Follow-up evaluations find that patients are almost always positive, and often euphoric, immediately after the surgery. And, more important, they experience satisfaction over the long term. In one study, two-thirds of patients who had not had the surgery said they needed it to establish their true identity. One patient, for example, said, "I felt like I was in the wrong body—that I am only complete with both my arm and leg off on the right side."[31] Some patients specify the precise location of the problem. They might say, "Not just above the knee, but four inches above the knee."[32] Almost every patient studied has described a feeling of relief after the surgery. They speak in terms of wholeness and liberation when they see the limb or limbs are no longer there.

Most people assume that anyone who wants to cut off a healthy limb has bigger problems than a faulty body part. Medical ethicists have expressed concern that after the first limb is amputated the patient will want to get rid of others. But there is no evidence of this except in cases where BIID involved multiple limbs from the beginning. Nor is there evidence of mental illness in general.[33] Michael First, a Columbia University clinical psychiatrist, conducted a survey of fifty-two BIID patients. Other than their BIID symptoms, the patients' test results were relatively normal. "They have families. They hold all kinds of jobs, doctors and lawyers and professors. They're not screwed-up people apart from this. You could spend an evening with them and never have the slightest clue," he observes.[34]

The cause of the problem seems to be a mismatch between their internal maps of their bodies and the bodies themselves. It is another example of the flimsiness of our proprioceptive maps.

***

There are really two problems in BIID. The most obvious is that a part of a person's body has become mislabeled as non-self. But the second and the more serious problem is patients' loathing of the alien part. Why such disgust? Just because it is not yours?

BIID is a rare affliction. Few of us can begin to imagine what might drive a person to such extremes. The feeling of disgust, however, has parallels we can all relate to. It is an emotion we often experience toward entities that cross the border from self to non-self. Psychologist Paul Rozin, the reigning expert on the topic of disgust, likes to ask people to think about how often they swallow their own saliva. This is something we do constantly, of course. Now, imagine instead of swallowing your saliva you spit it into a sparkling clean cup. How would you feel about drinking what's in the cup? Care for a gulp of your own saliva? No thanks, right? But why? We even give the liquid a new name. In our mouths, it was "saliva." Now it's "spit."[35]

Where, exactly, does the transformation occur? (Should you happen to be eating right now, you might want to take a break.) If you began drooling, a really thick drool, but sucked it back into your mouth before it disconnected, that probably wouldn't offend your taste. But if a piece broke off and someone suggests you put it back in your mouth? Uh, no thanks. Or, consider this: You are chewing a freshly baked chocolate chip cookie. You momentarily stick your tongue out, then back in, and resume chewing. The food would still taste fine, right? But what if you accidentally spit the wad onto a plate? Would you put it back into your mouth? Not so fine, I suspect.

The disgust level is even higher for other materials that leave our bodies. Snot in your nose? Fine. Once out of your nose, however, would you put it back in? What about your blood? Urine? Feces? But here's something else to consider. These things *are* in your body. Always. Snot and feces accompany us—no, are part of us—when we're out on a walk, talking to a friend, having sex, eating dinner. How do we manage to not let that disgust us? And what logic convinces us to be more disgusted by their presence outside our bodies than inside our bodies? Fortunately, however, we have learned not to think about these realities. Chalk it up to the creativity of evolution.

It gets even worse when you take in something that was once in another person's body. Consider feces. Could anything be more disgusting than someone else's feces entering your body? Well, sorry to say, you're absorbing bits of them all the time. "The world is covered in a fine patina of feces," as Stanford microbiologist Stanley Falkow so elegantly puts it. Each time a toilet is flushed, some of the leavings are aerosolized. Fecal particles end up in house dust and on objects anywhere in the vicinity. ("You want to keep your toothbrush a minimum of six feet away from a toilet," one researcher advised.)[36]

Before you start sterilizing with a blow torch, here's something to think about: those microbes are essential to your health. It is well established that the bacteria in our gut have wide-ranging influence on our physiological functioning. They effect digestion, allergies, and metabolism, for example.[37] Some of these bacteria are even used as medicine. The most effective medical treatment for certain chronic digestive disorders—notably an antibiotic-resistant intestinal pathogen named *Clostridium difficile*, which kills fourteen thousand people annually in the United States alone—is a fecal implant. The procedure involves exactly what it sounds like. The physician inserts someone else's leavings up your rectum or—bear with me on this—into your nose. Or, in a new medical breakthrough, you can now swallow it in pill form.[38] (Up the rectum, in the nose, or down the hatch? Decisions, decisions.)

Our digestive systems contain trillions of microbes—an estimated 100 trillion of these totally foreign life forms by the time we are five years old. The microbes, in turn secrete an enormous number of chemicals that are critical to the well-being of our bodies. This we have known for some time. But it is not just our physical well-being that is affected. There is mounting evidence that the microbes in our gut also play important roles in how we think and feel. A wave of recent studies have found that "our" bacteria can, for example, directly influence moods and emotions like anxiety and depression. "Directly" is the key word here. Everyone knows that the state of our guts is related to how we feel. When you have an upset stomach, it makes you feel lousy. But the remarkable new findings concern how this comes about.

The microbes in our gut, it turns out, secrete some of the same neurochemicals that our brains use to regulate moods and feelings, including serotonin, dopamine, and gamma-aminobutyric acid (GABA). Serotonin, for example, is important for regular bowel functions. But it is more famously known as "the happiness hormone." It is the target of many of the most popular antidepressant drugs, such as the multibillion dollar–selling Prozac, Zoloft, and Lexapro—the so-called serotonin reuptake inhibitors (SSRIs). GABA is, on the one hand, critical for muscle tone. But it is also the target of the most common antianxiety drugs, such as Valium and Xanax. These neurochemicals—serotonin, dopamine, and GABA—are manufactured by bacteria like *Bifidobacterium* and *Lactobacillus rhamnosus* that reside aplenty in our guts.

This raises therapeutic possibilities that scientists are just beginning to explore. Can the bacteria found in our guts be mined for therapy as psychiatric drugs? There is accumulating evidence that they can, although most of this comes from animal studies. In one often-cited example, a research team led by John Cryan, a neuroscientist at the University College of Cork in Ireland, fed one group of mice a broth containing *Bifidobacterium* and another group a dose of Lexapro. They then subjected the mice to a series of stressful situations and found that the microbe was as effective as the drug on every test: the two groups showed equal reductions in hormone levels related to stress and equal increases in behaviors that demonstrated perseverance.[39]

Stephen Collins, a gastroenterologist at McMaster University Medical School in Hamilton, Canada, has experimented with bacteria transplants. In one series of studies, he and his research team replaced the gut bacteria in a strain of anxious mice with the bacteria from a strain of fearless mice and vice versa. The result: The fearless mice became more anxious, and the anxious mice became more fearless. In another study, the researchers transplanted the feces from humans suffering from irritable bowel syndrome (IBS), an intestinal disorder with no known cause, into germ-free mice. IBS sufferers were chosen because people with the disease often have co-occurring psychiatric disorders such as anxiety and depression. Once again, the recipients took on aspects of their donors. The mice developed leaky intestines and other symptoms of IBS and, more important to the researchers, they displayed anxious behavior where they hadn't before.[40]

Findings like these will require replication with humans. But there is great enthusiasm among a rapidly growing group of researchers around the world who believe that our bacterial ecosystem will prove to play crucial roles in the treatment of autism, anxiety, depression, and other disorders. "There's been an explosion of interest in the connections between the microbiome [as the bacterial ecosystem is known] and the brain," observes gastroenterologist Emeran Mayer, who has been studying these questions for the past five years.[41] The National Institute of Mental Health has also come on board, having in 2015 awarded several million dollars in grants to further our understanding of the role of gut microbes in our mental health. Is it possible that the next generation of psychiatric drugs will be composed of bacteria from peoples' guts? Will the feces from happy people become the Prozac and Valium of tomorrow? Up the rectum, in the nose, or down the hatch? Stay tuned.

The point is that disgusting outsiders—bacteria (dare I say feces?)— can be good for you. But, of course, knowing this makes it no more appetizing. (I'm done. You can start eating again.)

***

There are differences between the iterations of proprioception that we have covered. In the case of phantom limbs, the brain thinks that a part is attached to its body when it is not. In BIID, it thinks that a part that really is attached to the body does not belong to that body. Both are generally disorders, whereas the revulsion to wastes outside our body, although sometimes illogical, is for the most part a healthy reaction. Each, however, are founded in the same dynamic that underlies the ease in taking mental ownership of a young woman's arm and Hugh Herr's success with prosthetic limbs. All underscore how arbitrarily we decide what constitutes *our* body and how intensely we distance ourselves from anything that fails to make the cut. The proprioceptive map is both "a tool and a weapon," philosopher Thomas Metzinger observes. "It's something that evolved to constantly preserve and sustain and defend the integrity of the overall organism, and that includes drawing a line between me and not-me."[42] The surfaces of our bodies are not simply border checks. They are also places of magiclike transformation from self to non-self.

The notion of "my body" is, like "my self," a story we tell ourselves. Body swaps? Phantom limbs? BIID? They are coded into the fiction. The character in Samuel Beckett's play *The Unnamable* puts it simply: "I say me, knowing all the while it's not me."

5
Parasites 'R Us

Hey, my bubble, my rules.
—Bart Simpson, *The Simpsons*

Perhaps it shouldn't be surprising that we—these minds of ours—have such a fickle view of what is us and what is not. As Norwood Russell Hanson once observed, "There is more to seeing than meets the eyeball."[1] Everything gets muddled when it passes through the filters of perception. But enough of this messy psychology-speak for the moment. Let us return to the lens of biological science. Certainly this discipline—which, I confess, we psychologists enviously refer to as a "hard science"—can offer a clearer description of the boundary between self and non-self?

***

Jerry Coyne is an evolutionary biologist at the University of Chicago. His research on population and evolutionary genetics has been widely published in professional and trade journals and his 2009 book, *Why Evolution Is True*, established him as a leading force in the study of evolution. Jerry is also an internationally famous defender of evolution against proponents of creationism and intelligent design. He is a highly respected scientist.

This, however, is a more personal story about Coyne. It goes back to 1973, when he was a mere twenty-four-year-old graduate student at Harvard. As he moved through the program, Coyne was becoming well versed in the intellectual tools of his trade—genetics, evolutionary logic, research methods, and the like. But when it came to real-life contact with nature, his experience was pretty much "limited to unexciting fruit flies crawling feebly around food-filled glass tubes."[2] He was even more frustrated working at Harvard's Museum of Comparative Zoology. This was the same museum that was founded by the great Swiss naturalist Louis Agassiz, under the guiding philosophy to "study nature, not books." But, aside from fruit flies in a sterile lab, the only nature Coyne was seeing were stuffed mammals in a display case on his way to the Pepsi machine. When given the opportunity to take a summer field course in tropical ecology in Costa Rica, Coyne didn't hesitate. He never imagined how close to nature he would get.

Toward the end of his stay in Costa Rica, Coyne was walking through the forest when he heard a mosquito getting closer and closer, and finally, it bit him on the head. "Not too far from the crown and I scratched it," he recalled.[3] But, unlike a usual mosquito bite, this one didn't want to go away. When, after a few days, the bump had grown to the size of a pea, Coyne consulted with a fellow student who was an entomologist. His friend got up on a bunk bed. "She looked at my head and pulled the hairs back, and she said, 'Oh my God, there is something moving in there,'" Coyne said. She spotted what appeared to be a tiny hose protruding from the mosquito bite. Then she realized the hose was wiggling. It was a breathing tube, like a little straw. That meant there was something live on the other side of the tube. The two biologists knew right away it had to be a maggot.

The maggot turned out to be a botfly, a hairy insect that lives in tropical regions in Central and South America. It has a biologically ingenious and, most humans would think, rather disgusting strategy for ensuring the survival of its young. The process works something like this: After a pregnant female lays her eggs, she flies in the air and grabs on to a mosquito. Then, in midflight, she glues her eggs to the mosquito's wings. The mother leaves. The mosquito, who probably has no idea anything has happened, continues doing what it always does, which is to fly around until it finds a warm mammal and sucks its blood. When the mosquito finds its prey, the mammal's heat triggers the eggs to hatch. One of the newly hatched larva—a tiny maggot—burrows its way inside the mammal through the mosquito bite, sets up a little home, and sticks its breathing tube out the opening. Botflies feed on the mammal's tissue until, after about six weeks, they've grown big enough to survive on their own, and then they exit through the hole in their host's skin. Coyne happened to be the host this time around.

He soon learned removing the botfly wouldn't be easy. The best solution would have been to cut it out with a sterile scalpel. But finding a good surgeon was a problem in a remote tropical forest. "There was a woman in the course who had botflies in her butt," Coyne recalled to me. She found someone to surgically remove them, but it wasn't a pretty scene. "This guy took her in a back room and started cutting them out with a Swiss army knife. I remember we could all hear her screaming when this was happening. I found myself thinking, 'Do I really want to go through this?'"[4]

He was tempted to try yanking the maggot out by pulling on its protruding spiracle. But Coyne knew that was probably the worst thing he could do. "Like all marvels of evolution the botfly maggot has devices to keep you from pulling it out because it makes its living in your body," he explained. "So it has a pair of hooks on the anal end, the other end, that are dug into your flesh so if you try to pull the thing out it just digs in and you'll break it in two. That's the thing you want to avoid because it can cause a serious infection."[5]

The most common treatment where Coyne was living was known as the "meat cure." He was told to strap a slab of meat—a steak, maybe—to his head. This cuts off the maggot's air supply, and the maggot, thinking the steak is part of Coyne's flesh, burrows into it searching for air. Once the maggot gets far enough, he would just have to pull off the steak with the worm in it. It made sense, but Coyne respectfully declined. "The idea of toiling in the tropical heat every day with a T-bone strapped to my head. It's not something that I wanted to do."

Meanwhile, the symptoms were getting worse. "It's a terrible itch and from time to time it would like move or twitch and you would feel this sort of sharp pain in your skull or you could feel it grinding up against it," Coyne recalled. "And when I went swimming or took a shower, it would sort of freak out because its airhole would be cut off, then it would really go nuts. You know, make a lot of pain. So I tried to avoid getting my head under water."

The lump was also getting noticeably bigger, and Coyne was all too aware why. "It was eating my muscles and tissues and scalp," he said. "It's turning human flesh into fly flesh." Like any normal person, Coyne was initially disgusted. "I freaked out completely," he said. But then the scientist in him took over. This was biology in its elegance. "You know, when you really think about it, it's amazing how an animal can take human flesh and turn it using its own genes into a fly."[6] How astonishing, he thought, that "something was transforming my molecules into their own. The idea that a fly could convert you into a fly. That really amazed me."[7] And the fact that this fly, by eating him, was in a very literal sense becoming him? "That's the part that made me like it," he says.[8]

***

Coyne returned to Boston a few weeks later and went straight to the Harvard health clinic. "Nobody had ever seen anything like this at Harvard before," Coyne recalled. Within minutes he was surrounded by about twenty doctors. "I had to explain it to them. They were all poking and prodding but none of them seemed to know what to do with this. So I figured it wasn't worth it to put myself in the hands of people who'd never treated anything like this before and were more likely to screw it up. The botfly wasn't that painful and I knew it was going to come out on its own after a while," Coyne told me.[9] He decided to just try to enjoy and marvel at what was happening inside him as much as he could.

"I know this might seem weird to a lay person," he said, but "I make my living on flies. I work with fruit flies. I'm a geneticist, and here is a fly making its living on me." Coyne was intrigued to find himself inside a food chain instead of on his usual perch as a consumer at its end. The botfly was fattening up on Coyne, and Coyne was becoming increasingly fond of the botfly. "I was getting more and more curious when it would come out. I didn't want to kill it."[10]

The botfly kept growing. Within a couple of weeks it had become the size of an egg, then a quail egg. Coyne started wearing a baseball cap. One night he was at a Red Sox game at Fenway Park with his girlfriend Sarah Rogerson. "Every once in a while I would rub my head, throughout the whole gestation of this thing, just to check on it. During the game, when I rubbed my head I felt something coming out of the lump. "Coyne kept saying, 'Oh my gosh. Oh my gosh. It's coming out. I can feel it,'" said Sarah. "A foul ball came up where were sitting and it hit one of those wooden seats in Fenway and we narrowly escaped getting hit because we really weren't paying much attention to the game at all."[11]

It didn't come out right away. Sarah and Coyne went back to his apartment. He kept checking to feel the lump. Sometime later in the evening, he reached up and said, "It's gone. It's out." He told Sarah they had to find it. "I turned on the light and there it was on the pillow and it was horrifying," Coyne said. It was a fat, white worm, about an inch and a half long. It was bulbous on one end and tapered to a little tail on the other. And it had little black teeth Forever the evolutionary biologist, Coyne was struck by the painlessness of the exit. "You know, it's painful when it's in there but when it comes out it does so very painlessly." This, he realized, was another evolutionary invention. "If the worm did it painfully, then the horse or the monkey or whoever it is infecting would just slap it and kill it."

But mostly he wanted to save the fly. He looked at his baby on the pillow and decided to try to rear it into an adult fly. "I'd prepared a jar of sterile sand and I took the worm and dropped it in the sand and put on a top with an airhole," Coyne said. "But unfortunately it died."[12] Looking back, he said that he was sorry he "didn't just put it into a jar of alcohol to preserve it."[13] Coyne felt extremely sad afterward. "You know in the temperature zone in Boston the botfly is not going to make it. It just can't live and so it was doomed from the start. I wanted to see it live its life cycle but unfortunately it didn't quite make it. I did the best I could with what I knew." He felt the loss. "It added some richness into my life. It did. People still get completely horrified when I tell them the story even though to me it's sort of a nice story."[14] And, he told me, "It was my botfly."[15]

***

Jerry Coyne's maggot was clearly an intruder—a hit-and-run thief who conned its way into Coyne's body, stole what it needed, and, when Coyne was no longer useful, went off to live an independent life. It was a parasite. But the maggot also raises difficult questions about the division between self and non-self. The maggot was never invited into Coyne's head. For those weeks it lived there, however, wasn't the maggot in many ways literally Coyne? After all, other than the tip of its breathing tube, the maggot existed completely inside his body. Besides, the maggot was flesh-and-blood Coyne in the most literal sense: Almost the entirety of its physical bulk consisted of Coyne's tissue. And then there was the boundary. To protect itself from infection, Coyne's body had encapsulated the maggot in a little pocket under the surface of the skin. The pocket became the maggot's home. The same physical boundary separating Coyne from the "lifeless" air outside himself—his epidermis—was now also separating the maggot from its own outside. So was the pocket more Jerry Coyne or maggot?

The psychologist in me loves watching the quirky ways people draw their personal boundaries. It's interesting how emotional we get when we believe somebody or something has crossed into our personal territory. But, the fact is, psychological feelings are trivial in cases like this. It didn't make much difference whether Coyne thought of his botfly as himself or his guest. Their relationship was a matter of life or death—certainly for the botfly and potentially for Coyne. Biologically speaking, all that mattered was that Coyne let the botfly survive.

And biologically is where the line between self and other is most critical. It is so important that we have, over the course of evolution, developed what is arguably the most complex biological system (other than perhaps our nervous system) in any living vertebrate to do the job: our immune system. The immune system is our border patrol. It consists of a roving bag of cells that patrol our body 24/7. Its job is to identify trespassers, assess their danger, and eliminate them if necessary. These watchguards are exquisitely tuned to distinguishing the fingerprints of intruders from their own body's cells and molecules. One of their specialties is spotting parasites.

Coyne's immune system had tracked the invader, labeled it as nonself, probably assessed that it was a temporary visitor who posed a limited danger, and decided it would be safer to contain rather than kill or remove it. Antibodies were dispatched to seal the maggot securely in a little pocket. All Coyne did was decide to let biology run its course.

***

The anatomy of the self sounds simple. There is my body and then there is everything foreign to my body. Not so, it turns out. When it comes to the self-other boundary, the anatomical lines can be as messy and confusing as the ones we draw in our minds. Perhaps even more so.

Consider, for example, what are known as "molecular mimics," a type of parasite whose very specialty is confusing self and other. "These parasites are really crafty," says parasitologist Paul Crosbie. "They get inside the host's body and stick some of the host's protein on the outside of their own cells."[16] It's how they survive. Some mimics even raid the macrophages, our combat troops, the very antibody cells whose job is to kill and devour parasites. The parasites then pull off pieces of the macrophages and stick them on their own surface as camouflage. Other parasites have learned to mutate their appearance to match that of the host's cells. As Crosbie says, these molecular mimics fool the host's immune system into thinking, "It's okay, that's one of my cells." These sneaks, these miniature secret agents, are the biological world's masters of disguise.

Don't go looking for the serenity of Mother Nature in the world of microbiology. This is a savage little jungle full of con men and killers. When Darwin argued that nature was a bad place to prove that God had a benevolent design, he pointed to parasites as primary evidence. "It is derogatory that the Creator of countless systems of worlds should have created each of the myriads of creeping parasites," he wrote.[17]

If you're looking for a lesson in con artistry, may I recommend a group of mimics known as intracellular invaders? These trespassers don't just disguise themselves as host cells. They sneak right inside the actual cells and wear the host's membrane as their disguise. The immune system, which is a network of cells itself, only interacts with the surface of other cells. Antibodies, which are part of the immune system, don't cross cell membranes. So once an assailant manages to get inside a cell, it's home free. It enters a safe haven where it can grow, reproduce, and, in some cases, plan its next attack.

Species of *Plasmodium*, the protozoa that cause malaria, are a good example of these parasites. They enter the host's body through a mosquito bite and immediately look for a liver cell to get into. Penetrating the cell membrane is a formidable task, but the parasites come well-armed for their invasion. Their heads contain a ring of chambers that operate like the barrel of a revolver. When the parasites find a liver cell, they shoot out a blitz of molecules that opens a hole in the cell membrane. These protozoa can't swim, but they are equipped with little hooks that they use to grab the sides of the hole and pull themselves through.

As they're doing this, the chambers on their heads shoot off another volley of molecules that clump into a protective shroud around the parasites, giving them cover as they work their way inside. When the parasites are completely in, the host cell's resilient meshwork conveniently—for the parasites, that is—seals the hole shut. The entire operation takes about fifteen seconds. It is a breathtaking military operation.[18]

Once inside the cell, the parasites start multiplying—eventually producing forty thousand or so offspring, called merozoites. The merozoites then spill out of the liver into the host's bloodstream to begin doing serious damage. But they face a problem: How can they escape the liver cell without getting killed by antibodies? The solution is a disguise. The parasite pulls off the membrane of the infected cell with its little claws and wraps the membrane around itself. Safely disguised as a wandering liver cell, the parasite can wander through the host's bloodstream to find new targets. Imagine this. It's like a B-movie prison break where the escapee mugs a guard and steals his uniform to make his getaway. When the parasites cut loose, however, they steal the guard's entire skin.

In the bloodstream, the protozoa pick out a healthy red blood cell to attack. Their military forces fire off another fifteen-second barrage of molecules as the parasite claws its way into its new home. Once safely inside, they strip off the liver cell costume and comfortably construct their lethal malaria factory. They begin drinking up the hemoglobin that fills the cell and, fortified with this precious nutrition, rapidly multiply. The growing horde of parasites eventually consumes the entire contents of the red blood cell, which turns into nothing more than a bundle of parasites surrounded by the original cell membrane. When there is no more hemoglobin to drink, the parasites, wrapped in the host's membrane, move through the bloodstream until they find another healthy blood cell to invade. The process continues from one red blood cell to another, accelerating its pace as the number of parasites exponentially increases at each new stop. Blood cells eventually become infected en masse, and the host falls ill with malaria.

Our immune system is supposed to be our foremost judge and jury for deciphering what is us and what is outsider. This remarkably complex and sophisticated biological system has been honed over the course of evolution to ensure that we and our species endure. It's a Darwinian masterpiece, homeland security at its finest. If this biological system is so easily misled, is it any wonder we get confused about personal boundaries on the far more subjective level of social behavior?

***

One might argue that mimics like the parasites that cause malaria are just a band of thieves. Their only interest in our bodies is to steal what they can use. Molecular mimics are simply more sophisticated at being sneaky. Just because they live inside our skin doesn't mean they are now us. This argument gets shakier when the parasite lives inside our actual cells but, still, one might say, a bloodsucker is a bloodsucker.

What, however, if the visitors didn't simply destroy you but fundamentally changed you? Parasites like those that cause malaria are akin to irresponsible hotel guests who could care less about trashing their suite. But there are other intracellular invaders who move in with the full intention of staying for the long run. These visitors act more like home buyers. Like most new buyers, they like to personalize the new place to suit their needs. There are, in fact, plenty of parasites like these who completely renovate their new quarters. For example, the larva of the parasite that causes trichinosis, a type of roundworm infection caused by eating raw or undercooked pork or wild game, move inside the host's cell and, over the next three weeks, first demolish and then reconstruct almost its entire interior: The trichina tear down existing filaments. They even rebuild the roads in and out by modifying the capillaries that control the blood flow to the cell. And the final takeover: They grow additional nuclei. They actually grow new nuclei.[19] The host's tissue is just a pile of lumber as far as these architects are concerned. The trichina don't just hide inside the host. They transform the host's insides.

***

My own nomination for the weirdest biological crossover is *Cymothoaexigua*, also known as "the tongue-eating louse." This frightening parasite destroys an entire organ in its host and then replaces it with itself. It invades the mouth of a fish, devours the fish's tongue and then squats down and neatly positions itself where the tongue was, attaching itself to the tongue's exposed muscles. The new tongue—the louse—does everything the old one did. It feeds its host just as in the preinvasion days, gripping and eating prey like a normal tongue. So, which is the host and which is the guest?[20]

The louse lives off the fish's blood and other fluids. It's—trust me—beyond nauseating to look at.[21] When the fish opens its mouth, in place of a tongue you see a slimy, multilegged creature kicked back in chaise lounge position, its beady eyes staring straight at you, its creepy claws reaching out to grab you or anything else that looks like food. But ugly as it may look, the louse doesn't appear to cause any significant damage to its host. In fact, it keeps the fish alive.

Imagine (apologies for the image) this hijacked fish were you. I'm sure you'd agree that the tongue you were born with is part of your self. But if a tongue-eating parasite moved in, you'd be acutely aware there was a foreign creature living in your mouth. Why, though, should you consider the parasite-tongue to be any less a part of yourself than your original tongue used to be? Is it because your new tongue once lived outside you, or that it has its own genes? Functionally, after all, it's the same arrangement as before: Both your old and new tongues take in food that keeps you alive, which in turn keeps your tongue alive. What if you had a disease that required your original tongue to be surgically removed? Once it was outside your body, lying pathetically across the room on a table, would you still consider it part of you? Probably not, or maybe you would say it used to be part of you. What if the doctors now fixed the tongue and sewed it successfully back in place? You would probably say it is part of you again, wouldn't you? So why is the parasite tongue forever an outsider? Just because it happens to have legs and eyes?

***

At what point do self and non-self merge? What if your own cells were built by an outsider and customized to house that outsider—who would be the tenant and who would be the landlord? Who makes that call? Richard Feynman once said about quantum mechanics, "Anyone who is not thoroughly confused just doesn't understand the problem." If you're not, by now, as confused as I am by what biology teaches us about the notion of a self, I offer one more organism: The mitochondrion.

Parasites are predators. It's a one-sided relationship whereby the parasite wins and the host loses. At first glance, the tongue-eating louse fits this definition. After all, the little critter invades its victim and bites off its tongue. But, soon after, the louse and its host enter into a remarkable collaboration, what biologists refer to as a mutualistic relationship. Unlike Jerry Coyne's parasite, the louse is there to stay. It had better, because separation would spell starvation for both parties. Mutualism—give-and-take relationships with outside organisms—is equally essential to human survival. Every one of our cells is a microcommunity, each populated by multitudes of hard-working organelles with their own DNA. Without their work, we wouldn't last a second. Perhaps the best example of these collaborators are the mitochondria.

Mitochondria are the tiny organelles that generate the ATP molecules that provide the cell with energy. The mitochondria are the cell's power plant. There are lots of them, anywhere from a few hundred in cells that don't use much energy to thousands in energy hogs like the cells in our liver, muscles, and brain. It is mutualism at its best. Our life depends on them. They in turn are provided with a safe haven and a steady source of nutrients. The two of us exist as one. Or so it seems.

The mitochondria are so ubiquitous and embedded in our cells' functioning that it's easy to forget they're not technically us. Biologically speaking, the mitochondria are independent organisms. Eons before the formation of complex organisms like our own, they foraged through nature as free-living bacteria. Nowadays the mitochondria live a more domesticated life, commingling safely within the comfort of our cells. But they remain, in the last analysis, not really us: The mitochondria are the only organelles in animal cells that carry their own genetic material, their own DNA (mDNA).[22] Mitochondria can grow, replicate, divide, and fuse independently of the cell surrounding them. And our own cells are incapable of manufacturing the mitochondria. Sure, they work for our welfare and we work for theirs, but where it counts—the perpetuation of one's DNA—they are autonomous agents. "They are much less closely related to me than to each other and to the free-living bacteria under the hill," observes the biologist Lewis Thomas. "There they are, moving about in my cytoplasm, breathing for my own flesh, but strangers." The mitochondria are, by definition, others.

Sort of, that is. "I was raised in the belief that these (mitochondria) were obscure little engines inside my cells, owned and operated by me or my cellular delegates, private, sub-microscopic bits of my intelligent flesh," Thomas remarks. But, as he learned more about these organelles, when he understood just how much claim they had to their own individuality, he was forced to alter his view of his own self: "Looked at this way, I could be taken for a very large, motile colony of respiring bacteria, operating a complex system of nuclei, microtubules, and neurons for the pleasure and sustenance of their families."[23]

***

Even if they don't share our genome, it is difficult to make sense of the mitochondria as outsiders. The fact is that the mitochondria were inside our cells from the beginning. From the *very* beginning. They are passed along at conception and accompany us on the entirety of our subsequent journey, prenatally to birth and on through death. They've apparently always been inside us—both as individuals and a species—and certainly will always continue to be.

The vast majority of our mitochondria—about one hundred thousand of them—are passed down through our mother's egg. A few of them, as we'll see later, manage to sneak through with our father's sperm. But most are maternal passengers, and these are the mitochondria that we have learned most about. The fact that a mother's mitochondria are passed directly down to her children means they have a traceable ancestry. Their DNA goes back to earlier generations, just as our own DNA does. And they've been with us for such a long time that, many geneticists believe, you can get as much information about your genetic ancestors by tracking mDNA as you would from tracking your own DNA. Often more, in fact.

I've always been interested in my ancestry. When retail genome labs began offering their services to the public, I was quick to send them my DNA sample. The labs ran a variety of tests. The one I was interested in, my ancestry analysis, tries to pinpoint one's genetic predecessors as far back in human history as possible. In my case, the best data came from my maternal side. My genome was traced to a "haplogroup"[24] that originated in Iberia sixteen thousand years ago. It was staggering to see my connection to people in the Ice Age.[25] The report described how this conclusion was derived from analyses of DNA. But it wasn't exactly my DNA. It was that of my mitochondria.

Mitochondrial DNA have made headlines in a number of high-profile forensic cases. It was used, for example, to identify the unrecognizable remains of many victims in the World Trade Center attacks. When Saddam Hussein was captured, mitochondrial analyses confirmed that American military forces had found the real Saddam and not one of his cadre of doubles. In a classic mystery case, forensic scientists were asked to identify the corpse of the last Russian tsar, Nicholas II, who had been lying in a grave with nine other skeletons for seventy-three years. They found the correct match by comparing mDNA samples from the nine skeletons to those of Nicholas's confirmed relatives.

Geneticists prefer studying our maternal mitochondrial genes when possible for several reasons. To begin with, mitochondrial DNA is cleaner to follow. Our own cellular DNA is a recombination of the genes from both our parents. Because of this, it gets remixed every generation. Mitochondrial DNA, on the other hand, is passed down pretty much unaltered from parent to offspring, which makes the connections easier to see.[26] Since almost all of them come from our mothers, the generational connections are that much simpler to follow. Second, the best way to determine ancestral heritage is by tracking genetic mutations—we all have these mutations—to their source, meaning the first time they appear in a genealogical history. Mitochondrial DNA offer another advantage here: They mutate more frequently than our own DNA, so there are more mutations that can be tracked.

Most important, they have been with us pretty much forever. One of the Holy Grails in genetics is finding "Mitochondrial Eve," the first woman to have dispensed her mitochondria to her children, who then passed them on to all the rest of us. M-Eve, it's believed, would be the most recent common female ancestor from whom all humans are descended. She's thought to have lived about two hundred thousand years ago, at the time when *Homo sapiens* were evolving separately from other human species.[27] In other words, these mitochondria, these genetic rogues, have inhabited our cells since practically the beginning of our species.

There is also the sheer blood-and-guts physical blurring between them and us. There are about ten million billion mitochondria in the average human body. Mitochondria account for up to 60 percent of the volume of muscle cells and 40 percent of the volume of heart cells.[28] They also make up a significant portion of our body weight. The exact estimates vary but, even conservatively, it's estimated that the mitochondria constitute about 10 percent of our weight.[29] (Should we be allowed to subtract this 10 percent when we weigh ourselves?)

Organisms living within organisms are nothing special in the world of microbiology. If you look inside many house plants, for example, you'll find a little insect called a mealybug carrying out a life of its own. Look inside the mealybug and you'll find collaborations of bacteria living their own lives. And inside these bacteria are smaller, separate bacteria.[30] And there are plenty of other outsiders. The mitochondria, like the mealybugs, mock the notion of a self. Squint into a microscope, and these organelles within organelles look like independent creatures, each going about its own work. Step back, however, and the mitochondria appear to simply be one of many elements that compose the single complex unit we call a cell.

Are the mitochondria us or them? It doesn't much matter how we answer this question. The fact is there are genetically independent organisms living, seamlessly enmeshed, throughout our bodies. Selves within selves. We're like those Russian matryoshka dolls that open to reveal a succession of progressively smaller dolls inside. There are the little mitochondria dolls inside the bigger mitochondria dolls inside the biggest doll of all—us. But, hold on, how can we be sure there's not a bigger doll yet? It's a tough question.

***

Is there anything in the mix we're left to call our own? Lewis Thomas leaves us with a modest plea: "I only hope I can retain title to my nuclei."[31] It will be interesting, as microbiologists dig deeper into our structure, to see whether even this turns out to be true. For starters, what about those trichinosis parasites who enter our cells and grow their own nuclei?

Besides, if Thomas were still alive, he would learn that foreign bacteria are no longer his only challengers. He would also be fighting against corporations and their lawyers. In one recent case, for example, the Supreme Court of the United States took on the question of whether a human gene can be patented. The justices ruled that it cannot, thus, for now at least, banning corporations from owning the DNA that lives in our bodies; but they left a gaping hole in their decision by, at the same time, ruling that edited or artificially created DNA *can* be legally patented.[32] There are also ongoing debates concerning issues like stem cells, euthanasia, and organ donation laws. How much does the self own itself? The answer, I'm afraid, may depend on how good a lawyer you can afford.

Where does one draw the line between self and other? In biology, the answer boils down to genetics. A self, as Richard Dawkins famously argued in his classic book *The Selfish Gene*, is nothing more than a set of DNA intent on replicating itself. Different DNA, different self. By this definition, my mitochondria are individuals separate from me. Yet, even to geneticists, my mitochondria's genetic individuality represents the essence of my own individuality, not simply who I am today but who I descend from. How can my ancestral fingerprint not be me?

But if the mitochondria are me, doesn't this mean I have two sets of genes? Aren't I a mosaic of both my own cellular DNA and that of my mitochondria? The fact is that all of the "others"—whether they are parasitic or mutualistic, cheaters or straight-shooters, long-term residents or one-night stands—have a significant characteristic in common: They each carry their own DNA. And this means that, for however long they are inside their host's body, two genetically distinct organisms are living under the same skin and, to one extent or another, are biologically intertwined. Deep down, at the core of our tissue, we are a gigantic, symbiotic array, a ragtag assortment of organisms. All of these are to some degree us.

Then again, results are more important than who gets credit for what. The fact is that somehow—miraculously really—when the pieces are tossed together, the machine we call our body actually works. And the reason it does has less to do with competing than cooperating. As evolutionary biologists Lynn Margulis and Dorion Sagan point out, "Life did not take over the globe by combat, but by networking."[33]

***

Jerry Coyne was convinced his maggot was *his*, not *him*. He quickly dismissed my suggestion that, for those few months, the botfly had actually become a part of himself. "I always knew it was a parasite. I always felt it was other than me," he told me.[34] But mental ownership and biological ownership are different matters. Coyne might feel like one person, but genetically—which, face it, is all that matters in the grander scheme of existence—he is something more.[35] And couldn't the same be said about all of us? Aren't we all human chimeras? We'll see some interesting answers in the next chapter.

6
Multiple Personalities, Multiple People

My inner self was a house divided against itself.
—St. Augustine, *The Confessions*

In 1995, Karen Keegan, a fifty-two-year old teacher and mother of three living in Boston, was told by her doctors that she urgently needed a kidney transplant. She was instructed to act fast. "They asked me who in my family might be willing to donate a kidney," Karen said.[1] Her husband, Pete, and her two older boys, Matt and Jess, all went in for DNA tests to find a matching donor. Karen was hoping for good news. Instead, she got the shock of her life. "A couple of weeks later I got a phone call from the hospital," Karen recalled, "and they said, 'Mrs. Keegan, uh, this is a very unusual situation that we're going to explain to you. It's something that we've never seen before but when the DNA testing was done on your sons we found that they didn't match your DNA.'" The boys' DNAs matched their father's but not Karen's.

In other words, Karen was being told she wasn't the mother of either Matt or Jess. Karen thought this was ridiculous. "I gave birth to these kids. I felt the pain," she told her doctors. "You better do the tests again because you're obviously wrong." The doctors ran the tests again. The results were the same. "The read was correct," recalls Lynn Uhl, a transfusion specialist who became interested in Karen's mystery. It was clear after the second set of tests that "there was not a laboratory error." The doctors were familiar with cases where the husband's DNA didn't match a couple's supposed biological child but, Dr. Uhl said, "we'd never had a mother whose DNA didn't match her children."

The first possibility they considered was there might have been a baby mix-up at the hospital, one of those infamous baby swapping stories. But a mix-up of both her babies? Besides, the father's DNA matched. How could Karen have ended up with the wrong children from the right father? Everyone was baffled. Margot Kruskall, the original doctor on the case, circulated the data to colleagues. It made no medical sense to any of them. "No one could quite figure it out," Kruskall recalled.[2]

This is when Karen's life took a nasty turn, as people began treating her with suspicion. They questioned her mental health, her honesty, and even wondered whether she might be up to something illegal. Maybe, some thought, she was one of those hysterical women who just wished she'd had a child. Kruskall's professional colleagues offered some creative explanations. "One suggested that [Karen] had secretly undergone fertility treatment using donated eggs," she recalled. "Another speculated that [Karen] and her husband had got her sister to conceive children with his sperm, and then pretended they were hers."[3] Worst of all, some people suspected that she had stolen the children. Karen recalls that people asked her questions like, "Could you tell us what hospital you had these children in?" They figured something was up "because obviously DNA is never wrong. It's never wrong." Even her sons were suspicious.

Karen's doctors were intrigued by the case. All they knew for sure was something didn't make sense. It took them two years to solve the mystery. The breakthrough came when lab technicians ran further DNA analyses and discovered that Karen's brother carried DNA that matched her two sons. "That really provided the spur that kept us going," Kruskall said. They were pretty certain now that Karen must also have the same DNA, somewhere. Perhaps they'd just been looking in the wrong place. All the tests had been done on Karen's blood. What if they examined other tissues? So the doctors now extracted a couple of Karen's hairs, scraped saliva samples from the inside of her mouth, took biopsies from her thyroid, bladder, and skin and samples from all sorts of other parts of her body.

The story now became even more mysterious. The new lab tests showed that Karen had different DNA in different parts of her body.

Some organs showed one DNA pattern while others showed a second pattern. If they didn't know better, the doctors would have thought the samples had come from two completely different people. And this second person, the tests showed, was the biological mother of Matt and Jess. Their DNA were a clear match.

It took a while, but the doctors believe they finally solved the mystery. The explanation, they think, goes back to before Karen was even born. Karen's mother most likely started off carrying two fertilized eggs in her womb, two girls gestating side by side in their own separate amniotic sacs. Normally, this would lead to nonidentical twins. But, in Karen's mother's case, at some point early on—probably a few days after conception—the two eggs collided with each other and somehow fused. They became one Karen. Or, if you prefer, Karen became two people. Either way you look at it, she is, biologically, twins. It's not that Karen had a twin. She is a twin—literally, nonidentical twin sisters. Karen isn't so much a mixture of the two as a mosaic. One of the twins, for example, staked out Karen's blood. The other took over her thyroid and her bladder. The two people "still had their own boundaries," Dr. Uhl observed.

It begins to make sense when you think about what used to be referred to as Siamese twins, a condition in which babies are born physically connected. The biological process that leads to conjoined twins is very much like what happened to Karen, only less extreme. In conjoined twins, the eggs only partially merge. In Karen's case, they completely fused. "If the eggs hadn't fused within four days, I would have become a Siamese twin," Karen said. "When you hear that you immediately have a more concrete vision of two selves. It brought home the reality that I really was a twin."

In medical parlance, Karen is known as a chimera. More specifically, she is a *tetragametic chimera*, meaning her body is derived from a total of four gametes—two eggs and two sperm. The term "chimera" comes from the Greek myth about an animal with the head of a lion, the middle of a goat, a dragon's rear, and a tail in the form of a snake. When Karen called her English major son, he recounted the unflattering Greek legend. The mythical chimera was a fire-breathing monster who is hunted down by the hero Bellerophon riding valiantly on his winged horse Pegasus. Karen didn't initially like her new label. She became more appreciative, however, when doctors explained it also meant her body contained double the normal number of HLA haplotypes (a term that refers to blocks of genes) and, as a result, she had twice the chance of finding a suitable donor kidney.

Some chimeras have striking physical abnormalities. In 1998, a patient was referred to doctors at the University of Edinburgh complaining of an undescended testicle. But when the doctors examined the boy, they couldn't find the second testicle. To their astonishment, they instead discovered an ovary and a fallopian tube in its place. Tests revealed the boy was a chimera formed from male and female embryos.[4] Most of the time, however, the difference in phenotypes is subtle. One girl was diagnosed because her eyes were different colors: one was brown, the other was hazel. Another chimera had a hitchhiker's thumb on one hand and a straight thumb on the other. Some chimeras have different hair patterns on opposite sides of their bodies. In most cases there are no detectable symptoms at all. As a result, chimeras "are probably dramatically under-diagnosed," Kruskall says.

Often chimeras only learn of their condition if they happen to encounter a uniquely demanding situation. This is what happened to Karen. It's also thought to explain why, for example, a patient may reject a bone marrow transplant from what appears to be a perfectly matched donor: if the donor is a chimera, she may also be passing on a small percentage of unfriendly cells from someone else inside. Chimerism may also explain the mystery of autoimmune diseases in which a body is attacked by its own immune cells: one twin may be sensing invasion by a foreign body; the second twin may then return the attack believing he's been invaded. It becomes a chimeric civil war.

Chimeras like Karen, who began as fraternal twins, are believed to be rare. As of 2007, thirty-six human chimeras of this type had been confirmed in the medical literature.[5] This isn't surprising if you consider the low probability of someone giving birth to even completely separated fraternal twins. We can expect an increase in twin-based chimeras in the future as more couples turn to fertility techniques that increase the likelihood of twin births. Still, these cases will undoubtedly remain scarce.

But it turns out there are other routes to chimerism that aren't limited to twins. Perhaps the most direct of these are surgical transplants—or, to be more specific, the unintended consequences of these procedures. A study at Innsbruck Medical University in Austria, for example, found that 74 percent of individuals who had undergone bone marrow transplants contained a mix of genomes—both their own and the contributions of their donors—nine years after the surgery. Forensic scientists are beginning to rethink their assumptions about DNA testing based on findings like these. In a recent sexual assault case, for example, chimerism helped the Washington State Patrol Crime Laboratory Division explain why the DNA in a suspect's saliva sample didn't match up with what they found in his sperm sample.[6]

The most common route of all, however, begins before birth. Ann Reed, chairwoman of rheumatology research at the Mayo Clinic, has used sophisticated DNA techniques to test for small amounts of foreign cells in people's bodies. Reed looks for much smaller amounts of foreign matter than you would expect to see in fused twins like Karen. She finds a lot of it: Reed has discovered, conservatively, that about 50 to 70 percent of healthy people have bits and pieces of others in their genetic makeup.

The process begins in utero. The blood of the mother and fetus are mostly kept separate during pregnancy, but we've long known that some cells may sneak through the gates. Biologists first recognized maternal blood cells in the fetus in the 1960s; the flow of blood cells from fetus to mother was first observed in 1893.[7] This, in itself, isn't particularly surprising. The placenta is not a closed barricade. It must, by its very nature, allow materials that are critical to the development of the fetus to be delivered. It's more of a restrictive border crossing. More surprising is how deeply rooted these acquired cells often become. Most cells in our body die off after a limited period, and, once the placenta is gone, there's no way new cells could migrate between mother and child. Somehow, though, the foreign cells manage to establish semipermanent residence inside their host's tissues. They often become vital to the functioning of particular organs and persist like this for decades.

The explanation, according to recent studies, is that at least some of the original émigrés are stem cells. Like any stem cell, these are capable of dividing into infinite new cells, each of which has the potential to transform itself into specialized cell types such as those you would find in a particular organ. J. Lee Nelson, an immunologist at the Fred Hutchinson Cancer Research Center in Seattle, puts it nicely: "I sometimes think of the transferred stem cells or stemlike cells as seeds sprinkled through the body that ultimately take root and become part of the landscape."[8] What seems clear is that many of us end up with a cadre of our mother's cells, and she gets some of ours. "It's pretty likely that any woman who has been pregnant is a chimera," observes Dr. Linda Randolph, coauthor of a 2013 review of chimerism in the *American Journal of Medical Genetics.*[9]

But wait. Consider what might happen if your mother had more children and if they, too, exchanged cells. Some of your wayward cells could end up in the body of your younger sibling; if more children came along, they might end up sharing both of your blends. Twins, especially those who share a placenta, are particularly prone to swapping cells during pregnancy. And your mother, of course, may already be carrying her mother's cells, which are also potentially exchanged with and between you and your siblings. A mother may even carry cells she received before a miscarriage or an abortion. In the end, "a single person can be a veritable menagerie of different cell types from different generations," observes the developmental biologist Claire Ainsworth."[10] Physicians refer to this condition as microchimerism.

Microchimerism is so common that many believe it must serve a biological purpose. In the case of the cells that pass from mother to fetus, one compelling theory is these cells work to keep the unborn child healthy. Nelson and his colleague Ann Stevens have presented evidence that our mothers' visiting cells play a key role in repairing some types of tissue damage, particularly during gestation.[11] In one study, for example, they found evidence of maternal cells working to regenerate the diseased pancreases of diabetic newborns.[12]

We should be even more thankful to those adventurous cells that sneak across the placenta in the other direction—from our bodies to our mothers. There is accumulating evidence that they help keep our mother's immune system from attacking the new little body who is invading her space. After all, the fetus probably looks like any other foreign organ to the mother's immune system, not unlike an organ transplant that stays around for nine months. And, we know from transplant research that transferring white blood cells from the donor to the recipient can, under the right conditions, encourage acceptance of the new organ.[13] Sharing breeds tolerance, and tolerance breeds acceptance: a fitting beginning to our relationship with our mothers.

Finally, at least in a mother's case, it now appears that these cells can end up not only in the skin, liver, and spleen but right smack in her brain. A recent case study by Nelson and his colleagues found evidence of fetal DNA in a mother's brain decades after her child's birth and, in a subsequent study, they autopsied fifty-nine female brains and found Y (male) chromosomes in multiple regions of these brains in 63 percent of the cases.[14] Is it possible that this connectedness enhances a mother's emotional attachment to her child?

How common is microchimerism? Many researchers believe there is even more than the already high numbers that have been uncovered. Increasingly nuanced tests of blood, bone marrow, and other tissues will, they suspect, reveal some chimerism in the vast majority of both men and women. "Our guess would be that it is probably universal," J. Lee Nelson says. Chimerism appears to be hardly the biological oddity we once thought. It is the norm, as in normal. And this, it appears, is a good thing. Without it, we might not be alive.[15]

There is a blurry line between singularity and multiplicity at our very biological core. In the previous chapter we saw how our bodies are inhabited by genetically distinct microorganisms. In this chapter we see that "our" portion of the genetic contents may be composed of a combination of human genomes. We are literally—chromosomally—multiple people.

**

The notion of multiple selves exists at many levels. Let us now turn to perhaps the most famous, and controversial, of these: the psychological phenomenon commonly referred to as multiple personality disorder.

I first encountered this condition a few years ago when a student, whom I'll call Jackie, came to my office to discuss her term paper topic. It was the first time we'd spoken privately, but I knew Jackie from lecture to be bright, well-informed, and hard-working. She had A's on both exams. Her comments in class were always intelligent and appropriate. The meeting started off well. Jackie was circling an interesting topic and, I thought, asking good questions. But I found it hard to take my mind off her appearance. She had all sorts of tattoos and an array of body piercings, neither of which were common at the time. Having spent my own college years at Berkeley in the sixties, however, I told myself she was just pushing the limits of normal deviance for a college student. But then I saw something more troubling. As she was talking, Jackie casually rolled up her sleeves and revealed a series of scars up and down both arms. There were dozens of them. I tried not to look alarmed, which I was.

Jackie caught me staring. When I looked up, her entire demeanor changed. Most noticeably, she began speaking in a young child's voice, what sounded like perhaps a shy ten year old. "These are where I cut myself," she said in an itty-bitty murmur. "I get really bored and so I get out a knife and I cut myself. Jackie doesn't know. Don't tell her, please. Please. Okay?" The changes of voice and demeanor were so startling that I initially thought it was a put-on. I would have laughed it off as childish playacting if not for the very real scars I was looking at on Jackie's arms.

This little girl in a woman's body had a lot to say. She told me about her unhappy childhood and strings of rejections and how she ended up in a mental hospital after mutilating herself. "You promised you won't tell Jackie about this, right?" About then my next appointment knocked on my door. Jackie suddenly sat straight up, switched back to her original voice and continued presenting her term paper proposal just where she'd left off before the young girl showed up. When I asked her what had just occurred, Jackie didn't understand what I was referring to. The moment I mentioned the voice change, however, she knew what had happened. "You must have met my alter ego," she said. She'd never met the girl herself, Jackie explained, but a lot of people had told her about the girl. "I can't reach her. She's destroying my life."

Jackie was suffering from a condition now known in psychiatric jargon as *dissociative identity disorder* (DID), a controversial psychiatric condition in which an individual is said to be invaded by one or more distinct personae with whom he or she feels no connection. Almost all of us experience mild symptoms of dissociation at one time or another. A majority of people, for example, report having sometimes had the experience of finding themselves in a place with no memory of how they got there. Surveys have found that it is also common to occasionally feel disconnected from one's body or even to hear voices inside your head telling you what to do or narrating what you're doing. In fact, studies show that 60 to 65 percent of us have had some type of dissociative experience at one time or another.[16] But these surreal fogs are usually momentary and quickly recede. In cases of DID, the dissociative experience is not only more extreme, but it may torment the individual for years or even a whole lifetime.

It is generally believed that DID originates from extreme childhood trauma. What is said to set DID apart from other stress-related disorders is that the trauma is recurrent and inescapable and, most critically, that it occurs before the individual has developed an integrated sense of self. As a way of coping, the helpless victim literally dissociates from the full impact of the trauma. The sufferer builds compartmentalized identities, each of which may have unconnected thoughts, feelings, and memories. Say for example, the problem is an abusive father. The suffering child would like to just escape but, unfortunately, he or she also depends on the man as a caretaker. With DID, the child might construct a persona that is denied access to memories of abuse; this persona is capable of carrying on an instrumental relationship with the father. It is a primitive, short-term solution that promises emotional and physical survival. But it demands a stiff price later in life.

Zoe Farris, a fifty-three-year-old Australian woman who was diagnosed with dissociative identity disorder in her early thirties, tries to explain what it feels like. "I had a friend who, in all her best and loving caring, offered to take me to her priest who did exorcisms," she recalls. "I said, 'No, they're not demons, they're part of me.' You know, they are my emotions and they are my memories that have just split off and formed little identities of their own. I'm one person but experientially they are different people, or personalities."[17]

Most people still refer to DID by the more colorful label of multiple personality disorder. The American Psychiatric Association officially switched to the term DID in 1994 because it seemed to more accurately describe what patients were experiencing.[18] The decision made good sense. Multiple personalities imply the presence of a troupe of fully formed identities. In actuality, people with DID are usually marked by the absence of *any* integrated identity at any given time. No single persona contains the full range of emotional responses or the access to narrative memories that you would expect in a more fully formed personality.

Ms. Farris is a poignant example. Zoe used to be a performer. When most people hear about this, they assume her multiple personalities must have served her well in this profession. They think of Robin Williams–types whose very genius involves seamlessly switching from one personality to another. After all, isn't great acting all about inhabiting multiple personalities and being able to call up the right one on command? But Zoe says her range of personae never entered into her acting. The Zoe who appeared on stage was always the same, singular, dissociated persona. The rest of her personae never even knew she was onstage. "There were times when I would be sitting backstage, waiting to go on," she recalls. "The show would finish but I hadn't realized that I'd already been on. That's the thing: I don't remember doing it."

Zoe has quite a cast of characters. "There's Linda who's about ten years old [for whom] everything is absolutely happy. She makes this 'wheee' noise but she's gone as soon as something upsetting happens. There's one I call the curled up one. There's a crying one and that's basically what she does. There's the angry one whose name I won't mention because I'm not allowed to. . . . She doesn't say much [but] if she does she might swear. All she wants to do is hit things. But she won't hit things when people are around."

For a long time Zoe kept a journal. She—what Zoe calls her "core self"—never knew what she had come across. Not only was the subject matter often a mystery, but Zoe couldn't even recognize the handwriting. There were entries from left-handers and from right-handers. Some were written left to right and others from right to left. There were some with big handwriting and some with "really tiny little handwriting."

Zoe expects to struggle with her multiple characters her whole life. She says, for example, that even now she's afraid to publicly say some of their names "or they'll freak out." With time, however, Zoe has learned to work around her burden. She is employed as a mental health worker and has published about her experiences in an effort to educate others. She has also managed to surround herself with a supportive and understanding family and friends. Her longtime friends "know if they say hello and I ignore them, it's another part of me," Zoe says. They understand that sometimes "I act differently. I look differently. I behave differently." When this happens, they accept that this isn't the "real" Zoe, the one who is their friend. "So they don't get offended anymore."

***

DID can be spooky for both the sufferers and those in their presence. This feeling is highlighted in popular books and movies. The classic, perhaps, is the Academy Award–winning film, *The Three Faces of Eve*, based on the true story of Eve White. Ms. White was a conventional, self-effacing wife and mother who suffered from severe, blinding headaches and occasional blackouts. She went to a psychiatrist who, upon hypnotizing her, unleashed Eve Black, a wild, hedonistic alter ego. The new personality "had a childish daredevil air, an erotically mischievous glance, a face marvelously free from the habitual signs of care, seriousness and underlying distress," according to her therapists.[19] As Eve's treatment continued, Ms. Black informed the therapists that she had been "coming out" in Eve's skin since they were children.

The creepiest part of the story is that Eve White was completely blind to Eve Black's existence. She first heard about her alter ego from her therapists. Their reports cleared up some mysteries for Ms. White, such as all the times she was punished for doing things she had no memory of doing. But, to the end, Eve Black operated completely out of Eve White's awareness. It was a very nice arrangement for Ms. Black, who got to enjoy a carefree life without having to pay the consequences of her self-indulgent behavior. Even when Eve White was "out," Eve Black took it all in. Eve White, on the other hand, hadn't the foggiest notion that Eve Black existed. Eve Black concealed herself not only from Eve White, but also from Eve's husband and daughter. Ms. Black despised the whole bunch of them. She denied being married to their husband, paid no attention to their daughter, and did all she could to make Eve White miserable. She even sabotaged Ms. White's therapy.

When her therapists propelled Ms. Black into the open it seemed, at first, to give Ms. White relief. Most notably, her headaches disappeared. But when her husband eventually got wind of Eve Black's carryings-on, he disappeared, too, as did most of the rest of the stable life she was familiar with. Eve kept at her therapy and eventually got to what she believed to be the root cause of her symptoms. In classic psychoanalytic style, this turned out to be a traumatic early childhood experience—in Eve's case, it was when she was forced to kiss her dead grandmother at the woman's funeral. After this cathartic breakthrough, a new personality, Jane, emerged. Jane was more responsible than Eve Black and more confident and interesting than Eve White. Pfft, Eve White and Eve Black were gone. Eve/Jane was again a whole personality and, happily, better than the one before. She married a new husband whom she met, as Jane, and reunited with her daughter. It's a nice ending, at least in the movie. Unfortunately, eighteen years after the movie was released, the real Eve revealed that she had actually experienced at least twenty-two other personalities both before and after her original therapy.

***

There is considerable debate about the number of true cases of DID. Some therapists report encountering hundreds of new DID patients a year; others say they've never come across even one. Skeptics like psychologist Nicholas Spanos believe that most cases diagnosed as DID are best understood as social performances that serve the needs of the patient and the therapist. This doesn't mean the performance is necessarily planned or manipulative. There is a school of sociology—epitomized in the title of Erving Goffman's seminal book, *The Presentation of Self in Everyday Life*—which argues that role playing is how we cope with any demanding relationship or situation (see chapter 13).[20] I might, for example, present myself as a more serious person when applying for a job, more fun-loving on a first date, more cerebral when talking to a teacher. There is not necessarily anything insincere about my different presentations. They are simply different facets of my self.

Spanos's explanation of DID pushes role theory to the extreme. He believes the personalities are a response to the excessive needs of particular patients and therapists. The patient, he says, is wrestling with painful repressed trauma and at the same time trying to please the therapist. The therapist, on the other hand, is eager to discover the syndrome. The multiple personae answer both their callings. How else, Spanos asks, do we explain why some therapists not only discover so many more patients with DID than others do, but that most of these multiple personae don't appear until the patient starts treatment? Spanos argues that it must be because the predisposed therapist encourages—indeed, brings to life— the multiple role playing.

Those who believe in the ubiquity of DID, on the other hand, contend that the illness is misunderstood and underdiagnosed by many professionals. Dr. Philip Coons, in the Department of Psychiatry at the Indiana University School of Medicine, for example, observes "there is a professional reluctance to diagnose multiple personality disorder [that] stems from a number of factors including the generally subtle presentation of the symptoms, the fearful reluctance of the patient to divulge important clinical information, professional ignorance concerning dissociative disorders, and the reluctance of the clinician to believe that incest [the most common trauma underlying DID] actually occurs and is not the product of fantasy."[21] This is a far cry from the accusation that psychiatrists are inventing the disorder.

Like so much of psychology, the truth probably lies somewhere in between. There has undoubtedly been overdiagnosis of DID by some professionals over the past few decades—owing in no small part to the impact of dramatic chronicles like *The Three Faces of Eve*. And, in some of these cases, the therapists have probably assumed more than a fair share of the responsibility for creating the very symptoms they went on to treat. On the other hand, there are clearly people whose suffering from the disorder has little to do with the urging of professional true believers. There are patients who enter therapy because they are indeed suffering from deeply fragmented personalities. Even Spanos says his conception of role playing doesn't mean the experience of multiple personalities is any less real or stressful to the patient.

In fact, the clients may not care much whether their multiple personalities stem from deep-rooted psychopathology or social role playing. The novelist Richard Ford once observed that there is no such thing as false happiness. The same holds true for suffering or any other emotion. No matter the cause of one's multiple personality disorder—whether it is based in organic brain pathology, stressful early experiences, or if it is simply adaptive role playing—the personal experience is a real one. And when we look at multiple personalities from this perspective, the boundary between personal pathology and social flexibility gets awfully fuzzy. There is a vast gray zone between the abnormal and the normal.

Jackie was doing much better the last time I spoke to her. She still suffers her demons but, with therapy, says that she has created more tolerant relationships among the group. If nothing else, she feels as if she has progressed to being able to "sort of communicate" with them. Most important, she's come to appreciate what each brings to the table. "I try to think of my 'people' as headstrong roommates in an apartment we share," she says. "Sometimes they're just control-freak bullies who I'd give anything to get rid of. But other times they do things for me that I could never do on my own. There's this really pushy, obnoxious one—I call her Leona Helmsley—who used to just embarrass me." Sometimes she still does. But, Jackie says, she's also learned to put Leona to good use. "For example, I'm such a pleaser that I freeze when I have to confront anyone. Now I sic Leona on these people. Sometimes, when it's someone who really deserves it, I hear myself cheering Leona on."

To one degree or another, we all transform into different people in different situations, sometimes almost unrecognizably different people. It is part of our social nature. Dissociation can occasionally be a clinical disorder, as in the cases of Jackie and Eve, but for most of us it's just another way to maneuver through life.

***

Multiple people. Multiple personalities. There is at least a smidgen of both in practically all of us. The purebred is the freak—and probably not a very healthy one. The notion of a singular, unwavering personality is even freakier.

7

Stranger in the Mirror

Who sees the human face correctly:
the photographer, the mirror, or the painter?

—Pablo Picasso

The older we get, the harder to relate to that face in mirror. Where did those lines come from? And that pouch under my neck? It gets really confusing when I end up in front of one of those multiple mirror setups that reflect from different angles. I might, say, be trying on a sports jacket in a store and see the back of this head with a hairline that recedes so far I'd need another mirror to find the end of it. The poor schnook, it seems, is bald. Sometimes I get caught up staring, thinking I should get better acquainted with this face, since it is apparently the one the world sees of me.

I hear this whining-at-the-mirror from my cronies all the time as we get older. "When did *this* disaster happen?" "My God, is that me or my mother?" "Hon, I think there's something wrong with our mirror." We all know it's normal to feel this way (right?). Just another bizarre twist in the journey brought to you from the architects of the aging process. It's normal, that is, as long as we recognize that the face in the mirror is, in fact, our own. The face I see may not be the one I want to see, or what I conjure in my outdated imagination, but I'm aware—all too well—of precisely whom I'm looking at. Most of us can't avoid recognizing our own face. You can scrunch it up, change angles or "make faces," but nothing short of a mask will delude you into thinking someone has switched places with you in the mirror.

Even chimpanzees recognize themselves. Psychologist Gordon Gallup devised a clever test of self-recognition that now bears his name. He started out by letting a group of chimps play with a mirror. The first few days they gestured toward the reflected image as if it was another chimp. After that, however, they started moving their hands around their own body while they stared at it in the mirror, seeming to sense the image was their own. To test more carefully that this was the case, on the tenth day of his experiment Gallup anesthetized the chimps and, while they were unconscious, painted bright red marks on the uppermost ridge of one of their eyebrows and on the top of their opposite ear, carefully painting the marks so they were outside the animals' direct vision. The red die was odorless and undetectable by touch. The idea was to be sure the spots could only be detected by looking in the mirror. When the chimps awoke, they were handed their mirrors. As soon as they saw the red marks they moved their hands to their own face and, using the mirror to guide them, tried to touch the spots. They recognized themselves.[1]

We humans learn to do this at an early age. Studies show that neurologically normal children can usually pass the Gallup test—being able to recognize that a spot on the face in the mirror is actually on their own face—between the ages of fifteen months and two years.[2] In other words, if chimps and two-year-olds know this, how big a deal can it be? Recognizing our own reflection seems to be an instinctive skill, like walking and talking. It's all too obvious, for better and for worse, who we see in the mirror.

∗∗∗

For some people, however, it's not so simple. Anyone who has spent time in a big city has seen people who talk to themselves. And if you've wandered deep enough downtown, you've undoubtedly met people who talk to other people that no one else sees. But what about a double whammy: a person who talks to himself and thinks that person is someone else? What happens when your delusion is your own reflection in the mirror?

Yolanda Santomarino is a seventy-five-year-old woman who lives in the Cherrywood Nursing Home in Reisterstown, Maryland. She was diagnosed with Alzheimer's disease six years ago. When Yolanda looks in the mirror nowadays, she is convinced she sees an entirely different woman by the name of Ruth. "Ruth is a friend that I met here," Yolanda says. "We talk to each other in the mirror." Ruth isn't always in the mirror. She seems to have a life of her own. In a video taken of Yolanda, she can be seen staring into the mirror and complaining to her caretaker: "I don't know, I think she [Ruth] went home." Yolanda tells her caretaker that Ruth "was really wonderful this morning. She got me dressed—in a new dress." Then, suddenly, Ruth seems to appear, because Yolanda begins talking directly to her in the mirror: "There's still clothes in here," she tells Ruth. "Do you have clothes in yours?"

Yolanda is asked if she's going to show Ruth the mask she made for her that morning. Yolanda says she wants to actually give it to Ruth. The caretaker gently advises that this would be difficult but suggests she should show Ruth the mask. Yolanda ignores the advice. Moments later she expresses disappointment that Ruth wasn't grateful for her gift. "She didn't say anything to me," Yolanda complains. The caretaker tells Yolanda that Ruth "looks like you. I think she looks like you." Yolanda disagrees. She waives aside the suggestion with an emphatic "No": Ruth doesn't look at all like her.

Yolanda is fond of Ruth, but she gets frustrated that Ruth doesn't want to get closer. Earlier that day, "I asked her to come over but she doesn't want to come over," Yolanda says. "She had me wait there and she never came out." Yolanda complains that, "I told her many times, be at your door and I'll be at my door." But Ruth always tells her she wants to stay where she is. Ruth, Yolanda explains, lives in the mirror. This clearly takes a toll on Yolanda. "I'm tired of talking to her through the window," she says.[3]

Yolanda has a condition technically known as "mirrored-self misidentification syndrome."[4] It is more common than you might think. One large scale study found that 2 percent of Alzheimer's patients exhibited mirror delusions. And it's not confined to Alzheimer's patients. The delusion also appears in other types of brain damage—most commonly following strokes or traumatic brain injury, particularly when there is injury to the right hemisphere of the brain.[5] The mirror syndrome is sometimes included under a broader category of delusions known as "phantom boarder syndrome," a term describing patients who are convinced an outsider has taken up residence in their home. What is un-usual about cases like Yolanda, however, is the boarder can only be seen in the mirror—or "through the window," as Yolanda prefers to say.

* * *

Only a small minority of people suffer from mirror delusions. When you think about it, though, it's a scientific miracle that any of us can recognize ourselves. It's a miracle we can recognize anyone's face, in fact. Facial recognition requires an extraordinary combination of skills. First, we need to perceive the features of a face. This is no easy task. Our brains must process an extremely complex and nebulous combination of shapes, textures, and colors. In addition, the faces are ever-changing—people move, they switch their expressions, the light changes. Somehow we need to filter, combine, and package this circus of inputs into an overall image that we can recognize as this person's face.

But recognition goes beyond perceptual acuity. We must then memorize what we've seen so precisely that we can later pick that face out of a crowd of other faces. A few people are able to retain eidetic images—so-called photographic memories—in their mind's eye. But how do the rest of us ever get it right? We certainly don't keep detailed measurements of the faces. We don't think "Mom's nose is 2.15 inches long and 0.82 inches from her top lip, but this woman's nose is only 2.08 inches long and it's too close to her lip. No, it's definitely not my mother." Even when we do recognize the face, we need to figure out who the face belongs to. This requires another set of mental processes in order to summon the memories, experiences, and emotions that enable us to identify who we're looking at.

All this requires the integration of multiple brain regions, ranging from the amygdala and hippocampus to a vaguely understood right hemisphere complex known as the fusiform face area. When there is damage to one of these regions, the result may be face blindness, or what's technically known as "prosopagnosia" (taken from *prosopon*, Greek for "face," and "agnosia" for "recognition impairment"), referring to the inability to perceive previously familiar faces. People with prosopagnosia have no difficulty perceiving faces. When looking at a face, they can describe the features as accurately as most people. But they fall apart in the memory phase. Prosopagnosia sufferers either can't retain an image of what they have seen or can't retrieve the image, or both. No matter how many times they see a face, it's as if they're seeing it for the first time.

Oliver Sacks, the brilliant and provocative neurologist, once described his own lifelong struggle with prosopagnosia, which, as is frequently the case, he was almost certainly born with. "My problem with recognizing faces extends not only to my nearest and dearest but also to myself," he says. On more than one occasion, he found himself apologizing to a tall, bearded man, "only to realize the large bearded man was myself in a mirror." He's also prone to the opposite problem. Once, "sitting at a sidewalk table, I turned toward the restaurant window and began grooming my beard, as I often do. I then realized that what I had taken to be my own reflection was not grooming himself but looking at me oddly."[6]

The ability to recognize faces falls on a continuum. Some of us are terrible at it. Others, known as "super-recognizers," are so good that they sometimes complain about not being able to forget a face. Most of us are somewhere in the middle. Clinical prosopagnosia, which usually involves damage in the fusiform face area, is estimated to affect as much as 2 to 2.5 percent of the population. In the most crippling cases, the sufferer has trouble recognizing anyone—even his or her children, spouse, or close friends.

**

On the surface, Yolanda's mirror delusion would appear to be a type of prosopagnosia. She, like Oliver Sacks, is unable to conjure up a memory of her face to match the one reflected in the mirror. But her underlying mechanisms take an added twist. Sacks's face blindness is neatly explained as a neurological problem. He inherited a faulty fusiform face mechanism and, as a direct result, is unable to recognize faces. It is possible that Yolanda also suffers from a neurological problem, but, even if she does, there is the issue of its selectivity. Here's the enigma: Yolanda has no trouble recognizing other people—actual other people, that is— either inside or outside the mirror. If I stepped next to Yolanda while she was looking in the mirror she would probably greet my image correctly. Then she would introduce me to Ruth. Like all cases of mirror-image delusion, the only face for which she has prosopagnosia is her own. There is obviously more going on here than damage to the perceptual processing circuitry.

Organic brain damage is, in fact, very common in patients with mirror delusions. Many sufferers have experienced a stroke or, as in Yolanda's case, are in the grip of Alzheimer's disease. But even when there is an organic problem, the patient's psyche can make all the difference. The fact is, Yolanda doesn't see just any random person in the mirror. It's Ruth and always Ruth. You don't need a PhD in psychology to surmise that, for better and for worse, the Ruth she has created tells us something about Yolanda's needs, fears, and desires. The form of the delusion may be triggered by a damaged neural structure, but the content, the particulars about Ruth, even her relationship to Yolanda, are offspring of Yolanda's idiosyncratic mind.

Yolanda is more fortunate than most people with extreme delusions, mirror or otherwise. Her imaginary creation is something of a friend, even if the friend isn't all Yolanda would like her to be. Typically, the mirror-phantom is considerably more ominous. Consider, for example, the case of a woman (whom I'll call Donna) who alleged she was being taunted by a woman who looked exactly like her.[7] Donna, a sixty-one-year-old married, well-educated New Zealander, said the woman had invaded her home, followed her everywhere, and spent every waking moment trying to make her miserable. But for some inexplicable reason, the only place she could see the intruder was in a mirror.

Donna's husband brought her to see a psychiatrist to whom Donna told her story. The boarder didn't have a name. Donna referred to her as the "old hag" or "ugly hag." The hag didn't speak to her, Donna said, but did taunt her with gestures and mimicry. The psychiatrist (Dr. Gluckman) put a mirror in front of Donna and asked her to make various body movements. He told her to smile, look angry, comb her hair and the like. Donna willingly complied. But she would become immediately upset and point furiously at the hag in the mirror who was mocking and insulting her.

Any shiny surface invited disaster. Her husband wouldn't take Donna in a car because she would go into a fit if she caught a glimpse of her nemesis in the body paint or windows. Eventually Donna stopped leaving the house altogether. But the house had its own problems. Donna and her husband had bought a shimmering, modern home that was lined with glass doors, built-in mirrors and glass-backed cabinets. Danger lurked everywhere. Donna refused to go in the kitchen because she was afraid she'd see the woman in the stainless steel bench. Her husband covered every reflecting surface he could find with heavy, opaque paper. But it was never enough.

Donna "believed the woman had invaded her life because she wanted her love and affection," Gluckman reported. But Donna said she was "incapable" of giving affection to this old hag and now the woman had turned on her. The woman both taunted and terrified Donna. When Gluckman asked Donna what other problems she had, Donna said she didn't have any. Just get rid of the hag and she would be fine. Her husband's life had turned equally dismal. No one visited them anymore. He complained that Donna's craziness had cost them all their friends. He felt bitter and helpless.

Medical tests indicated that Donna had signs of cerebral atrophy—probably an early stage of dementia—but "remarkably little deficit of the higher cerebral functions." And despite her organic damage, Donna "could interpret the mirror image of every gesture or facial expression or action made by me perfectly normally," Gluckman noted. But "she could not be persuaded the mirror image of herself was not a real person. She would say emphatically that it was not her but that terrible ugly old woman who followed her everywhere and frightened her."

Donna felt trapped, stalked. Her pursuer was slippery. Donna said she didn't know where the woman slept. Donna "could not escape, try as she would, from the presence of this hag," Gluckman reported. Why, Donna pleaded, did "the thing" keep taunting her? She would sometimes throw objects at the mirror to get the old hag to leave. She even heaved a bucket of water at her once. But the woman wouldn't leave her alone. Ever. Donna eventually gave up. "She lost all interest in life and spent her days sitting and moping, avoiding any room where there was a reflecting surface," Gluckman said.

***

Donna's persecution complex is, unfortunately, the norm in mirror delusions. The neurologist and psychiatrist Todd Feinberg has written extensively about the connection between brain circuits and the experience of self. He describes a patient of his own, an older woman who was brought to his office a few years ago by her frightened husband, whose emotional experience was remarkably similar to Donna's. The woman, whom he called R.D., was a church-going mother and wife who, her husband said, had been the epitome of mild-mannered womanhood, prim and proper as long as he'd known her. Recently, however, she had been having episodes of sudden, violent fits. The strangest part, he said, was that the fits occurred in only one circumstance: when she saw her reflection in the mirror. R.D. became agitated and hostile every time she caught a glimpse of herself. She was totally convinced the image in the mirror was a "strange and malevolent" person who for some reason was stalking her.

R.D. would begin ranting as soon as Feinberg placed a mirror in front of her. On one occasion in Feinberg's office, for example, she shouted:

"That's her, that's her. Yeah, that's her." . . .

". . . Did you hear the story? Eh? Did you hear it?" she asked Feinberg.

". . . [I've] had a lot of problems with her."

". . . She starts calling me these names. Streetwalker. [I] can't stand her."

". . . She's just an old bag. Yeah, she's a bag."

The stalker was sneaky, too. "I never heard her name. Never! Never! She never told me her name."

R.D. became furious and threatening when she addressed her tormentor directly:

"Now you get out . . . get home where you belong. You don't belong here. You don't live here. Out!"

". . . No, no. . . . You can't go in the house! No, you can't go in the house!"

". . . We know where you live."

". . . You're a good for nothin'. . . . You little bitch. . . . Now, you know where you're gonna' go? You're gonna' go home."

Later, she turned to Dr. Feinberg:

"When we get home, you know what? We're gonna' . . . find her waiting right around the windows. In the windows where she watches. [She] listens to what we do. I can't stand her.

". . . She's been walking around the house, around the area, for a long time. . . . All the time she bothers everybody."

"...I always wanted to hit her! I'm gonna' kill her."[8]

When we usually think of multiple personality disorder it is about people like Eve and her three faces. But Eve's trio at least inhabited the same body. Yolanda, Donna, and R.D. have created alter egos that are entirely separate people. These are multiple personalities acted out on a stage with mirrors to create special effects—special effects that they alone can see. The productions are remarkably inventive, from script to presentation. The problem is they're too good. They are so well-crafted that the writer-performer-audience (aka the patient) is trapped in the illusion that it's real life.

**

Neurologists often diagnose patients with mirror delusions—mistakenly, as we've seen—under the category of prosopagnosia. Psychiatrists and clinical psychologists, looking through their own lenses, tend to see what's known as Capgras syndrome. Classic Capgras refers to a person who is convinced that someone close to him or her—usually a friend, spouse, or some other intimate family member—has been replaced by an impostor, a person whose appearance and behavior is identical to the original but who is actually someone else. In extreme conditions of Capgras, the patient sees multiple impersonators. Sometimes, everyone looks suspicious.

Do mirror delusions fit the Capgras diagnosis? Does your reflection in the mirror qualify as another person? It's a good question. If you see someone other than yourself, what difference does it make whose reflection it is? The bottom line in all these delusions seems be a breakdown in what the Buddhists would call our illusion of uniqueness. There is a blurring of individual identity, be it your own or someone else's.

**

Can we create the mirror delusion in a normal person? Cognitive psychologist Amanda Barnier and her colleagues decided to test this question. They hypnotized eight highly suggestible subjects and told them they were going to see a strange person when they looked in the mirror.[9] "When you look to your left, you will see a mirror," she told them. "The mirror you will see will have properties of a normal mirror, with one major difference. The person you see in the mirror will not be you. It will be a stranger." To complement this suggestion, some subjects were given slightly different instructions: They were told the mirror was a window and that they would be seeing a stranger when they looked through the window.[10] The subjects were all psychologically normal and they were, in fact, looking into regular mirrors.

We know that a subject under hypnosis can be induced to believe in nonrealities described by the hypnotist. To a degree, that is. We also know there are considerable limitations to the power of hypnotic suggestions. Research shows that subjects are perfectly capable of saying no or ending the session when they want to. And there is no evidence someone under hypnosis can be induced to perform otherwise impossible feats of cognitive or sensory acuity.[11] In other words, people can only be pushed so far under hypnosis. Is seeing a stranger in the mirror pushing too far? The answer is no, Barnier found. It turned out to be remarkably easy to get subjects to accept the delusion. Seven of the eight subjects (88 percent) were convinced they were looking at a stranger. All seven began referring to their reflection in the third person.

With hypnosis, there's always the question of experiencing versus playacting. Every test Barnier ran, however, convinced her they were enduring "a subjectively real and compelling delusion." She describes one particular subject, for example, who "displayed initial surprise at seeing the person in the mirror and appeared so convinced that it was a stranger that he frequently looked behind him in an attempt to find the person in the room." Here is part of a transcript from the subject:

HYPNOTIST: Tell me, what do you see?

SUBJECT: (The subject looks in the mirror and then behind him). Who's that?

HYPNOTIST: Tell me about what you see.

SUBJECT: Another person.

HYPNOTIST: Tell me about the person.

SUBJECT: They're wearing a purple shirt, they've got a big nose, got a mole on their neck. . . . They've got short, curly hair, brown eyes, brown hair.

HYPNOTIST: Have you ever seen this person before?

Chapter 7

SUBJECT: No.

HYPNOTIST: Does this person remind you of anyone?

SUBJECT: I think I've seen him before at school. . . . I think he was in the year below me.

HYPNOTIST: What do you think his name is?

SUBJECT: Anthony (Not the Subject's name).

HYPNOTIST: In what ways does this person look like you?

SUBJECT: Same colored hair.

HYPNOTIST: In what ways does the person you see look different to you?

SUBJECT: Different colored eyes. I think my nose is smaller . . . got bigger lips . . . and I've got more freckles.

HYPNOTIST: What is he doing at the moment?

SUBJECT: Looking into the mirror. I don't know where he is though. (The subject looks behind him and around the room).

HYPNOTIST: Is he doing anything in particular or saying anything in particular?

SUBJECT: Just looking at me. He's saying something but I can't understand.

As a challenge, the hypnotist asked subjects to describe how an outside observer could tell them apart from their mirror/window image. Easy. Most pointed out that anyone could tell the difference just by looking at their features; a few said people would just know. Almost none of the subjects enjoyed the experience. Eighty-three percent described it as strange and/or uncomfortable. "I just thought he was an idiot," one subject said. "He just kept looking at me from the corner of the mirror. . . . I just wanted him to go away."

The subjects, in other words, sounded pretty much like actual mirror-image patients. Don't get me wrong. A temporary hypnotic state is hardly the same as a deep-rooted psychotic delusion. The point is that, for all of us, physical identity is more fragile than we like to assume. Kierkegaard once observed, "The greatest hazard of all, losing the self, can occur very quietly in the world, as if it were nothing at all. . . . Any other loss—an arm, a leg, five dollars, a wife, etc.—is sure to be noticed."[12] But the self is so vague and intangible. It's that ghost. And how can you tell when you've lost a ghost?

***

Any type of delusion, by its very nature, strains the boundaries of self and identity. Someone with, for example, a delusion of grandeur—imagining he is Jesus Christ or the king of England—has lost a grip on who he is and who he is not. But mirror delusions, more than any other, strike point blank at identity. Where is the line between self and other when your reflection is a stranger? Worse yet, when you don't like each other?

Making peace with one's imaginary companion may not be so different from making peace with oneself. One moment we like who we see in the mirror; the next moment we don't. All of us struggle with inner demons we would prefer didn't exist. Some just happen to see these selves in three dimensions. At what point does a fantasy in your mind's eye become so intense that it manifests as visual reality? This is the vast gray zone between vivid imagination and delusional thinking. It is often hard to say where normalcy ends and pathology begins.

Let us give the last words in this chapter to a mirror delusion patient known as T.H. who, in the middle of a testing session with his neurologist, broke out with this poem:[13]

When you get what you want in your struggle for self
And the world makes you king for the day
You go to the mirror and look at yourself
And see what that man has to say.

He's the fellow to please, never mind all the rest
He's with you clear up to the end
And you've passed the most difficult dangerous test
If the man in the glass is your friend.

8
Two Bodies, One Self
Or, What if You Met Your Identical Twin?

Because they knew each other's thoughts,
they even quarreled without speaking.
—Bruce Chatwin, *On the Black Hill*

In the case of mirror delusions, people see someone else when they look at themselves. Some people, however, experience a 180-degree flip: They see a copy of themselves when they look at a different person. And, in the case of one small group of people, this is barely a delusion. They have come face-to-face with a remarkable semblance of their flesh-and-blood double.

Consider the story of Barbara Herbert. Barbara grew up in a modest home in a working-class neighborhood north of London. Her father was a groundskeeper in a public park. Her mother died while she was still in school. When she was a young adult, Barbara needed to get a copy of her birth certificate as paperwork for a retirement plan. The clerk at the records office at first couldn't find anyone with Barbara's name. Finally, she came across a file for a girl named Gerda Barbara Jacobson, the daughter of a Finnish woman named Helena Jacobson, who had been born in the same hospital on the same day as Barbara. Further research revealed that Gerda had been adopted by the Herbert family. Barbara, to her astonishment, had been adopted.

When her birth certificate arrived, Barbara discovered something even more astonishing. The delivering doctor, it turned out, had jotted down Barbara's birth time. In Britain, this is only done to distinguish between twins. When Barbara pressed for more information, she learned that not only was it true she had a twin, but it was an identical twin. Helena Jacobson had given birth to identical twins, immediately put both up for adoption, and the two girls were adopted by different families. Barbara had entered the records office to expedite her retirement documents; she left having learned the secret of her birth—and with knowledge of her twin sister.

Barbara set out to learn more about her twin. She first tried putting advertisements in newspapers but got no credible responses. Then she petitioned the courts to release Daphne's adoption papers. The courts, following a policy originally designed to keep mothers from finding a child they had put up for adoption, refused. Barbara hired lawyers and fought a long battle to have them make an exception, explaining that the policy didn't make any sense in her case. Finally, the registrar general offered her a compromise: he wouldn't release the papers, but he would be willing to track her sister down and tell her that Barbara was searching for her. He asked Barbara if she would be prepared to meet her twin. Barbara said she was. The registrar general contacted Daphne's family, who relayed the request to Daphne. Daphne agreed to a meeting. They set up an appointment to meet at London's King's Cross railway station. And so, at the age of forty, Barbara and Daphne finally set eyes on each other.

The reunion began awkwardly. The women didn't hug or shake hands or even look each other over at first. Both felt the peculiarity of the encounter. By all usual standards, they were complete strangers but, biologically, they were about as close as two people can get. Neither knew how to act in the first moments. But their wariness was quickly replaced by astonishment. To begin with, they finally greeted each other by holding up matching crooked pinkies. They now stared more carefully at each other. It was like looking in the mirror. Both knew beforehand that there would be an acute likeness but, still, to meet a stranger who looked so much like oneself was a startling experience. They looked at each other's outfits: Both of them were wearing beige dresses and brown velvet jackets.

Physical appearance was just the beginning. Over time the twins discovered that they both preferred cold, black coffee; had the same favorite color (lilac); the same favorite actor (Brad Pitt); and liked the same books. They shared the same phobias, including a fear of heights, falling down stairs, and the sight of blood. Both laughed constantly and in the same distinctive way. (Psychologist David Lykken from the University of Minnesota twin project, where Barbara and Daphne were later studied, referred to them as "the giggle twins"). Both had wanted to become opera singers, but neither, it turned out, could carry a tune.

Their adoptive backgrounds were very different. In contrast to Barbara's working-class background, Daphne was raised in an upper-middle-class family, attended private schools, and frequently traveled abroad. Yet their lives had followed remarkably similar patterns. Both women had left school at age fourteen. At sixteen, they both met their future husbands at town hall dances. Both women had miscarried in the same month. And both eventually gave birth to two sons and a daughter, in that very order. Each had fallen down stairs when she was fifteen. When the Minnesota researcher probed the twins' political views, it turned out that both had only voted once in their lives, in both cases when they were employed as polling clerks. They scored almost identically—only one point apart—on IQ tests.[1]

***

There are an estimated three hundred pairs of identical (monozygotic) twins worldwide who, like Barbara and Daphne, were reunited after being raised apart.[2] Far and away the largest bank of information about these pairs is the Minnesota Study of Twins Reared Apart (MSTRA), which was established in 1979 by psychologist Thomas Bouchard as an offshoot of the University of Minnesota twin family project. The research project has studied more than two hundred of these reunited twins since that time. Each of them are subjected to a week of intensive psychological and physiological tests and interviews. Not every twin pair turns out to be as alike as Barbara and Daphne. But one of the most remarkable findings of the study is how often they do. Bouchard and his colleagues have accumulated a long list of sometimes extraordinary similarities— what they refer to with the refreshingly unscientific label of "spooky coincidences." Bouchard created the MSTRA, in fact, after meeting perhaps the most startling of these cases of spooky coincidences, who have become known as the Jim twins.

Jim Springer and Jim Lewis are identical twins who were adopted soon after birth by different parents. A court official recalls being taken aback when the Lewises unknowingly assigned their baby the same name the Springers had given to theirs days earlier. Both sets of parents knew their sons had been born twins, but they had been told the other twin had died in childbirth. The Springers and their Jim always assumed this to be true. The Lewises, however, learned early on that their son's twin was alive and told this to their Jim. As he got older, Jim Lewis became increasingly curious about his brother but said he was reluctant to find him because he was "afraid it might stir up some problems."[3] Finally, in 1979, at the age of thirty-nine, Lewis decided it was time. His first attempt was to contact the original adoption court and, unlike Barbara Herbert, he received the information he needed after little more than a month. Jim Springer, it turned out, was a records clerk in Dayton, Ohio, less than one hundred miles away from Jim Lewis's hometown of Lima, Ohio. They arranged to meet at Springer's home.

Like Barbara and Daphne, the two Jims were nervous about the meeting. Lewis, in fact, arrived late because he'd stopped off for a "last beer" to "shore up his courage." Springer was chain-smoking as he waited. He had started wondering whether Lewis might be after money or a kidney transplant. "There had to be some reason for this meeting," he recalled thinking.[4] Springer was waiting with his wife when Lewis walked in the door. The awkwardness dissolved almost instantly. "Jim and I shook hands and then we all looked at each other for a few seconds. Then we broke out laughing," Springer recalled. It was as if they'd known each other forever, Lewis added. "Right off the bat I felt close. It wasn't like meeting a stranger."[5]

Their similarities have become legendary in twin research. Biologically, they were almost clones. Both weighed 180 pounds. Both had put on ten pounds for no apparent reason at the exact same period in their lives, and both lost the ten pounds for no apparent reason at the same age. They shared the same health problems: Both started having migraines, with virtually identical symptoms, when they were eighteen. Both had high blood pressure—identically high blood pressure—and had experienced two heart attacks. They had both suffered from hemorrhoids. They had a "lazy eye" in the same eye.

They had a wide range of similar habits, interests, and behaviors. Both, for example, preferred Miller Lite beer and chain-smoked Salems. They had each built white benches around the trunk of a tree in their gardens. They liked stock-car racing but disliked baseball. Both men had worked part-time as a deputy-sheriff; both had worked for McDonald's; both had been gas station attendants. They both liked to scatter love notes to their wives around the house. Both were compulsive nail-biters. When Bouchard interviewed the Jims for MSTRA, he said he couldn't distinguish between many of their body movements—how they sat in a chair, shook hands, and the body language they used to express themselves.

The twins scored almost identically on psychological tests administered by MSTRA. "In one test, which measured such personality variables as tolerance, conformity, flexibility, self-control and sociability, (the Jim twins') scores were so close that they approximated the totals which result when the same person takes the test twice," Bouchard reported.[6] Their IQ scores were also almost identical.

There were initially criticisms that Bouchard and his team were overstating the similarities between the Jim twins. They weren't exactly accused of lying. But could they have fallen into the classic trap of seeing only what they wanted to see? It's human nature to search for information that supports our beliefs while casting a blind eye on anything that doesn't. Psychologists refer to this as "the confirmation bias." Perhaps, critics thought, Bouchard's group was trying too hard to discover the Jims' similarities but forgetting to count up their differences. There were also other criticisms. A case was made that most of the similarities were caused by particularly precise genetic programming; and, although the Jims were raised in different homes, their social environments—unlike those of Barbara and Daphne—may not have been all that different.

But then some really spooky coincidences emerged that no one could explain. Both, it turned out, had married a girl named Linda, from whom they were later divorced. Both remarried, this time to a woman named Betty. Lewis had named his oldest son James Alan; Springer named his oldest son James Allan. When they were boys, both Jims owned dogs whom they had named Toy. As adults, both spent their vacations on a stretch of beach only three hundred yards long—the same beach near St. Petersburg, Florida. They drove there in the same kind of Chevrolet. The list went on. Some of the coincidences crossed into the ridiculous, like the fact that both grew up with an adopted brother named Larry.[7] Most of the skeptics threw in the towel at this point.

The Minnesota researchers have discovered many other pairs who were shocked by their similarities. There is even a paradoxical uniqueness to the sameness in many cases; the similarities that defined a pair of twins were what often set them apart from other pairs. For example, in the more than two hundred pairs the Minnesota researchers studied there were only:

- Two "dog people"—an obedience trainer and a dog show competitor.
- Two people who became frightened if the door was closed in the soundproof physiology lab; they refused to enter unless it was left open.
- Two fashion designers.
- Two fire department captains.
- Two people who had been married five times.

And, guess what? In every one of these cases, and many more like them, both people were from the same pair of identical twins who had been reared apart. Over and again the researchers were "flabbergasted by the similarities, the unheard-of coincidences, and the counterintuitive findings" that their interviews and tests turned up. "We were not ready for what we found," observed Professor Bouchard. Even when there were differences between twins, they were often "variations on a theme more than anything else," he concluded.[8]

***

What are the chances that these are simply statistical anomalies? Twin expert Peter Watson calculated the statistical probabilities that many of the similarities in the Minnesota twin pairs could have occurred by chance.[9] He looked, for example, at the likelihood that five of the prominent concurrences between Barbara and Daphne (wearing the same outfit to their first meeting; their preference for cold, black coffee; their preference for vodka; their fear of heights; and having fallen down the stairs at age fifteen) might occur by chance. Even after liberal corrections for possible confounding factors (for example, shared physical anomalies), Watson determined that the probability all five similarities would appear by chance is 0.000,000,150—or 1 in 6.7 million. When we add the similarities between the Jims and those in other twin pairs, these odds grow exponentially.

We will probably never know precisely how much the similarities between Barbara and Daphne, the Jims, and many other reunited twins were determined by their genes versus how much was shaped by their upbringings. These nature-nurture questions always seem to defy precise answers. And we certainly can't prove which are more random than spooky. Then again, these issues are usually a lot more important to the researchers in the MSTRA than they are to the twins who were reunited. What matters to the twins is that they have met their near-doubles and their lives will never be the same.

∗∗∗

What is it like to have an identical twin? To begin with, there are practical benefits. Abigail Pogrebin, author of the book *One and the Same*, loves how seamlessly she and her identical twin Robin can fill in for each other. "I auditioned for her once when she was sick. We can use each other's passports in a pinch," she says. And Abigail describes even more mundane advantages. She can easily slip past her sister's doorman, for example. "He just nods when I walk by, never questions why I'm entering a home that isn't mine."[10]

What if one of you enjoyed a chore that the other one hated? Identical twins have advantages here, too. Debra and Lisa Ganz, for example, have developed an arrangement for clothes shopping. Debbie says she can't stand to shop. Lisa, fortunately, loves it. So Lisa has become the designated shopper for both. "I buy two outfits of everything," she says. "Debbie doesn't come with me. So unless a store has two, I won't buy it. I'll walk in the store and say, 'Can we try this on?' And I see the sales lady look around, like, 'Who are you referring to? Who is the *we?*' I'm the only one standing there." And Debbie is happy to report, "I haven't gone shopping in twelve years."[11]

Twins describe using each other as stand-ins for events they want to avoid, of signing in for each other at roll calls, of being able to appear in two places at once. One pair of identical sisters I spoke to, Harriet and Gertie Goldfarb, laughed about having secretly split a job for almost fifteen years. It was ideal for raising a family, they said, because they could exchange hours anytime they wanted. There are also health benefits. Abigail Pogrebin refers to her identical twin Robin as "my backup copy. She shares my blood-type, is my marrow match, my stunt double." You would have an organ donor on call.

Clearly, a twin can have practical benefits. For most twins, however, these are details in the bigger picture. Having a twin alters the texture of your every experience. It colors the entire quality of your life. When identical twins are asked to describe these more profound consequences, they tend to focus on several issues.

First of all, they say, your twin will probably become the closest relationship in your life. This is hardly surprising for twins who grow up together. After all, they've probably been constant companions their entire lives. But it also usually turns out to be true for identical twins who were brought up separately. Bouchard and his colleagues asked sixty-five reunited twin pairs who had been brought up in separate families how close they now felt to their reunited partner. Almost 70 percent said they felt "closer than best friends" to their twin. Notably, only 27 percent of these same twins said they felt "closer than best friends" to any of the adoptive siblings whom they had known their entire lives.[12] The closeness is often described in the most extreme terms. Identical twin Tiki Barber, for example, describes his relationship to his twin as "the strongest bond that there possibly is."

Second, there is usually a price to pay for this closeness. To begin with, many identical twins—both those who were raised together and separately—say it interferes with forming other intimate relationships. Marriage can be the biggest problem. "When you're married to a twin, essentially, whether you like it or not, you're married to the other one, too," Barber says. This is a lot to ask from a spouse. "I almost married once," says fifty-one-year-old Sam Zarante, another identical twin. But "Marie, my fiancée, didn't understand my being a twin. She thought my twin brother, Dave, and I were too close." Zarante's intended may have been right. Barber believes that for most twins, including himself and his brother, the bond is "greater than marriage." He notes, "I'm closer to Ronde [his twin], without a doubt. And that will never change." Although there is no systematic data reflecting the divorce rates for identical twins, many talk about the toll their twinship takes on their marriages. At the least, they often point out, the outsider spouse needs to know what he or she is getting into. "A lot of times being a twin causes divorce because spouses don't understand the closeness," says identical twin Sandy Miller.[13]

Third, competition is a commonly mentioned burden. Many identical twins describe rivalries with their partner. If you've grown up with your twin, the competition has been there all your life. Identical twin Caroline Paul, for example, talks about the perpetual challenge of competing with her twin sister. "Somebody who is born single doesn't have a measuring stick next to them," she says. "But twins always do. So either you don't stand next to each other and you have totally different lives or when you do stand next to each other, you make sure you're just as good."[14] In her memoir, Paul writes: "What you could be walks right next to you all the time."[15]

For separated twins who meet up later in life the competition is often more acute. Many say their first meeting is like holding up a mirror and being confronted by the person you could have become. Identical twins Elyse Schein and Paula Bernstein met for the first time at the age of thirty-five. "Imagine a slightly different version of you walks across the room, looks you in the eye and says 'hello' in your voice," they write in their coauthored book, *Identical Strangers*. "Looking at this person, you are able to gaze into your own eyes and see yourself from the outside. This identical individual has the exact same DNA as you and is essentially your clone.... It's hard not to think about what this person has done with what she was given. And how you measure up."[16]

Finally, the most profound problems of all: individuality and uniqueness. "For so many twins I've talked to, identical or fraternal, establishing separateness seemed to be *the* primary stumbling block," observed Abigail Pogrebin. She describes her own experience as typical: "It isn't unusual for me to be mistaken for Robin on a weekly basis in Manhattan," she says about her twin. "And this means I'm regularly reminded that I'm someone's double. What does it mean to be a copy of another person, for there to be two of you, for you to impersonate or replicate someone else just by existing? Physical likeness is what most people focus on when they encounter identical twins, but doubleness manifests itself more ambiguously from inside the twinship." It can, she concludes, "muddy your clarity of self. When you look like someone, spend all your early years with them, are assumed to resemble them, and are compared to them, you have an ingrained sense of being not just one, but two."[17] When Pogrebin wrote a book about her experiences, she titled it *One and the Same*.

How does it change a person's image of "I" and "me" when his or her uniqueness is so bluntly challenged? Is there personal validation in finding another like you? Does it offer relief from the loneliness and alienation that are so-often a by-product of uniqueness? Or does it diminish your self-worth? Does it mean you're redundant? These are the questions all identical twins face. They are especially profound for reunited twins who meet up later in life.

To find yourself looking into a human mirror, "is the most narcissistic encounter imaginable," observes Lawrence Wright, who researched a wide range of twin experiences for his book, *Twins: And What They Tell Us about Who We Are*. What an astounding experience, "to stand aside and really look at your almost-self, to talk to someone else who is inside the same physical package, to experience your almost-self as others must experience you." What does it feel like? Wright captures the tensions elegantly:

> No doubt it is exhilarating to discover another individual who is uniquely able to understand you, who seems to anticipate your thoughts before you form them. . . . But at the same time, seeing yourself replicated is a shocking confrontation with the finite nature of who you really are. . . . After you've explored the variety of ways that you are alike, it is the differences between you that capture your attention. Perhaps that is a way of holding on to your separateness, your particular identity. . . . But some of your selfhood has been appropriated. There is one side of you that wants your twin to be exactly like you in every detail, a perfect replica, but another side of you is struggling for air. You feel like you are being smothered by the sameness. Your specialness is being erased with every thrilling landmark of recognition.[18]

When all is said and done, does having an identical twin enhance or diminish the quality of one's life? Do the advantages outweigh the burdens? There is little consensus on these questions, either from twins or the researchers who study them. Nor do I expect there should be. Like all happiness questions, it's going to depend on the particulars of the person and the situation. There is an old *Seinfeld* episode in which Jerry begins dating a woman who is exactly the same as him. At first, he thinks he's hit the jackpot. "She's incredible," he says. "She's just like me. She talks like me. She acts like me." Then it hits him. "I hate myself. I need to get the exact *opposite* of me." So is having a twin a good thing or a bad thing? In the end, it may very well come down to Jerry's question: Do you like yourself?

9
The Art of Self-Cloning

"Ditto," said Tweedledum.
"Ditto, ditto!" cried Tweedledee.
—Lewis Carroll, *Through the Looking Glass*

Identical twins aren't the only people who see doubles. Consider the case of a patient I'll call Alexandra, an eighteen-year-old Greek woman who was admitted to a hospital with unusual psychiatric symptoms. Her psychological history had, until recently, been relatively unremarkable. People described her as "reserved, sensitive, stubborn and religious." She had maintained generally good relationships with her mother, father, and three siblings. Alexandra did have a tendency toward "misinterpreting" her relationships with other people. Sometimes these led to false memories. For example, she recalled being acquainted with people when this was not the case. None of this, however, had created alarm until now.

Her difficulties began the year before, when she experienced a high fever during an illness. Since then, Alexandra reported, she had developed insomnia, depression, agitation, and painfully ambivalent feelings toward her relatives. She was also convinced that she was being shadowed by a double of herself. The culprit, she said, was a female neighbor who used elaborate techniques—involving special makeup, a wig, and a mask—to make herself look exactly like Alexandra. She had the "same face, same build, same clothes, same everything." Alexandra had seen the woman's metamorphosis with her own eyes.

She described her tormentor in a letter to her father: "In here there is a girl as fat and as tall as I am. At night when everyone is asleep she puts on a wig and a mask and walks from room to room stealing things in order to incriminate me. One night I woke up and saw her with my own eyes. It is unfortunate that due to my confusion I failed to run to the window to shout to the people, 'Look here, this is me, and this is my double with a wig and a mask.'"

During a stay as a hospital inpatient, Alexandra began seeing multiple doubles. "She insisted that she had seen at least two female patients transformed into her own self," her psychiatrist said. Alexandra became extremely unstable emotionally. During a subsequent stay, she became agitated and irritable, and she could be violent with her doubles. In one incident, for example, she started pulling the hair of one of them (in reality, a confused fellow patient). When the double ran away, Alexandra pleaded with her doctors to catch the impostor and remove the woman's mask to reveal her true identity. Clinical interventions—psychotherapy, drugs, electroconvulsive therapy—offered only temporary relief from her symptoms. At last report, Alexandra was still under long-term hospitalization.[1]

***

Alexandra suffers from what is called "subjective double syndrome," a condition that is often classified under the heading of the better-known Capgras syndrome. It turns out, in fact, that doubles may have been very much what Jean Marie Joseph Capgras—the French psychiatrist after whom the disorder is named—originally had in mind. He initially called the disorder *phénomène de sosies*. The French word *sosie* means "look-alike" or "double" in the sense of identical twins.

It is an unusual illness. Psychiatrist Joyce Kamanitz and her colleagues found records of just twenty reported cases of the double delusion from 1900 to 1989.[2] My own search came up with about (depending on the criteria) ten more. They are often extraordinary. For example:

- A twenty-three-year-old woman who was convinced her double was the queen of a gang of criminals.

- A singer who believed her double was an Italian princess.

- A fifty-year-old woman who believed a double of herself was sleeping with her husband.

- A thirty-two-year-old man who reported an impostor who had replaced him in his hometown and eight other impostor-doubles of other family members in other cities.

- A forty-one-year-old woman who believed she had multiple doubles that included her son, husband, and theologians, who used the resemblance to withdraw her money from the bank.

- A fifty-three-year-old woman who reported duplicates of herself, her husband, her neighbors and, most of all, her daughter, who had more than two thousand doubles.

- A thirty-two-year-old woman who was convinced she had one double who was being groomed to be president of the United States and another who was running around the hospital performing sadistic sexual acts.

It is not clear how much these delusions result from organic brain damage and how much they stem from psychological problems. What is certain is that something is terribly wrong.

***

The double syndrome has provoked the imaginations of writers and other artists who often refer to the syndrome by the term "doppelgänger," from the German words *doppel* ("double") and *gänger* ("walker" or "goer"). Writers from Goethe and Oscar Wilde to Philip Roth (in his 1993 novel, *Operation Shylock*) and Mike Myers (aka Austin Powers and his nemeses Dr. Evil and Mini-Me) have molded the concept to suit their creations. They rarely paint pretty pictures.

Edgar Allan Poe's 1839 short story "William Wilson" was perhaps the first work to tackle the double experience head-on. William Wilson, the story's narrator, tells of leading a perfectly comfortable childhood until the day a new boy showed up at school. The boy quickly becomes William's rival as he pushes William to the limit both on the playground and in the classroom. But the eeriness begins when William sees how much the new boy looks like him. Worse yet, he bizarrely shares the same name, had entered school the same day and was even born the same day (January 19, which also happens to have been Poe's birthday). Over time, his new rival starts copying William's gestures. He begins dressing and talking like him. One night William sneaks into the boy's bedroom and is horrified to see that his rival's face now looks exactly like his own.

The boy, William tells us, was his absolute double: "His cue, which was to perfect an imitation of myself, lay both in words and in actions; and most admirably did he play his part. My dress it was an easy matter to copy; my gait and general manner were, without difficulty, appropriated; in spite of his constitutional defect, even my voice did not escape him. My louder tones were, of course, unattempted, but then the key, it was identical; and his singular whisper, it grew the very echo of my own." This double spells disaster for William. He follows William everywhere and destroys everything he does. William's life plunges into a downward spiral that leads to his "later years of unspeakable misery, and unpardonable crime."[3]

Alexandra and William would surely have understood each other.

***

Dostoevsky, in his novella *Dvoynik* (*The Double*), takes the doppelgänger to new levels. William Wilson simply ended up miserable and in prison. At least he could still narrate a book. Dostoevsky strikes at deeper pathology: his protagonist completely loses his mind. *The Double* centers on Yakov Petrovitch Golyadkin, a neurotic, anxious bureaucrat who fluctuates from assertiveness and arrogance to utter self-doubt. Nowadays, we would probably label him with bipolar disorder.

On the morning we're introduced to Mr. Golyadkin, he begins his day by looking in the mirror. And, we're told, he is "evidently quite satisfied with all that he saw there." Not for long. That night he sees a man coming toward him. As the stranger comes into view, Golyadkin notices the man is dressed and looks curiously like himself. Golyadkin calls to the man but, when the man approaches, Golyadkin panics and runs home. As Golyadkin nears his house, he spots the man running in the same direction. He follows the stranger and, to his astonishment, watches the man walk into his house, climb the stairs to his apartment, and sit on his own bed. The man smiles at Golyadkin as if he's an old friend. Golyadkin now recognizes his nocturnal acquaintance. It was, Dostoevsky writes, "none other than himself, Mr. Golyadkin himself, another Mr. Golyadkin, but exactly the same as himself." Golyadkin is terrified. "His hair stood on end and he collapsed into a chair, insensible with horror."

Golyadkin wakes up the next morning questioning his vision from the night before. He suspects his enemies have played a trick on him. When Golyadkin arrives at work, however, he sees his alter ego sitting "staidly and peacefully" across from him. Dostoevsky describes the man: "This was another Golyadkin, a completely different one, and yet at the same time very like the other—of the same height and build, dressed in the same way and with the same bald patch—in short, nothing, absolutely nothing, was lacking to complete the resemblance, so that if they were taken and placed side by side nobody, absolutely nobody, would have taken it upon himself to say which was the old and which the new, which was the original and which the copy."[4] The stranger's name is Golyadkin, Jr. He's there to stay. Junior slowly but surely begins to infiltrate Senior's life, at first for better and for worse but eventually simply for the latter. Over time, Golyadkin, Sr., helplessly watches his double insult his colleagues, run up bills in his name, and do everything he can to destroy his own already decaying reputation and social standing.

Golyadkin, Sr. becomes obsessed with his double and descends slowly but surely into paranoid madness. He even develops a case of mirrored-self misidentification syndrome along the way that would fit right in with the delusions of Yolanda and Donna (in chapter 7). When he looks in the mirror, Golyadkin, Sr. now sees a door—a door that always leads him to Golyadkin, Jr. His vision sounds like the experimental creation of mirror delusions in Amanda Barnier's hypnosis study.

But one double was just the beginning for Dostoevsky. Golyadkin, Sr. is eventually surrounded by hordes of them. (Dostoevsky was, psychiatrically speaking, ahead of his time with this vision. We now know that multiple doubles frequently appear to real patients with the disorder.) He hallucinates a crowd of "precisely similar Golyadkins . . . running after one another as soon as they appeared, and stretched in a long chain like a file of geese, hobbling after the real Mr. Golyadkin." He finds himself trapped by "perfect counterfeits of himself." Golyadkin becomes unhinged at this point, and his doctor sweeps him off to an asylum.[5]

***

To psychiatrists and psychologists, seeing doubles is a symptom of mental illness. To writers like Poe and Dostoevsky, it is emblematic of the hopelessness of the human condition. For all of them, it equates to pain and suffering. And, of course, there is much to back up their viewpoint. After all, if your friend tells you he's being followed by doubles, it is something to be concerned about. But just because the double syndrome *can* be an illness doesn't mean it always is. With most purely physical illnesses—say, the flu or the measles—you just want your symptoms to go away. The idea of meeting another version of you, however, isn't simply like a disease. There is also something alluring about it. It carries possibilities.

What would it be like to have a double? We conducted a survey to see how people felt about the notion. Our sample consisted of 108 college students and other young adults whom we told: "Imagine you were to meet someone who is your virtual double. The person has the same name, looks like you and even acts like you. In fact, people who know both of you often mix you up." We asked them to consider two scenarios. In the first, "You see this person from time to time but he/she is not highly involved in your immediate life." In the second, "This person is highly involved in your immediate life. He/she is a fellow student in many of your classes and is in the same circle of friends." The students were instructed to rate how much they liked the idea on a scale of 1 to 7.

They varied considerably. Many expressed curiosity. Some, to our surprise, loved the idea. ("Cool! I can't believe it but that's awesome," one commented). Many were attracted by the practical applications—for example, having a stand-in to fill in for them. A few saw the makings of a new best friend. Overall, however, more people were generally opposed to the idea than in favor of it: Of our sample, 57 percent said they either mildly or strongly disliked the notion of having a double who was a peripheral character in their life, and 67 percent were opposed to the idea of having a double who played a central role in their life.[6] When we looked at those with the most extreme opinions, the differences were more pronounced: Three times as many people said they "hated" the idea of any kind of double compared with those who said they "loved" it.[7]

The negative responders used words like "uncomfortable," "awkward," "confusing," "weird," "shocking," and "invaded." They also expressed fears that mirrored the reports we heard from identical twins in the previous chapter. These reservations fell into several categories.

Some feared mistaken identity:

- "I already share my name with someone I run into every once in a while and a little part of me dies each time I hear him called by my name."

- "I'd hate it that my double could get credit for things I'd accomplished. And that I'd get blamed for her screwups."

There were some who saw benefits. One respondent observed: "If I ever did anything wrong I would just blame it on the other person who looked like me."

Others were wary of the competition:

- "I'd hate it the most if she excelled in the things I excel in. For example, if she were the girl in my class the Professor liked. It would kill me."

In the case of a double who was central to their lives, some feared it would challenge their self-worth:

- "It would bother me the most that she had the same circle of friends as me, almost as if I wasn't enough, like they needed a double of me."

Every comment in one way or another touched on the fear of losing one's individuality or, worse yet, of realizing it was never fully there to begin with. People expressed anxiety about no longer feeling "special" or "unique" or "irreplaceable." One person summed up it up nicely: "I don't think so, buddy. There is only one me!"

***

The thought of an exact copy of oneself can be creepy, to be sure. But it also raises profound questions: Would you still be an individual? Would you be two individuals? What would your double think of you? Would you complement each other? Dilute each other? Get along?

Until recently questions like these were strictly hypothetical for all but a handful of psychotic individuals. A double could only exist through a delusion inside a person's head. But science and technology have changed all that. Before long almost anyone will be able to have his or her own double. And, unlike the delusional type, these will be ripe with possibilities that we are just beginning to grasp. The technology that gets the most attention is cloning. If biologists could create Dolly the Sheep, how far off is the prospect of cloning humans? You could grow your own identical twin. And, with the improved technology that will certainly follow, you'll surely be able to edit your clone's DNA: Perhaps make him a little prettier than you. Smarter. Someone to fight your fights. A little of this, a smidgen less of that. You are the artist.

But there is now an option that offers even more potential. You can build your own virtual self, what's known in geek-speak as an "avatar." For anyone who missed the movie with that title, an avatar is the character who represents you in computer games and virtual reality worlds like *Second Life*. (If you have no idea what I'm talking about, you might want to ask the nearest adolescent to explain it before you read on. Any adolescent will do.) The technology for this is already here. Today's sophisticated animation studio operates more like a medical school physiology laboratory than like the old Disney cartoon factory where animators drew their creations with pens on sketch pads. The new breed of cartoonists are modern-day Leonardos, scientist-artists who use sophisticated anatomic observation to create artistic images.

Say a computer gaming company wanted to create a high-tech avatar that captures your image. Their technician-scientist-artists could reach for any of a variety of "motion-capture technology" tools to recreate you with dazzling precision. They might begin by attaching LED, magnetic, or reflective markers to the joints of your body. You would then be asked to perform a wide variety of movements. The reflected signals would easily capture the most infinitesimal details—every point at the tip of every finger and toe—and how each bit worked together. Within a few minutes, the tracking mechanisms will have captured millions of bytes of information about you: what you look like, how you move, your tics and nuances. If you were hooked up to high-resolution equipment for two hours, there would be more data than you could fit on a typical hard drive.[8]

Once uploaded, the relevant pieces can be mixed and matched to create a three-dimensional image of you in motion. I can ask the computer for a version of you sitting in a chair, looking relaxed, wearing a smile on your face, and your eyes half-closed. Or I might call up one of you running on a track with sweat pouring from your body, a grimace on your face and your eyes wide open. Download the image and abracadabra. "There you be," as my friend Lenny says.

* * *

You might think cyberscientists overvalue their virtual creations. After all, when people hallucinate a double, they truly believe it exists. This inability to distinguish fantasy from reality is, in fact, what makes the experience so frightening. With a virtual avatar, however, one is well aware it's not real, no matter how convincing the image appears.

But are the two experiences actually so different? How much more "immersive"—a popular term in virtual technology—is one than the other? Neurologically, the evidence shows, often not much. Studies find that our brains frequently don't bother distinguishing between virtual and real experiences. For example, an almost or totally identical pattern of neurons is activated in a man's brain when he sees a virtual recreation of a gorgeous woman as when he meets the same woman in person.[9] If you see a hammer come down on a virtual hand that appears to be your own, it is no less terrifying even when you know it's not yours. In fact, after reviewing dozens of experiments comparing virtual and real experiences like these, researchers Byron Reeves and Clifford Nass concluded that our minds are simply not sufficiently evolved to distinguish between the two sources of information.[10]

There is mounting evidence that experiences in the virtual world can even spread to the real one. In one study, for example, cyber-researcher Nick Yee and his colleagues assigned people either an attractive or unattractive avatar to represent them in a "collaborative virtual environment"—a virtual room that looked just like the real room their real selves were in. Their avatars were paired with an avatar of the opposite sex with whom they then got to talk about their personal lives for the next twenty minutes. The avatars weren't exactly doubles, but nonetheless, participants were quick to take mental ownership. More attractive avatars disclosed more personal information about themselves, were friendlier, more extroverted, spoke with greater confidence, and were more assertive in their nonverbal behaviors. They even "walked" up closer to the other avatar. The better-looking avatars, in other words, behaved just like better-looking people do in real life.

Then Yee found something more remarkable. About twenty-five minutes after the virtual experiment, participants took part in an "unrelated" experiment during which they filled out a dating profile and chose blind dates for themselves on an online dating site. Those who had worn more attractive avatars, it turned out, rated themselves as more attractive and chose better-looking partners. In other words, their "real-world" selves behaved as their avatars probably would have. Their virtual confidence carried over to their physical selves.[11]

A number of studies find similar crossing over. For example:

- People who don taller avatars during virtual business negotiations are then more aggressive and work out better deals in real-life negotiations.[12]

- Wearing an avatar who is physically active leads people to later exercise more.[13]

- People who watch a virtual image of themselves selling a brand of a product later say they prefer the brand they were selling.

Younger people are especially prone to mix the virtual with the real:

- Young people who wear an older avatar become more concerned about practical matters like their future security. They are more attentive to saving money, for example.

- Children who watch a virtual doppelganger are prone to later recall these experiences having happened to themselves. It creates false memories.

New technologies are obliterating the boundary between the virtual and the real. It won't be long before virtual reality will feel so real that it literally becomes physical experience. There are already, for example, so-called haptic devices that attach to your body and then convert the appearance of touch in the virtual world to actual tactile sensation. You can feel your avatar's handshake or a hug.[14]

∗∗∗

Even these technologies will soon seem primitive Devices are being developed that will create vastly more detailed maps of your neuro/skeletal/musculature systems—every minute twitch, every movement of your vocal cords, even the firings of individual neurons—as you move through three-dimensional space. It will be like upgrading from X-ray machines to MRIs.

The longer-term future promises to be even more boggling. Within a few decades we can expect devices that not only capture appearance and superficial sensations but our essence as individuals. Jim Blascovich and Jeremy Bailenson, who direct cutting-edge virtual human interaction laboratories at the University of California, Santa Barbara and at Stanford, have followed these developments as closely as anyone. Having seen what is in the works, they matter-of-factly predict, "Sooner or later, artificial-intelligence technology will permit implementation of one's personality traits and other idiosyncrasies."[15] After decoding the person you are today, the new technology will be able to project your behavior into the future.

Say you are a movie star. The technology will have all your old performances in the data bank. This would be especially easy, because films are virtual to begin with. Your new e-self could then perform new roles. You could even play new parts after you were dead. Consider the business possibilities. You could sell your on-screen rights into eternity.

And you could improve upon your actual self. This is, in fact, already being done on a primitive scale. At the time of this writing, Orville Redenbacher was still the on-screen spokesperson for his popcorn company. The thing is, Orville had a heart attack and drowned in 1995. Yet there he is starring in the company's commercials—new commercials—touting products and saying things he never did when he was alive. These models not only look and sound exactly like the pre-death Orville. but they have been programmed so it appears he's acting out new scripts. At this stage of technology, the movements appear a bit "animated," which they entirely are. But wait a few years, and my guess is that he will be giving more believable performances—Orville was hardly a polished actor—than when he was alive.

Imagine what this could mean to a professor like me. I could create an avatar that looks and sounds like me, but better. I could dress him better. He could be younger or older, thinner or fatter. We could program an Obama voice when I wanted to sound inspiring or a Robin Williams delivery when I needed to liven things up. How about all those bad habits I couldn't resolve in psychotherapy? A few keystrokes and they're gone. And I could be off sipping a cappuccino while all this was happening. Incidentally, the appeal of virtual eternity hasn't escaped the entrepreneurial crowd. There are now companies that anyone, actors or otherwise, can pay to have an avatar created for them and stored for eternity.[16]

The predictions go on and on. Jim Blascovich, Jeremy Bailenson, and other scholars believe that, in another thirty or forty years, our avatars will feel like extensions of our bodies. We'll no longer need an artificial controller, keyboard, or even vocalization to operate our doppelgangers. They will be controlled via everyday thoughts, automatically and effortlessly, like a character out of *The Matrix*. "Wearing an avatar will be like wearing contact lenses, with people unaware that they are wearing anything," Blascovich and Bailenson write. Eventually, avatars will "walk among us." They will be like holograms, but more complete and realistic. We will intermix routinely, jostling one another in lines and in shopping centers. Moreover, as long as your avatars survive, you will, too. "After one passes on, his great-great-great-grandchildren can enter a 'holodeck,' sit on the long-deceased ancestor's lap, tell him about their day, experience his avatar tell a story, give a hug and provide advice," Blascovich and Bailenson dreamily predict.[17]

I may be getting ahead of myself here. Creating the future *you* with perfection will require considerable advances in technology. But these advances are surely coming, and, when they do, your avatar will become a parallel you. It will be eerily alive.

***

Sigmund Freud, who had a special fascination with doppelgangers, argued that people who see imaginary doubles are projecting their repressed, unconscious needs and memories, typically those too painful for them to face in conscious awareness. Freud may very well have been correct when it comes to individuals who live in the grip of delusional doubles.

But the avatar-doubles envisioned for the future shift from the pathological to the normal. Rather than projecting your fears, they will allow you to create a new, improved version of yourself. In fact, as many versions as you desire. You'll be able to tweak and revise them as you wish as easily as you might change your outfit before leaving home. Multiple personalities, once thought of as a disorder, will now—excuse the pun—be made to order. You will have doubles at your beck and command. Hallucinations are a problem. Avatars are a gift.

10
Who Thinks the Thoughts?

Poet at Work

—Sign that the French Surrealist poet Saint-Pol-Roux
hung on his bedroom door each night before retiring

I was giving a lecture a few years back when a student interrupted me with a question that challenged my entire argument. He was a hostile student. But he had a good point. And what he'd said, I quickly recognized, negated the rest of the lecture I had prepared. I paused to consider my options. Blank. Rumblings of panic. Then, seemingly out of nowhere, I heard myself ask a question that challenged *his* logic. It was slightly lame but, hearing it, led me to see a deeper flaw in his argument, which led me to launch a more formidable challenge. I then began explaining why my original argument was important. This led me to an array of psychological concepts that I hadn't considered before. Now I was on a roll. I began spelling out ideas that were shrewder than the ones I'd been preparing all morning. One thought led me to the next. I was still going strong when class ended some twenty minutes later. Connections kept coming to me even as I walked toward my office. When I got there, I wrote down everything I could remember saying before I forgot, which I knew I would.

Later that day I was basking in my morning breakthroughs. How clever of me, I thought. Then, however, I considered the facts. I—my "I" of awareness, the one who was reflecting on what I'd done—hadn't broken through much of anything. As best I could tell, I wasn't even thinking when the ideas came to me. *I* was barely present, in fact. It felt as if there was a very clever fellow somewhere inside me, a guy who came up with better ideas than I ever could. What right did I have to pat myself on the back? I was little more than a recording secretary.

***

Where do our ideas come from? Consider this simple exercise: Close your eyes and try to think of nothing for the next thirty seconds. When you're done, reflect on what happened. If you're like most people, thoughts entered your mind well before the half minute was up. You didn't decide to think them but, alas, there they were. Social psychologist Eric Klinger and his colleagues wanted to measure how often this happens in a normal day. They had people carry around a handheld device that beeped periodically. The participants would then immediately answer several questions about what they were thinking at the moment. Extrapolating from these moments, Klinger estimated that peoples' minds wander about two thousand times per day.[1]

Two thousand times a day! Assuming one sleeps, say, eight hours a day, that works out to a new thought popping into your head every thirty-two seconds. Compare this with the number of thoughts you generate through your own volition. How many times a day, for example, do you consciously try to think about something, as in those moments when you say, "Let me think about this"? If you're anything like the people I know, it is rarely more than a handful. On a busy day, it might be closer to zero. There is obviously a very active someone inside us and this someone does a lot more of our thinking than we—our aware selves—do. Where is this other? Who and what is it?

Let's push the question. Are you, the *you* that is aware, even capable of originating an idea? Philosophers have been asking this question for ages. More recently, however, scientists have begun offering hints at answers, and what they are finding is humbling. When we are pressed to act quickly, it has become clear, conscious thought is significantly slower than the "thinking" that goes on below the level of awareness. In one highly cited study published in 1985, for example, the neuroscientist Benjamin Libet devised a clever race between the two. Participants were assigned a simple task: to flex one of their fingers when they were inclined to do so. Libet wanted to measure the time that elapsed between the conscious decision to make the movement and the spike in inner brain activity that accompanied that decision. To measure the moment of conscious choice, participants were placed in front of a precise clock with a dot rotating around its dial. They were told to note the exact position of the dot on the clock at the instant they decided to make the movement. Inner thinking was measured by an electroencephalograph (EEG) that monitored what is known as the "readiness potential," an electrical signal that precedes physical action. Not surprisingly, there turned out to be a brief lag—on average one-fifth of a second—between the moment they decided to move their fingers and the actual movement. But here is what seemed at the time a startling finding: When Libet looked at the participants' EEGs, he found that their readiness potential spiked on average a full half second before they indicated they were deciding. In other words, they decided before they were aware of deciding.[2]

There's more. The readiness potential originates in the sensory motor area (SMA), a region of the brain concerned with motor preparation. Is it possible the work in the brain begins even earlier? Fast forward to 2008 as John-Dylan Haynes and his research team at the Max Planck Institute for Human Cognitive and Brain Sciences set out to find activity in other regions of the brain that might precede conscious decision making.[3] They designed a more precise replication of Libet's original study. Participants were told to fixate on a screen on which a stream of letters were presented. While doing this, they were to decide whether they wanted to push a button in front of them with their right or left hand and, as a measure of when this occurred, to remember the letter that was on the screen at the moment they made their conscious decision. More important, inner thinking was measured by functional magnetic resonance imaging (fMRI), a considerably more nuanced and powerful tool than Libet had available twenty-three years earlier.

The results: Haynes and his team found activity in several regions of the brain, most of which were localized in the frontopolar and parietal cortex, that preceded activity in the action potential by a large margin. Libet reported spikes in the readiness potential a half second before the moment of awareness. Haynes's group discovered rumblings of activity in the frontopolar and parietal cortex up to ten seconds beforehand. They found, in fact, that there was sufficient activity in the frontopolar regions to accurately predict which hand a person would choose up to seven seconds before that person became aware of his or her choice. Awareness, they concluded, is the endpoint of a cascade of processing steps that occur below the surface. "By the time consciousness kicks in, most of the work has already been done," Haynes understatedly observes.[4]

Who is operating the controls? "You are allowed to think that adult life consists of a constant exercise of personal will; but it wasn't really like that," a character in Julian Barnes's novel *Staring at the Sun* observes. "You do things, and only later do you see why you did them, if ever you do." The most dramatic insights arrive so suddenly and out of the blue that it can be startling. We may even scream out, as when Archimedes shouted "Eureka!" when he stepped in the bath and saw the water rise. Ezra Wegbreit, who studies the insight process in controlled experiments, says that he routinely sees people "bolt up in their chair and their eyes go all wide." It's as if they've received a revelation.[5] Psychologists refer to this—with refreshing lack of jargon, I might add—as the "aha" experience. And, make no mistake, the insight occurs before we proudly shout "aha." There is always a burst of electrical activity in our brain before we become aware of "our" brilliant insight.[6]

Who thought the thought? We cling to a belief in the power of consciousness, that our mental breakthroughs emerge when we are most fully tuned to the here and now. Awareness arrives all right, but it is usually after the show begins. We pull our hand from the hot stove before we consciously feel the pain. We jump out of the path of the oncoming car before we're aware that we need to. Our conscious selves are just another member of the audience.

Consider a train metaphor. Conscious thought, some philosophers argue, is like the steam whistle on an old locomotive. It reveals activity inside the engine, but it doesn't make an iota of difference to the moving train.[7] How frequently is this the case? Cognitive psychologist John Bargh has gone so far as to offer an exact estimate: "Our psychological reactions from moment to moment . . . are 99.44% automatic," he has calculated.[8] The precision of Bargh's estimate is arguable, but his point is well taken.

***

All is not lost, however. That half a percent can, with proper attention, be expanded and applied to disproportional effect. You can trick your unconscious thinkers to do your bidding.

Permit me to offer a personal example. Earlier in my career I would beat myself up when I was trying to begin a new manuscript. I would invariably spend a painful first morning struggling to draft a first paragraph. Worst of all was the first sentence. I would write something, erase it, write something else, revise that a few times, then erase it, too. Before long I'd be standing up, sitting down, organizing my desk, deciding whether to buy a new desk organizer, and eventually would start thinking about alternative careers. At the end of the morning, I never—not once—had an acceptable first sentence to show for my self-flagellation.

My first morning's output hasn't improved much over the years. I still go through a series of false starts. But I've learned through experience that it is an essential stage in my writing process. So, rather than fighting the unproductive experience, I now actively recruit it in my wake-up-the-muse scheme. I get up early and start failing. When I've put myself through sufficient pain—two to three hours usually does the trick nowadays—I quit for the day. When I wake up the next morning, the first sentence is almost always waiting for me. I type it, and the first paragraph invariably follows. It's uncanny. But, I've also learned, complete non-accomplishment on that first morning is essential. If I end the morning with a sentence—which is rarely very good, anyway—all I get when I wake up the next day is a slightly better version of the lousy sentence.

I know this appears pathetic. The take-away message sounds like doublespeak out of Orwell's *1984*: "Failure is success." But it's not as crazy as it seems. There is a wealth of research demonstrating that, when a problem has you stumped, the worst thing to do is try to force the answer. This flies in the face of what we were taught: That when the going gets tough the tough get going, and such—that we must focus, work through every detail, ignore distractions and, most of all, persist. The smartest strategy, however, is to tell yourself to forget the problem.

"Just look at the history of science," observes Jonathan Schooler, a leading researcher in the field. "The big ideas seem to always come when people are sidetracked, when they're doing something that has nothing to do with their research."[9] Consider the famous case of the mathematician Henri Poincaré, whose groundbreaking insight into non-Euclidean geometry came to him while he was on vacation and getting on a bus. "At the moment when I put my foot on the step, the idea came to me, without anything in my former thoughts seeming to have paved the way for it," Poincaré later wrote. He was so confident about his insight that he didn't bother checking it until his vacation was over. Finally, "On my return to Caen, for conscience's sake, I verified the result at my leisure," he said. When you're stuck on a problem, he observed, the only good solution is to distract yourself. His own suggestion was "a walk or a journey."[10]

Thinking about a problem can, in fact, be worse than useless. It may be counterproductive. We all know the frustrating feeling of trying to recall a name. The answer is on the "tip of the tongue" but keeps eluding your grasp. Perhaps you run through the letters of the alphabet. Then your address log. But you can't get it no matter how hard you try. You finally give up and move on to something else. And, when you do, the name appears in your head. You couldn't think of it until you stopped thinking about it.

The lesson is that awareness has limits. Descartes's assertion that "I think, therefore I am" is arguably *the* bedrock of Western epistemology. Philosophers refer to it as the "cogito." But the more we learn about neuroscience, the clearer it becomes that "I" isn't the only one doing one's thinking. It might be more accurate to say, "We think, therefore we are."

***

Westerners love originality. Be it a new book, an innovative theory, or a revolutionary corkscrew, we revere the fresh and inventive. When someone simply improves an old classic, we might call him "clever." When it is an original idea, however, she is "creative." The most original of the original warrants our ultimate compliment: he is, we say, a "genius." But creative people, and geniuses often most of all, tend to be painfully aware of their limitations. We applaud them for their insights, but they are often as ambivalent about taking credit for their creations as I was for the insights I delivered to my class. The writer Henry Miller described an artist as someone with good antennae—hardly the attribute we associate with creative genius.

Writers, in particular, have offered colorful descriptions of the mysterious process. These masters of words, wizards of articulation, are often struck dumb when trying to explain the source of those words. In some cases, they tell of entire scripts being delivered out of nowhere. William Blake, for example, described going into hallucinated states during which he would hear outside voices. Blake said about his poem *Milton*: "I have written this poem from immediate dictation, twelve or sometimes twenty or thirty lines at a time, without premeditation, and even against my will."[11] Charles Dickens spoke of "some beneficent power" that told him what to write. An early biographer said of Dickens during the writing of *A Christmas Carol*: "It seized him for itself . . . he wept over it, and laughed, and wept again, and excited himself to an extraordinary degree . . . and walked thinking of it fifteen and twenty miles about the black streets of London."[12]

Contemporary writers give similar accounts. The children's story writer Enid Blyton describes her creative process this way:

> I shut my eyes for a few minutes, with my portable typewriter on my knee; I make my mind a blank and wait—and then, as clearly as I would see real children, my characters stand before me in my mind's eye. . . . The story is enacted almost as if I had a private cinema screen there. . . . I don't know what is going to happen. I am in the happy position of being able to write a story and read it for the first time at one and the same moment. . . . Sometimes a character makes a joke, a really funny one that makes me laugh as I type it on my paper and I think, "Well, I couldn't have thought of that myself in a hundred years!" And then I think: "Well who did think of it?"

Blyton, it turns out, had a flesh-and-blood partner who had his own silent partner: One of her illustrators, the artist Van der Beek, said he, too, received his images from some mysterious place. As he was drawing for Blyton's "Noddy" book series, Van der Beek recounts, "Little Noddies would appear from everywhere and crawl all over my desk."[13]

Others talk about being fooled by what they write. "I can't remember exactly how a given play developed in my mind," recalls Harold Pinter. "I've got an idea of what might happen—sometimes I'm absolutely right, but on many occasions I've been proved wrong by what does actually happen. Sometimes I'm going along and I find myself writing 'C comes in' when I didn't know that he was going to come in; he had to come in at that point, that's all."[14] Pinter says of his play *The Homecoming* that it essentially wrote itself. He remembers "being surprised by the process and laughing a lot at the toxic, belligerent family" that he found being written in front of him.[15]

Singer/songwriter Tom Waits tells about sometimes having to stand up to his muse. Waits recalls how frightened he became when the beautiful first lines of what was to become one of his masterpieces, "Picture in a Frame" ("The Sun come up. It was blue and gold . . ."), popped into his head. The problem was he was stuck in traffic at the time with no recorder or even a pencil or piece of paper to transcribe what he'd heard. He began to panic that he would lose his revelation and it would haunt him forever. Then Waits backed off. He looked up at the sky and said: "Excuse me. Can you not see that I'm driving? If you're serious about wanting to exist, I spend eight hours a day sitting in the studio. You're welcome to come visit me while I'm sitting at the piano. Otherwise, leave me alone and go bother Leonard Cohen."[16] The writer Robertson Davies summed it up neatly: "I hear the story, I am told the story, I record the story."[17]

***

Reports like these—not only from writers, but from other artists, scientists, scholars and a multitude of others engaged in creative endeavors—underscore the thin line between inventive genius and diligent secretarial work.

But perhaps these artists are selling themselves short. Yes, one's insights arrive neatly packaged from outside awareness. They are, however, neither sudden nor from out of nowhere. Any epiphany worth its weight has a backstory. And, here again, that meager half a percent called awareness can be stretched and exploited to make all the difference. Consider the case of Robert Louis Stevenson, who not only extracted fine literature from the back of his mind but turned the disparate fragments of his unusual personality into a successful business organization.

Stevenson's most famous novella, *The Strange Case of Dr. Jekyll and Mr. Hyde*, is arguably the archetypical portrait of a divided self. The Jekyll-

and-Hyde notion of a nice guy on the outside who masks a wacko monster on the inside has become part of our language. It has been one of the most frequently adapted stories in film history, beginning with a 1908 version, followed by at least six other releases through 1920 (three in that year alone!) and remakes and parodies every few years that continue today. There have been versions by everyone from John Barrymore and Spencer Tracy to Bud Abbot and Lou Costello.

The Jekyll and Hyde tale has been critically acclaimed as a remarkable piece of creative fiction. Scratch the surface of the author's actual life, however, and you wonder whether imagination is the right word for his work, or whose imagination it is we're even talking about. There is a maxim in writing that you should write about what you know. *The Strange Case of Dr. Jekyll and Mr. Hyde* could be Exhibit A for this argument. If there is one thing Stevenson knew, it was what it meant to lead a double life.

From early childhood, Stevenson was unusually focused on playing roles and assuming personae. He and his friend Charles Baxter, for example, took on entire alter egos—"Johnson and Thomson"—that conveniently deviated from their everyday characters. Whereas Stevenson and Baxter were relatively reserved and obedient children, Johnson and Thomson were described by one of Stevenson's biographers as "heavy-drinking, convivial, blasphemous, iconoclasts."[18] Playacting is, of course, common in children. But there was a deeper split in Stevenson that was as acute as night and day—in fact, literally so. There was one Stevenson during his waking hours. And there was what he believed to be an entirely other version that took over when he went to sleep.

This second life, his dream life, was a ferocious place. In his essay "A Chapter on Dreams," Stevenson writes of himself in the third-person, describing how he had always been "an ardent and uncomfortable dreamer. When he had a touch of fever at night, and the room swelled and shrank, and his clothes, hanging on a nail, now loomed up instant to the bigness of a church, and now drew away in a horror of infinite distance and infinite littleness, the poor soul was very well aware of what must follow. . . . Sooner or later the night-hag would have him by the throat, and pluck him, strangling and screaming, from his sleep."[19]

These dreams would be classified today as "night terrors." One of my colleagues who suffers from chronic night terrors describes how, in his own dreams, he might, for example, leap out of bed convinced there is an alligator in the bedroom trying to eat his family. He would then run around the room screaming and tossing objects at the savage intruder. His wife would try to talk him back to reality, explaining there is no alligator and that he's just having one of his night terrors. The image of the alligator would be so vivid, however, that my colleague will remain convinced he must persist or they would all be eaten.

Most night terrors take place during the REM (rapid eye movement) stage of sleep and quickly terminate when the REM period ends. The sleeper, upon awakening, usually remembers no more than an overwhelming feeling or a single scene, if anything. This was initially true for Stevenson. Sometime during his student days at Edinburgh College, however, he began "to dream in sequence," meaning that his dreams were now unfolding in complete stories. They had a narrative. And when he awoke, Stevenson now seemed to remember everything.[20]

This was also when Stevenson started talking about "the Little People" who managed his "internal theatre." The Little People produced plays in his mind after he fell asleep—writers, set designers, directors, actors and, presumably, anyone else needed to put on an original performance. Their initial stories were sloppily constructed. These were "tales where a thread might be dropped, or one adventure quitted for another, on fancy's least suggestion," Stevenson observed, writing like a critic of another author's plays.

Stevenson was more than a little unusual. But he was an astute talent scout. He recognized right off that the Little People possessed a terrific raw genius. They simply needed coaching. He taught them, he recalled, that "the stories must . . . be trimmed and pared and set upon all fours, they must run from a beginning to an end and fit (after a manner) with the laws of life." He even gave them lessons in marketing, urging them to keep an eye on the "crass public" and the nitpicking "thwart reviewer." The Little People were excellent students. Stevenson recalled being carried away by their stories. They even left books in his dreams. The tales were "so incredibly more vivid and moving than any printed book" that Stevenson said he became disappointed when he tried to read "real" literature.[21]

This is when Stevenson began sounding like a cross between a CEO, a drill sergeant, and a paranoid schizophrenic. He started referring to the

Little People as his "brownies." In Scottish legend, the brownies are hairy, brown, good-natured little elves who attach themselves to people and try to help out however they can. The brownies like to do their work invisibly, usually at night. They ask for nothing in return, although they're grateful for maybe a few oatcakes or a little bowl of creamy milk (and, if their hosts can spare it, perhaps a wee lager now and then). But don't offer to pay them, "'cos they will get affy upset and bugger off forever," the legend goes.

Whenever he needed money, which was pretty much always, Stevenson would instruct the Little People to produce a sellable story. As Stevenson wrote of himself: "When the bank begins to send letters and the butcher to linger at the back gate, he sets to belabouring his brains after a story, for that is his readiest money-winner; and, behold! at once the little people begin to bestir themselves in the same quest, and labour all night long, and all night long set before him truncheons of tales upon their lighted theatre."[22] The work order came in the form of a ritual. When he was ready to go to sleep, Stevenson would lie down on his bed, careful to keep his feet off the mattress, close his eyes, and raise one arm.[23] This was his signal to the Little People to get to it. (We can probably add obsessive-compulsive disorder (OCD) to Stevenson's list of psychological struggles.) He referred to the operation as his story mill.

The collaboration was a resounding success, culminating in Stevenson & Co.'s greatest triumph: *The Strange Case of Dr. Jekyll and Mr. Hyde.* Stevenson's wife, Fanny, described the crucial dream to Stevenson's first biographer, Graham Balfour, in 1899. "Louis wrote Jekyll and Hyde with great rapidity on the lines of his dream. In the small hours of one morning, I was wakened by cries of horror from him. I, thinking he had a nightmare, waked him. He said, angrily, 'Why did you wake me? I was dreaming a fine boguey tale.'" The problem, Fanny learned, was that she had woken him right in the middle of what would turn out to be a crucial scene, the first episode where Jekyll transforms into Hyde. Stevenson sent Fannie away and went back to sleep to continue watching the transformation scene. He was like a theatergoer returning from intermission. Stevenson wrote out the first draft of *Jekyll and Hyde* as soon as he awoke the next morning.

Before his dream, Stevenson had been working on his own story about a double life. But the Little People's version was very different and, he was certain, way better than his. Fanny, whom Stevenson trusted as a critic, read both versions. She mostly liked what the Little People had written but believed a great deal in Stevenson's pre-dream version was better. Stevenson, however, would tolerate no criticism of the Little People's story. He told Fanny these were things "he couldn't eliminate because he saw it so plainly in the dream." When Fanny returned a while later, Stevenson "pointed with a long dramatic finger to a pile of ashes on the hearth of the fireplace." He had burned his original manuscript.[24]

Jekyll and Hyde was published in 1886. It was an instant popular and critical success beyond anything Stevenson could have imagined. In its first six months, 40,000 copies were sold in Great Britain and an astonishing 250,000 copies, legal and pirated, were bought up in North America. "It was read by those who never read fiction, it was quoted in pulpits, and made the subject of leading articles in religious papers," Stevenson's biographer wrote.[25] Stevenson not only had his first best seller. He was internationally famous.

***

How much credit should one take for an insight in a dream? Consider the case of Don Newman, a then-young mathematician teaching at the Massachusetts Institute of Technology in the 1950s. One of Newman's colleagues at the time was the boy-genius John Nash—the same John Nash portrayed in the book and subsequent movie *A Beautiful Mind* who was to become a Nobel laureate as well as a victim of paranoid schizophrenia. Newman had been frustrated by a difficult math problem. "I was . . . trying to get somewhere with it, and I couldn't and couldn't and couldn't," he said. One night he had a dream in which he was struggling with his problem when Nash appeared and asked if he needed help. Newman described the difficulty and Nash quickly explained how to solve it. Newman knew he had his answer the moment he woke up, and he immediately began writing what was to become an important mathematical paper.

The best part is that Newman remained convinced for the rest of his life that it was Nash's solution at least as much as his own. "Don actually included a footnote thanking me in the paper," Nash recalled, "and he kept acting grateful, like I'd actually helped him when it was his dream."[26]

Think about this. Newman got his answer from a person in his dream who he believed was more intelligent than himself. "It was not my solution; I could not have done it myself," was all Newman could say.[27] (Sidebar: The real John Nash spent most of his adult life tormented by hallucinated voices, a condition we will explore in the next chapter. He was convinced that his own thoughts were being spoken by other people. Should Newman have thanked them, too?)

Stevenson thought about questions like this. A reporter from the *New York Herald* once asked him how much credit the Little People deserved for his writings. Stevenson began by estimating that they "do one-half my work for me while I am fast asleep." But he then went on to question whether his waking self contributed very much or anything at all. "And in all human likelihood," he said, they "do the rest for me as well, when I am wide awake and fondly suppose I do it for myself. That part which is done while I am sleeping is the Brownies' part beyond contention; but that which is done when I am up and about is by no means necessarily mine, since all goes to show the Brownies have a hand in it even then."[28]

✳✳✳

These sorts of boundary issues weren't always so confusing. The ancient Romans, in particular, would have had little problem deciding who deserved credit for what. The Romans believed that ideas came to you from a mysterious spirit who followed you through life as a guide, protector, and all-purpose intermediary to the higher gods. They called this spirit a *genius*.

The Roman genius had little in common with today's definition of creative brilliance. Theirs was more like a personal assistant—a to-die-for personal assistant, to be sure—who would pop up as needed. There were arguments about exactly where this guardian spirit resided. Some believed it just hung around your vicinity—say, lounging in your studio or your office while you worked. Others thought it lived inside your head. According to one popular theory—a terrific one, in my opinion—it resided in your knees (*genua*).[29] No one talked about being a genius. You were simply fortunate to have one. Your genius was a first-rate gofer who knew where and how to get you the information you needed—

kind of like an early version of Siri (of iPhone fame).[30] The two of you shared the credit for your successes and the responsibility for your failures.

I'd like to think that Robert Lewis Stevenson would have been easier on himself if he had lived back then. In darker moods, Stevenson could be painfully self-critical. He once described himself as "a creature as matter of fact as any cheesemonger" who didn't have the talent for writing such imaginative stories, "a realist bemired up to the ears in actuality." He practically called himself a phony: "The whole of my published fiction should be the single-handed product of some Brownie . . . some unseen collaborator, whom I keep locked in a back garret, while I get all the praise and he but a share."[31]

***

Perhaps the most quoted line from *Dr. Jekyll and Mr. Hyde* is Jekyll's observation: "Man is not truly one but truly two"! Few of us suffer the harshness of the Jekyll and Hyde split. But we are all part self, part other; part *me*, part *I*. We are at once the authors who write the words, the actors who speak the words, and the audience that hears the words. Are these one and the same person? The great Argentine writer Jorge Luis Borges captured the conundrum elegantly in this excerpt from his essay "Borges and I":

> The other one, the one called Borges, is the one things happen to. I walk through the streets of Buenos Aires and stop for a moment, perhaps mechanically now, to look at the arch of an entrance hall and the grillwork on the gate; I know of Borges from the mail and see his name on a list of professors or in a biographical dictionary. I like hourglasses, maps, eighteenth-century typography, the taste of coffee and the prose of Stevenson; he shares these preferences, but in a vain way that turns them into the attributes of an actor. It would be an exaggeration to say that ours is a hostile relationship; I live, let myself go on living, so that Borges may contrive his literature, and this literature justifies me. It is no effort for me to confess that he has achieved some valid pages, but those pages cannot save

me. . . . Years ago I tried to free myself from him and went from the mythologies of the suburbs to the games with time and infinity, but those games belong to Borges now and I shall have to imagine other things. Thus my life is a flight and I lose everything and everything belongs to oblivion, or to him.

I do not know which of us has written this page.[32]

11
The Voices

If I knew where the good songs came from,
I would go there more often.

—Leonard Cohen, speech at the Fundación
Principe de Asturias (October 21, 2011)

For the first twenty years of his life, Herbert Mullin was described as an intelligent, high-achieving, likeable, and psychologically normal young man. He was a Boy Scout and played Little League baseball. He had numerous friends at school and was voted "Most Likely to Succeed" by his high school classmates. Just after graduation, however, one of his best friends died in a car accident. Mullin was devastated and, soon after, began acting strangely. He built a shrine to his deceased friend and would spend hours on end staring at it in silence. He began acting increasingly inappropriately in public. In 1969, when Mullin was twenty-two, his parents committed him to a mental hospital, where he was diagnosed as suffering from paranoid schizophrenia. Mullin spent the next few years drifting and moving from job to job. He checked into and out of a series of mental institutions.

Around this time the voices entered his head. They ordered him around, often telling him to do peculiar things. At one point they told him to shave his head and, on another occasion, to burn his penis with a cigarette lighter. Mullin listened to the voices and did as told. In October 1972, the orders took a horrendous turn. Mullin was living in Santa Cruz, California, which lies near one of the most ominous earthquake faults on the planet. The voices told him an earthquake was imminent. They also told him there was only one way California could be saved:

Mullin had to go out and kill people. Albert Einstein himself, Mullin was informed, had chosen him for this assignment.

On October 13, Mullin clubbed his first victim, a fifty-five-year-old drifter, to death. The voices applauded his work and told him he needed to keep on killing or the earthquake would occur. Two weeks later, Mullin picked up a female hitchhiker, stabbed her to death, and, apparently on orders from one of the voices, cut out her intestines and strung them on a tree branch to inspect them for "pollution." Four days later, Mullin went to confession, during which the voices told him the priest, Father Henry Tomei, had volunteered to be his next sacrifice in order to stop the earthquake. "I saw the light over the confessional and the voice said: 'That's the person to kill,'" Mullin later said. He beat and stabbed the priest to death. Over the next two months, Mullin went on to massacre, killing an old high school friend and his wife, four teenaged boys camping in a remote park, and an old man quietly weeding his front lawn. In all, Mullin murdered thirteen people. He was sentenced to life in prison for ten of these murders.[1]

***

We are all prone to hearing sounds that don't exist. In a hallucination, however, the fantasy becomes confused with reality. In cases of severe schizophrenia, the individuals may become convinced that they are literally hearing the voice of another person. There is, however, considerable variation in the form of the experience. A British study of one hundred voice hearers who had been diagnosed as schizophrenic discovered variations in, for example:

- The tone of the voices. Most said the voices usually spoke in a normal conversational tone. But 13 percent said they mostly shouted, and 14 percent said they generally whispered.

- Where they seemed to be coming from. The majority said they heard the voices through their ears coming from an outside source. However, 38 percent said they almost always originated inside their own heads—usually from around the center of the forehead, although a few heard the voices speaking from other parts of their bodies, such as the chest or abdomen.

- The number of speakers. More than half said they sometimes heard "crowds of people mumbling or talking together."

- How long the voices lasted. About 25 percent said the voices lasted on average less than a few minutes but, at the other extreme, 42 percent said they usually persisted for more than an hour at a time.[2]

Clearly, it is unwise to generalize about the hallucinations of schizophrenics. Different as they may be, however, there is the common thread of an inability to distinguish between delusion and reality. In severe cases, the voices become so intense and persistent that it becomes difficult or impossible to distinguish between one's own thoughts and the voices of others. This is why voice hearers sometimes seem to be talking to themselves or shouting out loud.

The intrusiveness can be frightening. The voice may sound as if it is being spoken by a person just inches away. A woman named Dolly, who was tormented by voices for many years, says she "could feel the breath of their mouth" when the voices spoke. Full-fledged visual hallucinations are, contrary to their portrayal in the media, much less common. Even when voice hearers don't "see" the speaker, however, they are prone to develop an accompanying mental picture. It could be just a rough sketch "like if they're tall or thin or if they are a person of color and even what they're wearing," says Dolly. "But some voices you kind of sense that they are wearing a suit and tie and some aren't. It's a bit like when you're on a bus and somebody sits next to you, you can't see them but you kind of guess what they are like just from them being next to you."[3]

Adam, who has also heard voices for most of his life, says he knows they are creations of his mind. The main voice is so intensely invasive, however, that, even though Adam never sees the man, he has developed a vivid mental picture of what he looks like. "He is the Captain, a World War II submariner," says Adam. "He looks like me, but he's got a big, big scruffy beard, the old naval, World War II German naval uniform on. Now and again he puts on a daft German accent when I mention he's a German submariner." The Captain controls his life, Adam says. He distracts and demoralizes Adam all day long. "It's like having a coach train you, but a coach who's an arsehole who sits there and says,

'Well, actually you are fucking useless, you're a fucking waste of space.' But if you're sitting having a conversation with someone, he'd be saying something horrible about them or picking out at what clothing they wear then really hone in on it, or their weight, or the way they look, their hair, stuff like that—he would just do anything to try and put you off. You're trying to talk in a conversation with this person and you've got some arsehole behind you saying, 'Fucking look at the state of their shoes, look at that.'"[4]

∗∗∗

John Nash, the genius mathematician who solved the seminal mathematical problem in John Newman's dream (see the previous chapter), is perhaps best known for his later struggles with inner voices, as famously described in *A Beautiful Mind*. If you are not familiar with his story, Nash was a brilliant, supremely confident wunderkind who burst onto the academic scene in 1948 at the age of twenty and, over the next decade, proved himself "the most remarkable mathematician of the second half of the century," in the words of his eminent colleague Mikhail Gromov.[5] Nash was admitted to Princeton University's doctoral program at the age of twenty, and he was hired as a professor at MIT at the astonishingly early age of twenty-three.

By the time he was thirty, however, Nash started hearing voices that no one else did. He rapidly descended into a debilitating paranoid schizophrenia that defined the remainder of his life. MIT forced Nash to resign his tenured position. He underwent numerous unsuccessful therapies, including drug and shock treatments, and a series of stays in mental hospitals in America and Europe. There were occasional remissions. But, in the end, he became "a sad phantom who haunted the Princeton University campus where he had once been a brilliant graduate student, oddly dressed, muttering to himself, writing mysterious messages on blackboards, year after year," his biographer Sylvia Nasar writes.

Ironically, this same man who became so detached from reality had, before his breakdown, been described as compulsively rational, empirical, and attuned to real life behavior. "He wished to take life's decisions—whether to take the first elevator or wait for the next one, whether to bank his money, what job to accept, whether to marry—into calculations of advantage and disadvantage, algorithms or mathematical rules divorced from emotion, convention, and tradition," Nasar observes. Works of mathematical genius are typically incomprehensible to us mere humans. But Nash's achievements in game theory and algebraic geometry, for which he was eventually awarded a Nobel Prize, were anything but obscure. He created a theory of human rivalry and conflict that captured subtleties of human nature that anyone could relate to.

Perhaps this exacerbated his problems. In Nash's mind, the same rational empiricism drove all his ideas, from his groundbreaking theorem to the delusional characters he believed were following him. The Harvard professor George Mackey once asked Nash, "How could you, a mathematician, a man devoted to logical proof . . . believe that extraterrestrials are sending you messages?" Nash looked up from his apparent stupor and replied softly, as if talking to himself, "Because the ideas I had about supernatural beings came to me the same way my mathematical ideas did. So I took them seriously."[6]

***

To both professionals and lay people, hallucinations are perhaps the clearest symptoms of psychopathology. When someone complains of swings in emotion, it can be difficult to draw the line between moodiness and bipolar disorder. But when a person hears voices in his or her head, and when that person is convinced the voices belong to someone else, we are quick to label that individual as schizophrenic.

In the 1970s, Stanford University psychology professor David Rosenhan conducted a now-classic experiment that challenged the system of psychiatric diagnoses. He asked eight associates—a psychology graduate student, three psychologists, a pediatrician, a psychiatrist, a painter, and a housewife—to try to gain admission to different psychiatric hospitals by feigning a single symptom: auditory hallucinations. The "pseudopatients," none of whom had a history of mental illness, all called different hospitals for an appointment and, upon arrival, complained that they had been hearing unfamiliar voices. They said the voices were hard to make out but seemed to be repeating the words "hollow," "empty," and "thud." They claimed no other psychiatric symptoms. All told, the stories were repeated in twelve varied hospitals in five states across the country. They included old and rundown hospitals in rural areas, premier university-run hospitals with excellent reputations, and one strictly private, very expensive hospital.

Every hospital admitted every patient on every occasion. Even more significant was what happened after they were admitted. Following Rosenhan's instructions, the pseudopatients dropped their act as soon as they were inside the wards. They began acting as they normally would and, whenever asked, told the staff they felt "fine" and were no longer experiencing any symptoms. They made it clear as often as possible that the voices were gone. The problem was that the staff didn't believe them. The pseudopatients were kept inside the hospitals an average of almost three weeks. It took fifty-two days for one patient to get released. The initial falsifications were never detected. It seemed everything they did, no matter how normal, was interpreted as evidence of mental illness. Once a kindly nurse found a pseudopatient pacing the corridors. "Nervous, Mr. X?" she asked. "No, bored," he replied to no effect.

Hearing voices not only became an unambiguous sign of insanity in these cases, but it created an impression in others so indelible that it couldn't be erased. When the patients were eventually released, it was, in every instance, with a diagnosis of schizophrenia "in remission." Rosenhan published his results in an article in *Science* under the memorable title, "Being Sane in Insane Places."[7]

***

Rosenhan's study underscores how quickly and definitively we label a person who hears voices as mentally ill. It wasn't always this way, however. Hearing voices has been reported in almost every culture throughout history, but it was rarely seen as a sign of mental illness. Often, in fact, the voices were accorded great importance. In ancient Greece, for example, mortals would seek out the voices of the gods for guidance; centuries later, followers in the great monotheistic traditions did the same. Auditory hallucinations, if you think about it, are tailor-made for those seeking guidance. Voices use language, meaning they can communicate with much greater precision than you would receive from, say, a visual hallucination. And, if you believe the voice is spoken by god, this is a guide you can trust.

The league of voice hearers is impressive. It includes the likes of Pythagoras, Mohammed, Merlin, Joan of Arc, Luther, St. Augustine, Loyola, and Pascal. We associate voices with religious conversions, but they have appeared in many contexts. A grieving Galileo, for example, was said to have listened on end to the voice of his deceased daughter.

Some historians believe that until around 1000 BCE, auditory hallucinations were a way of life for practically everyone. The most impressive—albeit controversial—of these arguments was proposed by another Princeton University professor, psychologist Julian Jaynes, in his memorably titled book, *The Origins of Consciousness in the Breakdown of the Bicameral Mind*. Our ancestors probably heard voices in their heads just as we do today. But Jaynes draws upon a wealth of historical, archaeological, literary, and neurological evidence to argue that, until about three thousand years ago, they believed the voices were coming from the outside. They heard criticisms, warnings, and instructions for future courses of action—the same sorts of babble that continue to fill our minds today. But their minds, through a combination of unevolved neurological wiring and normative thinking, were unable or unwilling to grasp the possibility that these messages were coming from inside themselves. Because the voices seemed spoken by an outsider, whom they couldn't see, they took on sacred meaning, Jaynes argues. This, he says, explains why the people of ancient Greece, Egypt, and Mesopotamia were convinced that the gods spoke directly to them. They would ask the god a question and listen for the answer.[8]

The most notable example may have been Socrates, the father of logic and rationality. Socrates was guided by a voice that he believed belonged to his personal *daemon*, the Greek word for "god." He trusted the daemon to the end. One of the principal charges leveled at Socrates during his trial for impiety was that his daemon wasn't sanctioned by the state. But the same daemon "stopped" Socrates from defending himself, and, when Socrates was later sentenced to death, "stopped" him from escaping. His obedience to the voice was so pronounced that it probably cost him his life.[9]

The word "hallucination" existed in Latin, but its original meaning was more benign than it is today. It referred to a person who confabulates or rambles. It described a way of thinking rather than a symptom of mental illness. The modern definition of the word "hallucination" didn't appear until the Enlightenment, more than two thousand years after Socrates, when philosophers and scientists began to discover physiological underpinnings to hallucinations.[10] Until then, "voices were not regarded as pathological; if they stayed inconspicuous and private, they were simply accepted as part of human nature, part of the way it was with some people," as Oliver Sacks observes in his book, *Hallucinations*.[11]

***

Even today, hearing voices is more acceptable and common in some cultures than in others. In a large study conducted in England, psychiatrist Louise Johns and her colleagues interviewed more than eight thousand Anglo and ethnic minority individuals about hallucinatory experiences. They screened out anyone with mental health problems. Among the remaining "normal" adults, Caribbean people were two and a half times more likely to report having experienced hallucinations than were Anglos; and Anglos were twice as likely to report hallucinations as were South Asians.[12] Think about this. If a person happens to be from the Caribbean, he or she is about five times more likely to hear voices than someone who comes from a place like India. Why should this be? There is no neurological evidence that people from the Caribbean have louder wires running through their heads. The answer, it seems, is steeped in cultural values. A behavior that seems crazy to one cultural group may be perfectly acceptable to another.

Even among the mentally ill, one's culture vastly affects the voice hearing experience. In one telling study, psychological anthropologist Tanya Luhrmann and her colleagues interviewed psychiatric patients in Accra (Ghana), Chennai (India), and San Mateo, California (United States). All had auditory illusions as their primary symptom.

The Americans, Luhrmann found, tended to describe violent, horrible voices telling them how hopeless and worthless they were. They were much like the schizophrenics in the British study whose voices barked commands ("Get the milk," "Go to the hospital"), were critical ("You're stupid," "You can't do anything right"), often abusive ("You bloody poof," "Ugly bitch") and tried to frighten them ("We are watching," "We're going to kill you"). Some of the American sufferers described the voices as the most painful aspects of their schizophrenia. One woman described the feeling as a "constant state of mental rape."

In Accra, on the other hand, almost half the patients said they usually or always heard a "good" voice. Most often it was God doling out benevolent advice. ("When I hear the voice, what the voice tells me, that's what I do.") The voices also tended to be more relational. ("They keep me company.") Even when the Ghana patients heard "bad" voices, the good ones often intervened. They might tell the patients to ignore the evil voices or assure them that they would take care of the problem.

The Chennai group was the most likely to hear voices of people they knew. At least half said they heard relatives and ancestors. This could be a mixed blessing. The voices often offered comfort and company. Some people reported rich back-and-forth relationships with the relatives who spoke to them. But the voices could also be annoying. Many in the Chennai group, for example, complained of voices that were meddling or overcontrolling. They described relatives who continually ordered them to clean up or change their clothing. In other words, they sounded a lot like real families.[13]

I don't mean to romanticize the hallucinatory experience in any culture. All the patients in Luhrmann's sample, no matter where they were from, suffered from their delusions. But it is important to recognize that hallucinations are the creations of individual minds and the cultures that shape them. Seen this way, they offer unusually vivid insight into a person's interior and exterior worlds.

***

There is no question that hearing voices is tightly interwoven with schizophrenia. All told, it is estimated that as many as 75 percent of schizophrenics hear imaginary voices.[14] Auditory hallucinations are clearly a common symptom of the illness. But this does not mean everyone who experiences auditory hallucinations is schizophrenic. In a survey widely cited in the scientific literature, psychologists Thomas Posey and Mary Losch constructed a list of fourteen examples of auditory hallucinations, most of which were taken from the case reports of schizophrenic patients. They then asked 375 healthy adult volunteers whether they had ever experienced something similar to each example. It was emphasized that they weren't being asked about hearing thoughts in their heads but of actually hearing voices out loud "as if someone had spoken." Seventy-one percent of the volunteers said they had experienced brief verbal hallucinations while they were fully awake. The most common hallucination—reported by 57 percent of the sample—was hearing someone call out one's own name.[15] Even these numbers probably underestimate the ubiquity of auditory hallucinations. Posey and Losch only inquired about hearing spoken words. If we add sounds like imaginary knocking on the door and phantom cell phone rings to the list, the frequencies would undoubtedly be higher.

These "normal" hallucinations can be jarringly vivid. In one survey, for example, an engineer told of sitting in a movie theater on a day he was trying to make a difficult professional decision, when a voice shouted out, "You can't do it you know." The voice, the engineer later commented, "was so clear and resonant that I turned and looked at my companion who was gazing placidly at the screen. . . . I was amazed and somewhat relieved when it became apparent that I was the only person who heard anything."[16]

Hallucinations are experienced less frequently in the normal population than they are by schizophrenics. One large-scale study found that 45 percent of normal people who reported verbal hallucinations said they heard them as often as once a month.[17] This is considerably less often than schizophrenics report. The U.K. study found that 48 percent of its patients heard voices on average one to "several" times a day. Still, these numbers underscore the ubiquity of the phenomenon in the general population.

***

If these statistics for normal people sound exaggerated, consider yet another study. In 1964, psychologists Theodore Barber and David Calverley told a group of seventy-eight students to close their eyes and prepare to concentrate on a recording of Bing Crosby's "White Christmas," which at the time was the biggest-selling record in history. They didn't start the record, however. After thirty seconds of silence, Barber and Calverley asked the students what they had experienced. Nearly half said they'd heard Crosby's voice singing "White Christmas" as clear as could be. They knew he wasn't singing, but, nonetheless, there it was.[18] You might want to try the experiment with one of your own favorite songs. Most of us have experienced getting a song lodged in our head like a little earworm. Now, observe what happens when you try to suppress it. In most cases, the harder you try, the more prominent the tune becomes. Forget about harmless earworms. You've created an obsession.

This doesn't happen just with music. Suppression can boomerang into obsession for almost anything we want to forget, even the most trivial thoughts. Consider another mental exercise. Sit back in a quiet, undisturbed place. Close your eyes. Now: Try *not* to think of a white bear. I dare you: DO NOT THINK OF A WHITE BEAR. Keep at it for five minutes and count each time you think of a you-know-what. Studies confirm the obvious: People who are told to not to think of a white bear report significantly more bear thoughts than those who are instructed to think of one. And, it seems, anything they try only makes matters worse. In one study, for example, people were first told to *not think* of the bear for five minutes and then told to *think* of the bear for the next five minutes. The result: Images of the animal accelerated to even more obsessive levels, far above that of another group that was told to think about the bear from the start.[19] All it takes is a simple suggestion, and you, too, can be obsessed by images you can't control.

Let us return to voices, however. There are so many otherwise normal people who struggle with the voices in their head that support groups have been created. One example is Intervoice: The International Community for Hearing Voices, an initiative with networks in twenty-six countries around the world.[20] Another is Hearing the Voice, a research-based group founded by psychologist Charles Fernyhough at Durham University in England. This international, interdisciplinary group explores voice hearing from a multitude of perspectives— normal thought processes, mental illness, public perceptions, cultural stereotypes, and cutting-edge neuroscience. A notable finding from both of these programs is that most voice hearers suffer less from mental illness than they do from the reactions of their peers. One study, for example, found that many of its clients say it is "not so much the voices that are the problem, but the difficulties that some people have in coping with them."[21] David Rosenhan wouldn't have been surprised.

Hearing voices is "a normal, and relatively frequent, component of consciousness for a large portion of the general population," multiple researchers have concluded.[22] It is a defining symptom of mental illness. It is also a normal experience. There is a fuzzy boundary between the two.

***

There is also a fine line between hearing voices and thinking them. Here is a typical beginning to one of my days: My alarm goes off. I'm not quite awake, but there are already voices in my head. Me 1: "Ooh, it feels so good under the covers. I want to stay." Me 2: "Get up. You've got work to do." Me 1: "Just two more minutes." Me 2: "Yesterday you said the same thing and fell back asleep." Me 1: "I'll set an alarm, okay?" This goes on for a while until my body pulls itself out of bed. How or when my body decided to make its move almost always occurs to me after the fact. It's the one part of the conversation I never seem to hear.

But these two characters are just the opening act. Before long, the media director in my cerebral cortex wakes up and begins the day's Levine-brain extravaganza. First up is a replay of selected events from the day before. Perhaps I again hear my son saying something I liked during a phone conversation. I play a role in what I hear, of course. I might, for example, "decide" to replay the key sentence a few times. I smile each time I hear it. Then the tape stops. I have no idea how, when, or where the decision was made to do this. I hear my own inner voice comment, like some after-the-fact news anchorman, "Go, Zach."

At some point, my head goes on break. I turn mindlessly busy for a few minutes. Then I find myself thinking about a tense exchange I had two days ago with a colleague. I again hear the man's voice accusing me of something I'd done, and I again hear myself babble some weak reply. Then my inner voice—the *I* with the voice of a news anchor—pipes in to tell me what a jerk the guy was and what a wuss I am for not letting him know it. I step into the conversation and find myself saying, perhaps aloud, that I agree. Then I hear myself rehearsing a beautifully controlled, articulate, and pointed rebuttal to the man. "That's what I'm going to tell him today," I tell myself in this back-and-forth between the two of us. I rework the wording a few times. Then I think, "No! Just leave it be and let the guy argue with himself." I snap back at myself, "You're hopeless.

A total wuss!" (Uh-oh, I think that last "wuss" leaked out loud. I quickly check that no real people are listening.)

You might object that I'm not literally *hearing* a voice. These are thoughts, not audible sounds. But is there really that much of a difference between the two? A research team at Hearing the Voice recently conducted the largest and most detailed account of voice hearers to date, in which 153 individuals, the vast majority of whom had histories of mental illness, were asked to describe their voice hearing experiences in their own words. Only about half the respondents described the voices as purely auditory, as "indistinguishable from hearing somebody in the room."[23] The others "heard" the voices either wholly or partially as thoughts. But these thoughts—the stuff of normal inner narratives—were sometimes as impactful as the purely auditory hallucinations we associate with mental illness. Even more so, in fact. As one participant observed: "I did not hear the voices aurally. They were much more intimate than that, and inescapable. It's hard to describe how I could 'hear' a voice that wasn't auditory; but the words the voices used and the emotions they contained (hatred and disgust) were completely clear, distinct, and unmistakable, maybe even more so than if I had heard them aurally."

A brain that is always "on," whether it speaks in sounds or thoughts, has kept our species alive. "Constant thinking is what propelled us from being a favorite food on the savanna—and a species that nearly went extinct—to becoming the most accomplished life-form on this planet," observes the neuroscientist Barry Gordon. We no longer face the ever-present life-or-death concerns our ancestors had to deal with—whether the object on the road was a branch or a snake, or if the rustling leaves were caused by the wind or a leopard. But our primate-style worrying continues today, Gordon argues. "As social animals, we must keep track of who's on top and who's not and who might help us and who might hurt us. To learn and understand this information, our mind is constantly calculating 'what if?' scenarios. 'What is the danger here?' 'What is the opportunity?'"[24] As a result, a brain that is wired correctly has narratives running through its mind.

The yammering is incessant. Some people find it as annoying as any uncontrollable noise—like the sound of traffic or someone else's loud music or a barking dog. But at least you can muffle noises from the outside. There are no earplugs for the nattering in your head. It is what drives some people to meditate. "The rationale for meditation is straightforward: If the self is too chatty, too intrusive, too catastrophizing, perhaps one should simply turn it down a bit," says social psychologist Mark Leary, a leading scholar on the topic of the self.[25] "Had the human self been installed with a mute button or off switch, the self would not be the curse to happiness that it often is," he adds.

If you've never done so, I suggest taking a couple of minutes out of your day and try listening carefully to the narration in your head. Find a quiet place, close your eyes, and just listen. At first you'll probably hear your own familiar silent voice. Perhaps it tells you to "Get back to work." Pretty soon, though, other peoples' voices will pipe in. Maybe your boss will tell you to get back to work. Or, you'll hear from your mother or your kindergarten teacher. These outsiders seem to hijack the microphones. Notice how seamlessly the voice melds from your own to those of others.

The voices aren't always unfriendly. They might praise or encourage you. They might, like good psychotherapists, help us understand a feeling we are struggling with. "You're just tired. Remember, you hardly slept last night." The voices can be lifesaving. Oliver Sacks recalls one such instance when he was dangerously stranded on a mountain with a badly injured leg: "I heard an inner voice that was wholly unlike my normal babble of inner speech. I had a great struggle crossing a stream with a buckled and dislocating knee. The effort left me stunned, motionless for a couple of minutes, and then a delicious languor came over me, and I thought to myself, Why not rest here? A nap maybe? This was immediately countered by a strong, clear, commanding voice, which said, 'You can't rest here—you can't rest anywhere. You've got to go on. Find a pace you can keep up and go on steadily.' This good voice, this Life voice, braced and resolved me. I stopped trembling and did not falter again."[26]

Sacks's experience is not uncommon. Mountain climber Joe Simpson describes a remarkable example in his book *Touching the Void*. Simpson had fallen off the vertical face of an ice ledge after climbing a twenty-one thousand–foot peak in the Andes. He spent the next three days trapped in a crevasse with a broken leg, starving, severely frostbitten, and with no good reason to believe help was coming.

I had never been so entirely alone. . . . I was abandoned to this awesome and lonely place, and although this alarmed me it also gave me strength. . . . There was silence, and snow, and a clear sky empty of life, and me, sitting there, taking it all in, accepting what I must try to achieve. . . .

It was as if there were two minds within me arguing the toss. The voice was clean and sharp and commanding. It was always right, and I listened to it when it spoke and acted on its decisions. The other mind rambled out a disconnected series of images, and memories and hopes, which I attended to in a daydream state as I set about obeying the orders of the voice. I had to get to the glacier. . . . The voice told me exactly how to go about it, and I obeyed while my other mind jumped abstractly from one idea to another. . . .

The voice, and the watch, urged me into motion whenever the heat from the glacier halted me in a drowsy exhausted daze. It was three o'clock—only three and a half hours of daylight left. I kept moving but soon realized that I was making ponderously slow headway. It didn't seem to concern me that I was moving like a snail. So long as I obeyed the voice, then I would be all right.[27]

The voices can be friendly in less dramatic ways. It is common, for example, to hear useful information, typically a detail—perhaps a name or an address—that one is struggling to recall. Or, it might be a reminder of the consequences of an action, for example: "If you finish that cake, you're going to feel lousy the rest of the night." Psychologist Eleanor Longden, who has struggled in her own personal battle with hearing voices, describes how the voices became more benign once she learned to accept them. "Sometimes they were even helpful," she says. "During one of my exams, one of my voices dictated the answers," she recalls. ("Does this count as cheating?" she adds.)[28]

Many say the voices ask them questions. These generally pertain to something the hearer is concerned about, for example, their mental states ("Why are you feeling so guilty about this?") or activities ("What are you going to do this morning?" "Do you want to find a job?"). They are rarely about things like the weather or the time of day. Many also direct their own questions to the voices. And the voices, in a throwback to bicameral thinking, usually answer back.[29]

Some voices provide entertainment. The most common example is music. Although these can be as unpleasant as any other compulsive hallucination, they can also offer pleasure. Some sing along with the voice. Oliver Sacks tells of a patient with a self-described "intracranial jukebox" that allowed him to switch from one "record" to another.[30]

***

There is a fine line between "thinking" and "hearing voices." In fact, the essence of what we usually envision as thinking *is* inner speech. Perhaps you are out on a walk or trying to get to sleep and you find yourself thinking about everything you need to do the next day. You are thinking with language, aren't you? You're hearing a voice, even if it is a silent one. In a telling study, people were "beeped" at random times throughout the day and asked what was going on in their heads at that moment. Up to 80 percent of the time it involved thinking in words.[31] Some people hear the words aloud. A few, like Herbert Mullin and John Nash, hear them spoken by another person. But, audible or not, the monologues, dialogues, and group discussions run through all of our minds.

Even when the volume is on mute, the words are "heard." I think of the advice my colleague Jack McDermott, a professor of English, once gave me. "You should always test your work out loud," he said, "because reading is an auditory activity." He's right. There is evidence that Broca's area, the language center of the brain, creates the "sounds" of words in our minds as we read them silently on the page.[32] You are probably doing this as you read this sentence. It doesn't usually make much difference whether the narration has literal volume. The same goes for all our thoughts. Narratives run through our consciousness day and night. We use language not only to communicate with others but to communicate with ourselves. It is difficult, in fact, to conceive of thinking—not simply observing, but thinking—that isn't verbal.

Consider how a child learns to think. Lev Vygotsky was an influential Russian developmental psychologist and polymath who is sometimes referred to as "The Mozart of Psychology." In his most famous theory, Vygotsky began with the assumption that inner thinking—per-

150

haps the most personal of activities—begins with "the drama that occurs between people." It is an offshoot of our earliest relationships. "Every function in the child's cultural development appears twice: first, on the social level, and later, on the individual level; first, between people (inter-psychological) and then inside the child (intra-psychological)," he writes.[33]

Young children are helpless. They learn to maneuver the world through the verbal guidance of their parents and other teachers: "This is how you make the letter T, Bobby." "Keep moving the pedals on your bike or you'll fall down." "Look both ways before you cross the street." Children are initially completely at the mercy of external voices. As children develop their own verbal skills, however, they begin reciting what they've learned. Drop in to recess in a kindergarten class and you'll hear kids talking to themselves at the same time. "You write a T with a straight up and down line and then a short line over the top." "Keep pedaling. Keep pedaling." "Look to the left. Look to the right. Okay, cross." It sounds like an insane asylum.

As children grow older, however, they are pressured to think their thoughts in their own heads and, over time, they learn to internalize the voices. It may happen in steps. The first time children are "shh'd" by a teacher, they might lower the volume to a whisper. After the next admonition, they mutely move their lips. Eventually, however, they learn to keep the words in their heads. Developmental psychologists refer to this stage as "private speech." According to Vygotsky, this is when true thinking begins.[34]

The point is that what we think of as adult thought, the most private of activities, began as a conversation, perhaps with your mom or dad or whoever else might have chirped in. Thinking is a shared activity. It "is something that happens between people," observes Charles Fernyhough. "If we can manage it by ourselves later in life, it is only because we have previously had someone close by to do it with us."[35] Our minds are populated by voices—our I, our Me, and a cast of other people. The voices can be problematic. But it is important to remember that they are tools of survival. "The word in language is half someone else's," writes the philosopher Mikhail Bakhtin.[36] This seems to me as good an estimate as any. To believe that the thoughts in your head are yours alone is its own particular delusion. It is normal but a delusion.

In fields like medicine, there is often a clear line between the normal and the pathological. When a cell turns cancerous or a bone cracks, something is unarguably wrong. In matters of psychology, however, normalcy may have many interpretations. Do we hear the words aloud or silently? Do they seem to come from inside one's head or from the lips of another person? The answers to these questions may be less important than what the voices are saying.

Besides, it probably won't be long before we are all speaking to oracles. With just a few tweaks of technology, we will be able to insert a chip into our ear and connect to an expert for any quandary. We can already ask our devices for information about items like driving directions and good restaurants. Eventually, however, virtual voices will supplant the role of the voices in our heads. They might tell us what we should say at a given moment or help us think through a problem. But instead of rehashing the advice we learned as a child—as we do through the current voices in our heads—we'll hear the accumulated knowledge of professional counselors, physicians, and other expert guides. They will be like the old voices except smarter. We may not even have to ask for advice. There will be an algorithm that identifies the problem before we do.

It will be a lovely irony: Technological progress will return us to the mindsets of the bicameral ancients. We, like our ancestors, will seek guidance from the wise ones. And we will hear their words as clearly as if they were standing in front of us. Our very own oracles.

12
Herding the Cats

I'm half-Irish and half-English. That means
every so often I have to occupy myself.
—Robin Williams

The engineer-futurist Ray Kurzweil has famously predicted that within a few decades we will be able to routinely scan peoples' brains and upload complete copies of their minds into computers. In fact, Kurzweil says, the process is already theoretically feasible. The main obstacle is cost, which will require a few years to work out. When the technology is perfected, however, it will free us from the limitations of a biological human body. We'll live forever on a computer chip.

Kurzweil's vision raises many questions. But the one I can't get out of my head is, Which version of me is going to be stored? I don't know about you, but the different me's who have existed through my time on this earth are hardly carbon copies of one other. I have more in common with most friends who are my age than I do with my selves as I remember them from earlier years. I look back fondly on many of those past me's—the five-year-old I was on my first day of kindergarten, the high school student I was on my first date. But, if we happened to meet, I really don't know what we'd have to talk about. I would probably offer them unsolicited fatherly advice that would annoy them to no end. So, Mr. Kurzweil, when my mind gets uploaded, to be preserved forever, which iteration is it going to be? Say I'm ninety-five years old (and alive) when the technology is ready. Will I have to endure eternity with the deteriorated old faculties I have left?

There is, in fact, no such animal as a self who exists outside of time. There have been endless iterations of our past selves and, if we live long enough, there will be as many or more of our selves in the future. The previous two chapters have focused on relationships within ourselves: the give and take in our thinking process and the voices that speak to us from within. Let us now turn to the relationships *between* our selves, between the person we were in the past, are in the present, and will be in the future. We understand that all these selves are blood relatives. Being family, it would be nice to think they are in harmony. Our own little rainbow coalition. The fact is, however, they often show little concern for each other's welfare. We are ridiculously divided in time.

***

Let me offer a personal example. I have a bad habit of making social arrangements I later regret. A couple of years ago, for instance, I was at a party while on a trip to New York City. Somehow I began talking to a nice couple from Romania who introduced themselves as Aurel and Elena Eminescu. We exchanged stories about our respective families and homes, theirs in Bucharest and mine in central California. At one point, I enthusiastically described the magnificent national parks (Yosemite, Sequoia, King's Canyon) that are only a couple of hours drive from my house. The Eminescus became interested and pumped me for more information.

As we prepared to part, I wrote out my contact numbers and invited them to stay at my house should they ever get to Fresno. We had plenty of space, I told them, with two empty bedrooms now that our sons had moved out. I didn't think much about whether they would actually come, but I felt generous making the offer. The truth is, I felt like a big shot. We shook hands and parted.

A few days later I flew back to Fresno. I'd been on the road for almost two weeks and was anxious to return home, to see my wife, and return to my own little cocoon of a life. I'm basically a private person. I love traveling and meeting people, but I get socially overloaded quickly. As we hit the runway at the Fresno airport, nothing sounded better than going through my mail, getting back to my little projects, and relaxing around my house.

I turned on my cell phone and had two messages. The first was from my wife welcoming me home and assuring me that, as I'd requested, we had no social plans for the next few days. The second message was from a guy with a heavy accent I couldn't quite make out. The first time I played it, I thought he was saying "This is Oral M&M's," and figured it was some prank call. Then I remembered: Aurel Eminescu, from that party in New York. I replayed the message. He and Elena had told their young sons—Pache, Dimitrie, and Radu—about this Prince of a guy and these fabulous national parks and the offer to stay at my house. They had decided to take me up on it. They had made plans to visit San Francisco this coming weekend and arranged to visit Fresno along the way. In fact, I should expect them tomorrow. The message ended with their flight information and a request to please pick them up at the airport, which I'd apparently also offered to do. They would be taking day trips to the parks and hoped I could be their guide. They would also like to stay with us for the week—five nights—if that was okay.

I wanted to punch myself. When I got home and told my wife, she wanted to punch me too. "Let me get this straight. Five Romanians you hardly know named Aurel, Elena, Pache, Dimitrie, and Radu are coming to stay in our house for five nights. You know I hate entertaining strangers. And, by the way, you know you hate it even worse. Why do you do these stupid things?" All I could say was, "I'm sorry. I'm an idiot." I meant it. "Well, I'm clearing out of here those days. The Eminescus are your problem." She meant it.

I'd like to say that I had been trapped into making an aberrant mistake. After all, it is protocol to make friendly invitations to fellow travelers, kind of like saying "Let's do lunch" to an acquaintance you run into. Shouldn't they have understood you're not supposed to take these offers seriously? And didn't they read their Lonely Planet guidebook? Fresno is not what you'd call a hot tourist attraction. But the truth is, I get myself into these binds all the time. I love making plans. I initiate appointments for breakfast, lunch, dinner, coffee, drinks, or whatever at the drop of a hat. I make commitments to deliver manuscripts, join committees, hear talks, and give talks. These plans always feel right at the time. What I can't seem to learn, however, is to anticipate what they will feel like when the actual date comes—which is, all too often, trapped. Afterward I recognize what an idiot I was. Then I go out and do it again.

I think of myself as basically a future-oriented person, ergo my planning-addiction. In a curious way, however, my planning for the future is generated by the pleasure it provides in the present. This, I believe, is where I often get myself in trouble. I'm more attuned to that immediate pleasure than to the realities of the future. It is not that I want to harm my future self. He's just not at the top of my worries list.

It is rather cruel of me when you think about it. I certainly wouldn't assign an unpleasant task to, say, my neighbors without asking them first. I can't imagine myself having said, "Please bring your family to Fresno, Aurel. The whole bunch of you can stay with my neighbors Kay and Richard as long as you want." But that's exactly what I did to my future self. Now I was left holding the bag for the actions of my irresponsibly myopic self from three days earlier. What kind of jerk leaves someone with a mess like this? I'd been screwed—by my self. And he felt no shame, no guilt, offered no apology.

Why should I feel worse about hurting a friend than hurting myself? How can I treat myself so coldly? I don't pretend to have a fully satisfying answer. But the core of the problem, I believe, is time. Our selves, at their very essence, are divided in time. The self we experience at any moment will never meet the self who follows. It is a basic tenet of evolutionary psychology that we act more caringly toward people we expect to encounter in the future. The entire concept of social exchange—cooperation for mutual benefit—is driven by the expectation that one's actions will be reciprocated at a later date.[1] It is no less than the Golden Rule. But our future selves are destined to remain physical strangers. How do you trust someone you'll never meet? It's like communicating with a shadow, like the "man behind the curtain" in *The Wizard of Oz*. Out of sight, out of mind. Here to today, gone tomorrow. Choose your own platitude.

***

I consider myself fairly adult at apologizing when I've done something wrong. But my phrasing can be sneaky. I hear myself saying things like, "I'm sorry, I didn't mean to say that"; or, "Forgive me, I wasn't thinking." I'm expressing sorrow but suggesting that my actions weren't the work of my real me. The me who is apologizing at this moment would never do or say those terrible things I'm apologizing for. That was another person. I sound like one of those CEOs who apologize for the scandalous behavior of their company without actually taking personal blame. "I take ultimate responsibility for this crisis. I am the CEO and the buck stops with me." He's sorry, but, he wants you to know, he's a victim, too. "I'm as angry at the real culprits as you are," he's implying.

It isn't only when apologizing that we refer to ourselves in third person. We do so almost any time we reflect on ourselves. Consider the language we use:

- I like myself.

- I hate myself.

- I'm not myself today.

- I scare myself.

It's as if a stranger shares one's cranium, a cohabitant. The other one is me, of course—who else could he be?—but at the same time he feels outside my control. He goes about his business with very much a mind of his own. And so, we casually throw around terms (and statements) like

- Self-deception ("Don't you see what you're saying?")

- Self-control ("Get hold of yourself, Buddy.")

- Self-reflection ("I was thinking about myself yesterday.")

- Self-punishment ("Don't be so hard on yourself.")

- Self-respect ("You should be proud of yourself.")

If visitors from another planet heard us, they'd figure we were insane. "Explain to me, Mr. Earthling, are you saying you live two people to a body on your planet? Does this mean everyone is what you refer to as "Siamese twins"? Or would you prefer we call you schizophrenics?" We speak to others this way, too. There is a wonderful scene from the show *30 Rock* where Alec Baldwin tells Tina Fey, "Don't ever say you're just you because you are better than you." If there were clinical psychologists among the extraterrestrials, they would probably send the whole bunch of us off for treatment. They would be wrong, or so we'd tell them. Because here on our planet this is normalcy.

***

Never put off till tomorrow that which you can do today.
—Benjamin Franklin

Never do today what you can put off till tomorrow.
—Aaron Burr

Never put off until tomorrow what you can
do the day after tomorrow.
—Mark Twain

Our extraterrestrial observers would become even more confused about other ways we treat our future selves. You might think that we would do everything in our power to enhance the well-being of our selves-to-come. But, in fact, we can be remarkably insensitive toward our intracranial successors.

The term "delay of gratification" refers to resisting a small immediate reward in return for a larger one at some future time. It is a skill that pays off. In a seminal study conducted by psychologist Walter Mischel, a friendly researcher placed a marshmallow in front of four-year-old preschool children and told them that, if they could wait fifteen minutes before eating the treat, he would come back with a second one and the child could eat both. Not surprisingly, not all of the children stuck it out for the duration.[2] More important, however, was what Mischel discovered about them later in their lives. Sixteen years after the original experiment, Mischel tracked down the children, now teenagers, and found that those who had been able to wait out the full fifteen minutes when they saw that first marshmallow turned out to have higher grades in high school, better SAT scores, and were more emotionally and social competent on a variety of measures. And the successes continued as they grew older. In another follow-up, this time four decades after the original study, Mischel learned that those who had resisted temptation as four-year-olds were more likely to graduate college, earned higher incomes, got into less trouble, and had more productive lives in many other ways.[3]

The value of self-control has been confirmed in many studies.[4] Of course, we don't need psychologists to tell us this. When someone you trust tells you that he or she will double your payoff if you wait, you obviously should. But there is a lot of that four-year-old in most of us that makes it awfully difficult to hold off for that second marshmallow.

Behavioral economists refer to this way of thinking as "hyperbolic discounting": we tend to put less value on rewards in the future than those in the present.[5] "A bird in the hand ..." and all that. This made good sense for our ancestors who foraged the plains for something to eat with no certainty of what the future held. Unfortunately, it remains our kneejerk response in a landscape with little resemblance to the one our ancestors faced. As a consequence, we often end up discounting future rewards when we shouldn't.

We show a curious disrespect for our future selves when we behave this way. It's as if "I" in the now is more important than the "I" we will be in the future. But this is only the beginning of our twisted logic. There is, at least, something to be gained by immediate gratification. It just happens to be short-sighted. In other instances, however, we sometimes inflict damage to our future selves without the benefit of a short-term payoff, or any payoffs at any time. We may actually punish ourselves in the present by virtue of the fact that we are hurting ourselves in the future. And, the more pain we inflict upon our future selves, the worse we may feel while doing it. I'm not referring to the kind of pain that feels oddly pleasant to wallow in—when, perhaps, we indulge ourselves in depressing music after a lover walks out on us; or we nostalgically roam the streets of our childhood recalling all we've left behind. I mean just plain suffering.

Consider the all-too-human problem of procrastination, where putting off the inevitable makes no sense at all.[6] A patient delays going to a doctor when he knows something needs fixing. A taxpayer pays penalties for missing the filing deadline. A writer avoids finishing his book by flitting from one unnecessary distraction to another. What makes procrastination so illogical—and such a fascinating window into human thinking—is that it results in more misery than you would experience by doing what you are avoiding. The longer we procrastinate, the worse the problem often gets. Say you are a person who tends to put off washing the dishes, for example. You know full well that not only will you eventually have to wash them, but, the longer you wait, the cruddier the job will get. You dump your dirty dishes on your future self, and, in return, you get to live with a dirty kitchen.[7]

As a professor, I'm surrounded by procrastination. Every semester I watch students torture themselves as the deadline for their term paper approaches. Why, I ask them, can't you be nice to yourself and just do the work you know you'll eventually have to do? I'm right, they usually tell me and then go directly back to torturing themselves. Our inclination to procrastinate is so common that the economist George Ainslie, who has written extensively on the subject, describes it to be "as fundamental as the shape of time." In fact, he adds, "It could well be called the basic impulse."[8] "Yes," we would tell our visitors from another planet. "This, too, is normal."

Cognitive psychologist Dan Ariely and his colleague Klaus Wertenbroch conducted a telling experiment. Ariely was teaching a class at MIT for which he required students to write three papers that would constitute most of their final grade. On the first day of class he offered them an unusual option: The students were free to set their own due dates for each paper, he announced. But there were several rules. First, all three papers had to be turned in no later than the last day of lecture. Second, students had to declare their deadlines by the next day of class. Third, once declared, the deadlines were binding. Fourth, overdue papers would be penalized 1 percent of the final grade each day they were late. Finally, although they would be allowed to set early deadlines, they would receive no extra credit for doing so.

The rational decision was clear: Set all three deadlines to the final day. There was no reward for early submissions and considerable penalty for late ones. By setting the latest possible deadline, you could finish the papers anytime you wanted while retaining the option to take longer if you needed to. There was nothing to lose and everything to gain. It was a no-brainer. And what did Ariely's students do with their newfound freedom? They set a grand total of one-third of their deadlines—one of their three papers, exactly what they would be required to do in any other class—to the final day. Only 27 percent of the students set all three deadlines to the last allowable date.[9]

We would be hard-pressed to call these folks stupid. They were MIT students, after all. How, then, do we explain why almost three-quarters of them decided against the logical choice? The answer, it seems, is they didn't trust themselves. They knew procrastinating would both make them miserable in the short run and hurt their performance in the long term; they would feel (1) guilt over not working and (2) anxiety over the grades they would end up with. The longer they procrastinated, the worse they would feel and the lower their grades would be. Yet they were convinced that, left to their own devices, they would procrastinate anyway.

***

"I don't trust myself." What a curious statement. The "I" making the statement understands that another "I" will take over the controls sometime in the future. And it is convinced that other I will act against both of their self-interests. Is this what we mean by lacking self-control? Wouldn't it be more accurate to say "one self lacks control over another self? Looked at this way, observes the journalist James Surowiecki, "the first step to dealing with procrastination isn't admitting that you have a problem. It's admitting that your 'you's' have a problem."[10]

The issue, we tell ourselves, is a lack of "self-discipline." It is so ubiquitous that we have normalized it with this everyday term. It's as if disciplining ourselves were no odder than disciplining your child or your dog. In truth, however, the process couldn't be more convoluted and bizarre. "Discipline" is rooted in authority and power. "Self-discipline" assumes we can completely control ourselves. But we need to remember what we are up against here. Our adversary—that shadowy executive who operates outside awareness—holds the trump card. The self of awareness can decide to take an action. "I'm going to walk up to this beautiful woman and introduce myself." But the bigger question is whether we will act. Sometimes we do. "Please don't think I'm rude, but I couldn't help but notice you and wanted to introduce myself." Other times, however, you can literally feel the resistance pushing against you from inside. "I'm just too scared to do this," you might tell yourself. In other words, conscious decision making has been trumped. It is as if the inner executive gave us no choice.

How, then, do we discipline ourselves? Bookshelves overflow with advice. Most of these programs promote grit and strength. If this strategy—what we like to call willpower—gets the job done, congratulations. But it often doesn't. When we fail in our quest, it is common to blame ourselves, to resolve to try harder next time, be stronger, sweat, keep at it. And so the cycle continues. Should you find yourself in one of these loops, it may call for a different approach. To paraphrase the investment guru Warren Buffet: if you find yourself in the same hole, it's probably a good idea to stop digging.

I suggest you begin as the MIT students did: Don't trust yourself. Design a strategy that accepts your personal limitations or, more precisely, both of your personal limitations: Those of the "I" who doesn't seem to have enough willpower and those of "myself" who is strong enough to resist but too much of a bum to change. It is best to imagine you are trying to change some other person. There are many possible strategies. The most psychologically nuanced employ subtle manipulation. Think of this as the carrot approach. The goal here is to sneak under your inner defenses without resorting to force. One clever variant of this approach is known as "structured procrastination." It is based on the idea that procrastination doesn't mean doing nothing. In fact, many proficient procrastinators are at their busiest when they procrastinate. My writer friend Stanton, for example, says you can tell how much he's written by how clean his office is. The cleaner it is, the less he's accomplished. The thing is—and this is the key to structured procrastination—if cleaning his office was at the top of his to-do list, Stanton would probably procrastinate about that.

Stanton isn't lazy. He's just not doing what he should be doing. Structured procrastination makes the attraction to less important tasks work in your favor. The philosopher John Perry, the reigning guru of the structured procrastination movement, suggests you develop a task triage. First, create a list of the tasks you want to complete, ranking them in importance from most to least. You do this knowing you'll want to avoid the job at the top of the list. But the tasks below that are probably also worth doing, and "doing *those* tasks becomes a way of not doing the things higher on the list," Perry says. With a carefully constructed triage, "you can become a useful citizen. Indeed, the procrastinator can even acquire, as I have, a reputation for getting a lot done," Perry says.[11] It's a ju-jitsu approach. The more you procrastinate, the more you get done.

***

Sometimes, however, subtle psychology may not be enough. When this is the case, it may be time to turn from carrots to sticks. To paraphrase the great psychologist Don Corleone in the *Godfather*, we need to make an offer we can't refuse. We need to threaten ourselves. I know this sounds like insensitive advice, but, as another character in the movie put it, "It's not personal, Sonny. It's strictly business." Ariely's young geniuses took this approach. They bound themselves to a contract that removed free will from the equation. Signed, sealed, delivered.

It is not a particularly inspiring way of thinking. But, to be sure, it is in the footsteps of an impressive tradition. In Homer's epic *The Odyssey*, the goddess Circe gives Ulysses the option of hearing the beautiful songs of the Sirens but warns him that he or any sailor who does so will be so mesmerized by what he hears that he will direct his ship toward the source of the song and end up crashing into the rocks and dying. Ulysses enacted a two-stage plan: First, he ordered all his men to stuff their ears with beeswax so they couldn't hear the songs. Then, he had them tie him to the mast of the ship so he'd be able to hear the songs but would be unable to change the ship's course. Arrangements like these, where free choice is replaced with binding rules, are referred to in legal circles today as "Ulysses contracts."

Nothing is too ridiculous when devising contracts. Victor Hugo, it was said, once became so frustrated with his lack of willpower that he started writing naked to ensure that he wouldn't bolt out of his study. For added security, Hugo instructed his valet to hide his clothes and promise not to reveal their whereabouts until he'd finished his day's work.[12]

The threats may escalate to self-blackmail. This has appeared often in the literature on game theory. In a 1971 paper, Thomas Schelling, a Nobel Prize–winning economist, describes how a Denver cocaine-addiction clinic catering to wealthy clients employed self-extortion as part of its therapy program: "The patient may write a self-incriminating letter that is placed in a safe, to be delivered to the addressee if the patient, who is tested on a random schedule, is found to have used cocaine. An example would be a physician who writes to the State Board of Medical Examiners confessing that he has violated state law and professional ethics in the illicit use of cocaine and deserves to lose his license to practice medicine. It is handled quite formally and contractually, and serves not only as a powerful deterrent but as a ceremonial expression of determination."[13]

Or consider the case of Zelda Gamson, a political activist who has dedicated her life to fighting social injustices. Gamson had a serious smoking habit. After many unsuccessful attempts at quitting, she devised a last-ditch strategy: She publicly pledged to donate $5,000 to the Ku Klux Klan if she ever smoked another cigarette. Then, to make absolutely sure she couldn't wiggle out of the deal, Gamson asked her close friend to be the enforcer: she gave her friend a signed check made out to the Klan and instructed her to immediately put it in the mail if she caught Gamson smoking a cigarette. Gamson never smoked again.[14]

The most effective strategies tend, like the examples above, to include other people (Can we call them third parties?) in one's self-conflict—either as supporters or referees or both. One informal study found that people were two-thirds more likely (62 percent vs. 37 percent) to keep a personal commitment when they engaged one or more people to monitor their progress.[15] If you have the resources, you could hire a personal assistant. I first tried this approach with a student, whom I'll call Lewis, who came to my office for help with his term paper project. Lewis explained to me that he had a miserable history of "flaking" when he had an entire semester to work on a paper. His pattern was to set a daily writing goal first thing each morning. He would then spend the rest of the day finding ways to postpone, ignore, and/or renegotiate the goal with himself, until it was time to go to sleep. He would spend the night obsessing over what a screw-up he was, wake up exhausted, and start the cycle gain. In other words, Lewis was a textbook procrastinator. When I asked how he had made it this far in school, he rattled off stories of a nagging mother who used to follow him around telling him to get back to work. A couple of years back he decided he'd had enough and told his mother to back off. This led to his current predicament.

I suggested a strategy that I borrowed from Ian Ayres, a professor of both law and management at Yale: hire a professional nagger.[16] It would fill the role his mother served but, it is hoped, without the collateral emotional damage. Lewis liked the idea and took it from there. He found "a really bitchy woman" (whom he nicknamed Wanda) who promised "not to put up with any of my bullshit" and worked out a contract. Lewis contracted to e-mail a minimum of 350 written words to Wanda by 9 p.m. each day. The first time he fell short, Wanda would e-mail a gentle nudge: "I haven't heard from you today, Lewis." If he continued missing the mark, however, she was instructed to begin a program of escalating harassments. After the second missed deadline, Wanda would barrage him with calls and texts. If that didn't work, she was to post his failures on Facebook. As a final option, Wanda would stalk and nag him everywhere he went "just like my mother used to do"—what he referred to as "the death sentence." Fortunately, Lewis later reported, it never came to that. He had slipped up a couple of times, he said, but nothing like the past two years of disastrous semesters. It wasn't the nagging itself that worked, he said, but the threat of being nagged (which is exactly what Ian Ayres predicted would happen). The program was a success and, Lewis recently told me, is one he has repeated with good results on other occasions.

If you are put off by having an actual person take this role, you might consider a website to do the pestering. One novel example, called The Resolution Solution, was designed by a group of tech-savvy rabbis to help people keep their Rosh Hashanah (the Jewish New Year) resolutions.[17] You type in your resolutions, and the website e-mails you daily, weekly, or monthly reminders of what you committed to. It "can nag you once a day. It can nag you weekly, monthly, but it rests on Shabbat," co-creator Rabbi Motti Seligson said about the site.[18]

For a more visual approach, there are websites that let you create a virtual nagger. A site in Japan allows overweight men to design a virtual wife to monitor anything from their diet ("Eat your vegetables") to more complicated habits. The subscriber chooses from one of four wives: a giggly maid, a stern businesswoman-type, a caring nurse, or a trendy nail artist, each with customizable faces and voices. The nagger is programmed to send messages that escalate from gentle nudges to obnoxiously annoying shoves when the man falls off his diet. The site is hopelessly sexist, but the psychology behind it is worth consideration. And think of how effective it will become with future technology.[19]

Chapter 12

***

You might think this style of self-management lacks dignity or, at the least, signals weakness of the will. But there is another way to look at it. They are extensions of our will. They are prosthetics. We rely on prosthetics for many mental processes. Say, for example, I ask you to solve a difficult mathematical problem without using a calculator: What is 14 × 18 × 13? You will probably reach for a pencil and paper to do the arithmetic. Is this cheating? Or, how about memory? I scribble out shopping lists when I go to the supermarket. My pockets are stuffed with names of people I would have otherwise forgotten before they got out the door. Then there's my computer. When I write, I think my thoughts through what I see on the screen.

I don't associate these "devices" with personal failure. My accomplishments are mine, and I take pride in them. Think of a blind man's cane. It doesn't replace his arm. It extends it. In the man's mind, the tip of his cane has become the tip of his sense of touch. It's the same with our pencils and paper and our computers. They become so well integrated in the loop "that we can say we 'use' them only in the sense that we can say that we 'use' our fingers to type," observe the philosophers Joseph Heath and Joel Anderson.[20]

Admittedly, the prosthetics can get pretty quirky when your target is willpower. But, if you design and carry out the strategy, why should that make the accomplishment any less yours? So what if asking your butler to hide your pants or tricking yourself with a made up to-do list sounds stranger than using a white cane? You *willed* yourself to have willpower. And it is this act of willing, I believe, for which we should be judged. The blind man deserves credit for the way he maneuvers his cane, not for the metal on the tip. I can't help it if I'm weak, but I can figure out strategies to be less so.

But, once again, I'm getting lost in intellectual terms like "will" and "willpower." In most of life, we don't will ourselves to get the job done so much as convince ourselves to do it. Ulysses used a hard sell. My friend Stanton works a soft one. Carrots or sticks? It's not important. In the end, as salespeople like to say, there is the bottom line: "Did you close the deal?" And, when we do, we should give ourselves as much credit for tricking ourselves as when we will it. More, in fact. We say we value innovation. And effective self-control calls for innovation at its creative best. What's not to be proud of?

***

If at times we appear absurd, bickering with ourselves, each side cajoling and manipulating the other like streetwise con-artists, just chalk it up to another chapter in the human comedy. Ian McEwan describes it nicely in his novel *Solar*: "At moments of important decision-making, the mind could be considered as a parliament, a debating chamber. Different factions contended, short- and long-term interests were entrenched in mutual loathing. Not only were motions tabled and opposed, certain proposals were aired in order to mask others. Sessions could be devious as well as stormy."

Or, as the writer Jay McInerney puts it, "You are a republic of voices. . . . Unfortunately, that republic is Italy."[21]

13
A Troupe of Performers

On the stage he was natural, simple, affecting;
'Twas only that when he was off he was acting.
—Oliver Goldsmith, *Retaliation* (1774)

Pick a job and then become the person that does it.
—Bobbie Barrett, *Mad Men*

I'll never forget my first day of college teaching. To a normal person in a normal profession this should have been a moment for celebration. Getting to this point, after all, had been a considerable achievement. I'd sweated my way through four years of a competitive undergraduate school, two more years at a second university to get a master's degree, and another four plus at yet another university to finally earn my doctorate. I'd struggled through countless tests, qualifying exams, comprehensive exams, a thesis, a dissertation, the indignities of being a teaching assistant, the demands of often quirky professors and supervisors. I'd landed an academic job during a viciously competitive market. I was a survivor, a finisher, a success story. It was all high-fives when I left my graduate student hovel of a life in New York City for my new one as a supposed big shot professor in California. "Make us proud, young man," one of my advisers told me. "All the doors are open to you."

But what I mostly felt sitting in my new office, waiting to begin my first lecture, was terror. Whatever in the world, I was asking myself, had possessed me to select a profession whose defining activity, speaking before groups, had been my lifelong phobia? Sure, I wanted to be a professor. It had been my dream for as long as I could remember. Right now, however, I was feeling like the proverbial man who had always wanted to be a concert violinist until he found out it would entail having to learn how to play the violin. How could I be such a moron?

So there I was, pacing back and forth across my little office, manifesting all the traditional symptoms of coronary artery disease—rapid heartbeat, shortness of breath, sweating like a hydrant—as my first lecture drew closer. It's odd what your mind reverts to when you feel cornered. Think positive thoughts, I kept telling myself. But when I—a man who had just received his PhD in psychology, mind you—tried this, the only words that came to mind were old Nike slogans: "Be all you can be," "Just do it," "There is no finish line." I'm not just a moron. I'm a cliché of a moron, a moron's moron.

Before long, the only image I could conjure was the frightened stutterer I'd been when I had to give oral presentations in high school back in Brooklyn. My mind kept replaying a particularly traumatic episode when a tenth-grade English teacher assigned each of us to prepare speeches critiquing classic books. I drew *Robinson Crusoe*. This created a special problem for my stuttering because I had a nasty problem with words that began with the letter R. Furthermore, I was told to deliver my talk with a British accent. This was a ridiculous challenge given that I recently had been diagnosed as having a bad case of "Brooklynese" (in a high school in Brooklyn!) by our school speech therapist. My talk was an absolute disaster. Now, a decade later, the nightmare was looping through my mind. There was that fifteen-year-old me stumbling to the front of the class, trembling, where I spoke with a British accent that made me sound like a left hemisphere stroke victim delivering an analysis of *Robinson Crusoe* while trying to avoid saying the word "Robinson."

And this first lecture would be just the beginning of a career defined by public speaking. Was I going to be torturing myself like this for the next thirty-five years? What could I have been thinking about all that time I was studying to be a professor? I decided to quit my new job right then and there. And I mean *right* then, because if I was going to put an end to this teaching delusion, I certainly wasn't going to put myself through that first lecture.

For some reason, however—your basic deer in headlights comes to mind—I walked to that first class and gave my lecture. The experience was mostly a blur, as was the rest of that initial week. But after the first frantic performances something remarkable occurred: a whole new me, a college professor, showed up at the lectern. The new self—I'll call him Dr. L.—was rather poised and confident and verbally at ease. One of the first things I noticed was how intellectual Dr. L. sounded. He spoke differently from what I was used to. Even the Brooklyn accent lost its edges. The students certainly seemed impressed. What was really odd, though, was how pleased I was by this new persona as well. There were times when I would hear words come out of my mouth and think, "How clever!" One time I heard myself suggest a clever experiment to test a concept I had been lecturing about. I found myself, like a good student, frantically scribbling down a sketch of the experiment as soon as my lecture was over.

I'd never been much of a storyteller. In fact, I have hardly any childhood memories of stringing together more than a few sentences when speaking. One early lecture, however, I began with what was planned as a brief anecdote. When I was done, students peppered me with questions, seemingly interested to know more. I started the story again and, this time, one image led to another, and to another and, when I looked up at the clock, I realized I had been telling my story for half the class. From then on, Dr. L. developed into a reliable storyteller, certainly a much better one than I'd ever known myself to be.

Then there was this sense of humor. I've always tried to be funny, but my usual style had been concise comebacks (attempts, at least). I now found myself performing extended riffs. One student complained he hadn't paid tuition to hear a stand-up routine—which I took as a compliment. Sometimes I would get into give-and-take with my audience. It felt as if I was doing improvisation. Where did that come from?

There were elements of my new persona I could trace to people I knew. Curiously, however, I didn't realize I was mimicking them until after the fact. Once, early on, an old friend had volunteered to critique my lecture style. Afterward, I asked him about my physical movements and gestures. "I love that John Lennon thing you do when you want to make a point," he told me. "You really nailed his moves." The fact is, I had no idea I was doing any such thing. When I lectured the next day, however, I saw that my colleague was absolutely right. I even said, "Thanks, mate," to someone who picked up my dropped pen.

From then on it was hard to get John Lennon out of my head. A few weeks later, my impersonation leapt to the ridiculous. I was lecturing about the effects of culture on childhood development. I decided to personalize my lecture by describing a memory from the fifth grade when my best friend Alan had shocked me by making fun of my Old World grandparents. My students seemed to be listening intently. This inspired the performer in me, and I felt myself raising the passion level as I proceeded. I finished by saying that this was what it was like "to be raised in a broken home in a tough section of Liverpool." It was an effective ending. But it was ridiculous. I was raised in a loving home by eastern European Jews in Brooklyn. Uh-oh. John Lennon had crept in again.

There were other cameos. One time I was delivering a lecture about Erik Erikson's eight stages of man. When I got to the stage of middle adulthood, what Erikson calls the period of "generativity versus stagnation," I talked about how important it is to pursue long-term life goals that have an impact on people other than oneself. I described middle-aged friends of mine who had made a lot of money but now complained that they had done nothing worthwhile with their lives. I felt very wise at that moment and said something like: "When I was young like you, it seemed as if money and success were all that mattered. But when you get to be my age, you understand how important it is to feel that you've made a contribution beyond yourself. You need to take time for your family and friends and causes you care about. Experience is a great teacher, and, if there's anything I've learned, it's that your time can never be replaced." It sounded good. But what in the world was I talking about? "*When you get to be my age*"? I was twenty-seven years old—nothing but a *pisher* ("a little squirt"), as my grandmother used to say in Yiddish.[1] And, "*Experience*"? I had been out of school for a full two weeks, oh great sage I was. But, even as I was giving my advice, I knew it sounded awfully familiar. It should have, because it was almost verbatim what my father had said to me just before I'd left for California. Another invisible scriptwriter had joined my ranks.

The noted biologist Robert Sapolsky describes a very similar experience in his book *The Trouble with Testosterone*. After his father died, Sapolsky found himself unexplainably adopting elements of this man he had loved. He began displaying his father's mannerisms, wearing his clothing, and even carrying around the bottle of nitroglycerin he'd kept at his side for his bad heart. The peak of Sapolsky's confusion came when he delivered the final lecture of the class he was teaching. He had intended to give a eulogy to his father. Instead, while dressed in his father's old flannel shirt, he found himself lecturing in the first person as if he were his father. Sapolsky recalls how he began "offering the frail advice of an octogenarian":

> I warned them, amid their plans to tackle difficult problems in life and to be useful and productive, that they should prepare for setbacks, for the realization that each commitment entailed turning their backs on so many other things—like knowing their children, for example. And this was not me speaking, still with a sheltered optimism about balancing parenting with the demands of science, but he with his weathered disappointments and the guilt and regret he expressed in his later years that he was always working when I was a boy. I told them that I knew they wanted to change the world but that they should prepare for the inconceivable—someday they would become tired.[2]

I know just what Sapolsky was talking about. It is like something actors describe when they become so enmeshed in a role that the boundary between the part they're playing and their actual selves seems to dissolve. The actress Annan Paterson told me, "There are times when I am so in the moment that I feel overcome by emotion during a scene that it feels like I'm there." She might get so lost in the script that she feels real hate or love for her onstage co-performer. Paterson recalls one strange occasion when, during a performance of a play set on a farm in Ireland, "a real-life huge fly landed on my knee and I killed the fly as my character but in real life, too. For a moment I really was on a farm in Ireland surrounded by pigs. It felt like 'me'— not like acting."[3]

But actors have a script in front of them. In my case, it was unclear where the words were coming from. If it was my father talking, was I just a dummy in a ventriloquist act? If I was speaking from a script, where was it stored and how was it activated? Who was the writer? Who was the director?

I never doubted that Dr. L. was me. But his style was so uncharacteristic. He was so animated and such a performer. And he talked constantly, sometimes an hour and a half (that is, a ninety-minute class) from start to finish, which I never, ever had done in my life. There were times when I wondered what he was going to say next. Nor did my new persona totally replace the old one. He just showed up at lecture time. I soon learned, in fact, that Dr. L.'s domain was rather limited. Once during those first weeks, I attended a colleague's presentation. I was sitting in the audience at a student desk. During the discussion period, I swaggered to my feet all-big-shot-like to ask a question. To my embarrassment, the doofus from my high school English class showed up instead of Dr. L. But when I lectured to my class in the very same room the next day, Dr. L. was back.

It was a confusing time for me. I liked this new self. Truth be told, I had a bit of a crush on him. But he also felt like a stranger. And I felt so fickle. Give me a new title and I send my old identity packing. Just like that. What kind of person was I?

***

A hundred and fifty miles up the road from me, social psychologist Philip Zimbardo had, coincidentally, just published a study that would recast social psychology's answers to these very questions. Zimbardo, who years later became a friend and collaborator, had set up a fake prison in the basement of the Stanford University psychology building. Ads were placed in the local newspapers: "Male college students needed for psychological study of prison life. $15 per day." Twenty-four intelligent, educated, middle-class, college-age men were selected. All were deemed to be "normal-average" on clinical interviews and personality tests. Half the men were randomly assigned to be guards and the other half prisoners. Selection was based on a literal flip of the coin. The two groups had similar scores on the psychological tests taken before the experiment began. "It is important to remember that at the beginning of our experiment there were no differences between boys assigned to be a prisoner and boys assigned to be a guard," Zimbardo said.[4]

The prison was hastily constructed. Three laboratory rooms were converted into "cells." Adjacent offices were converted into housing for the guards and bedrooms for the warden (a Stanford graduate student) and the superintendent (Zimbardo himself). A small, dark storage closet was made into an area for solitary confinement known as "The Hole." A long corridor was converted into a prison "yard." This was the only outside place other than a toilet down the hallway that prisoners were allowed to go (blindfolded, "so as not to know the way out of the prison"). The experiment was planned to last two weeks.

On the morning of August 14, 1971, squad cars—real squad cars, and real police, by arrangement with the Palo Alto Police Department—swept through the city, sirens blaring, picking up the prisoners in a surprise mass arrest. The prisoners were "charged," warned of their rights, spread-eagled against the car, frisked, handcuffed, and tossed in the back of the squad car to be booked at the police station and then transported to the "Stanford County Prison" in the basement of the psychology building. Upon arrival, they were stripped naked, searched, and deloused. They were issued uniforms consisting of a smock that was worn without undergarments, a stocking cap made from a women's nylon stocking that covered their hair, and a heavy chain that was to be worn around their ankles at all times. Their prison IDs were printed on the front and back of their smocks. They were addressed by these ID numbers rather than their real names throughout the experiment.

The guards' outfits were designed to psychologically simulate what real guards experience. To remove any sense of individualism—what Zimbardo called "deindividuation"— they were made to wear identical khaki uniforms and silver reflector sunglasses that kept them out of eye contact (a touch inspired by the movie *Cool Hand Luke*). To promote a feeling of power, they carried billy clubs, handcuffs, whistles, and the keys. They received no specific training as to how they should play their roles. The guards "were free, within limits, to do whatever they thought was necessary to maintain law and order in the prison and to command the respect of the prisoners," Zimbardo said.

Such was the design of the experiment: a hokey prison, an ivory tower professor playing warden, and psychologically normal, volunteer students playing prisoners and guards. The biggest fear most subjects had at the start was that they would be bored.

Day one passed uneventfully. On the morning of the second day, however, a prisoner rebellion broke out. Prisoners removed their caps and numbers and barricaded themselves inside their cells. They began to taunt and curse the guards. When the morning shift of guards arrived, it was decided that something should be done. Zimbardo was startled by what occurred next. "At first they insisted that reinforcements be called in," he recalls. "The two guards who were waiting on stand-by call at home came in, and the night shift of guards voluntarily remained on duty (without extra pay) to bolster the morning shift. The guards met and decided to treat force with force. They got a fire extinguisher that shot a stream of skin-chilling carbon dioxide and forced the prisoners away from the doors; they broke into each cell, stripped the prisoners naked, took the beds out, forced the prisoners who were the ringleaders into solitary confinement, and generally began to harass and intimidate the prisoners."

The prisoners became increasingly despondent and resigned to their condition. They even took responsibility for the treatment they were receiving. Tape recordings of private conversations between the prisoners revealed that 85 percent of their evaluative statements about fellow prisoners were derogatory, in essence suggesting that they had brought it on themselves. Even more surprising was what they talked—and didn't talk—about. There was almost nothing about their lives outside the prison. Ninety percent of their conversation was about prison topics— the bad food, complaints about guards, ingratiation strategies to get a cigarette or other favor. In other words, they sounded like real prisoners.

Some prisoners broke down. In less than thirty-six hours, the staff had to discharge Prisoner 8612 because of "extreme depression, disorganized thinking, uncontrollable crying and fits of rage." The guards released him reluctantly, because they were suspicious he was trying to "con" his way out. "It was unimaginable that a volunteer prisoner in a mock prison could legitimately be disturbed to that extent," says Zimbardo. But over the next three days, three other prisoners had to be released with similar anxiety symptoms. A fifth prisoner was released when he developed a psychosomatic rash over his entire body, an apparent reaction to his parole appeal being rejected by the mock parole board.

Almost all the guards flexed their power to one degree or another. Prisoners were forced to perform tedious, pointless work, such as moving cartons from one closet to another or continuously picking thorns out of blankets (an unpleasant task created by the guards' having dragged the blankets through thorny bushes). They were made to sing songs or laugh or stop smiling on command and were sometimes ordered to curse and malign each other publicly. "The guards had prisoners do push-ups, jumping jacks, whatever the guards could think up, and they increased the length of the counts to several hours each," Zimbardo said. In one case, prisoners were ordered to clean out toilet bowls with their bare hands.

Some guards limited their aggressiveness to a few relatively harmless acts. Others, however, exhibited sinister inventiveness as the experiment proceeded. One particularly aggressive guard explained how he had become caught up in testing the limits of his power: "I was running little experiments of my own. I wanted to see just what kind of verbal abuse people would take before they started objecting, before they started lashing back. . . . And it surprised me that no one said anything to stop me. No one said to me . . . 'You can't say those things. Those things are sick.' . . . I said, 'Go tell that man that he's the scum of the earth' (and they would). They'd do pushups without questioning. They'd sit in the hole. They'd abuse each other. . . . And no one questioned my authority at all. It really shocked me. I started to abuse people so much and started to get so profane—and still no one said anything."[5]

The apparent facility with which guards' behavior changed from good to evil astonished the experimenters. Perhaps the most telling account of this transformation is seen in excerpts from the diary of Guard A:

Prior to start of the experiment: "As I am a pacifist and nonaggressive individual I cannot see a time when I might guard and/or maltreat other living things."

After an orientation meeting: "Buying uniforms at the end of the meeting confirms the game-like atmosphere of this thing. I doubt whether many of us share the expectations of 'seriousness' that the experimenters seem to have."

First Day: ". . . I evolve my first basic strategy—mainly not to smile at anything they say or do which would be admitting it's all a game. . . . At cell 3 I stop and setting my voice hard and low say to 5486, 'What are you smiling at?' 'Nothing, Mr. Correctional Officer.' 'Well, see that you don't.' (As I walk off I feel stupid.)"

Second Day: "5704 asked for a cigarette and I ignored him . . . After we had count and lights out (Guard D) and I held a loud conversation about going home to our girlfriends and what we were going to do to them."

Fourth Day: ". . . The psychologist rebukes me for handcuffing and blindfolding a prisoner before leaving the (counseling) office, and I resentfully reply that it is both necessary security and my business anyway."

Fifth Day: ". . . The real trouble starts at dinner. The new prisoner (416) refuses to eat his sausage . . . we throw him into the Hole ordering him to hold sausages in each hand. We have a crisis of authority; this rebellious conduct potentially undermines the complete control we have over the others. We decide to play upon prisoner solidarity and tell the new one that all the others will be deprived of visitors if he does not eat his dinner. . . . I am very angry at this prisoner for causing discomfort and trouble for the others. I decided to force-feed him, but he wouldn't eat. I let the food slide down his face. I didn't believe it was me doing it. I hated myself for making him eat but I hated him more for not eating."

Sixth Day: "The experiment is over. I feel elated but am shocked to find some other guards disappointed somewhat because of the loss of money and some because they are enjoying themselves."[6]

For all the players—prisoners, guards and, perhaps most telling of all, the psychologist who designed the study—the line between playacting and reality had become dangerously blurred. All became consumed by their make-believe roles. The final straw was the emotional breakdown of Prisoner 819, who went into a rage and then an uncontrollable crying fit. Zimbardo was preparing to prematurely release 819 when one of the guards forced a group of prisoners to stand in a line and chant, "819 is a bad prisoner. Because of what 819 did to prison property we all must suffer," over and over. When Zimbardo realized 819 was hearing this, he rushed to the room where 819 was supposed to be preparing for his release, only to find the young man crying and preparing to go back into the prison to prove to his fellow inmates he wasn't a "bad" prisoner. "He had to be persuaded," Zimbardo says, "that he was not a prisoner at all, that the others were also just students, that this was just an experiment and not a prison and the prison staff were only research psychologists." It was now clear that the experiment had to be stopped.

And so, after six days and nights—"Was it only six?" Zimbardo later asked himself—the planned two-week experiment was aborted. Zimbardo's own transformation was critical in the decision to terminate. "I had become a Prison Superintendent," he observes. "Over time, that role became primary. It was 'My Prison' that I had to secure against rebellion by prisoners, or from alleged break-ins by friends of the prisoners. I began to talk, walk and act like a rigid institutional authority figure more concerned about the security of my prison than the needs of the young men entrusted to my care as psychological researcher. I ended the Stanford Prison Experiment early because I, like my guards, had fallen into the role assignment so thoroughly that it was not clear where my identity ended and the role began." The usually compassionate social psychologist found himself turning into "a Dr. Mengele in the making, a mold into which situational evils were being poured," as he put it. Fortunately for Zimbardo, he was able "to break the mold before it broke me."[7]

***

The Stanford prison brought out the worst in people. My early days of teaching brought out my best. But the psychology in both instances is much the same. New roles create new characters. When the role is unfamiliar and high-pressured, there is no telling who will show up.

Some psychologists conceptualize personality through the metaphor of "man the rat"—the Skinnerian notion that we are basically the sum total of our reinforcement history. Another school of psychology prefers the image of "man the scientist"—that people confront life by methodically applying the scientific method to each new situation. The metaphor currently in vogue is "man the computer"—that we are systematic data processing engines.

With no disrespect to any of these conceptualizations, I believe the human personality is best understood through a different metaphor—that of "man the actor." Social behavior can be thought of as theatrical performance. Backstage, we prepare scripts and develop characters. Onstage, we give our social performances. The sociologist Erving Goffman referred to the process as "the presentation of self in everyday life." The skilled among us know how to read our audience, gauge the part they want us to play, and bring forth the right actor to recite the right script.

To say one "performs" a role sounds more superficial than it is. The original twelfth-century definition of the word "person" was "a character in a drama" or, more to the point, "a mask." It was understood that the roles we play are more than games. They are the essence of who we are and how we relate to each other. Our masks tell the world who we believe ourselves to be or, perhaps, who we'd like to be. In a very real sense, they are us.

Philip Roth eloquently captured people-as-actors in his novel *The Counterlife*, when his alter ego Zuckerman tells his lover:

> There is no you, Maria, any more than there's a me. There is only this way that we have established over the months of performing together, and what it is congruent with isn't "ourselves" but past performances—we're has-beens at heart, routinely trotting out the old, old act. What is the role I demand of you? I couldn't describe it, but I don't have to—you are such a great intuitive actress you *do* it, almost with no direction at all, an extraordinarily controlled and seductive performance. . . . It's *all* impersonation—in the absence of a self, one impersonates selves, and after a while impersonates best the self that best gets one through. . . . All I can tell you with certainty is that I, for one, have no self, and that I am unwilling or unable to perpetrate upon myself the joke of a self. It certainly does strike me as a joke about *my* self. What I have instead is a variety of impersonations I can do, and not only of myself—a troupe of players that I have internalized, a permanent company of actors that I can call upon when a self is required, an ever-evolving stock of pieces and parts that forms my repertoire. But I have no self independent of my imposturing, artistic efforts to have one. Nor would I want one. I am a theater and nothing more than a theater.[8]

***

What begins as acting may, in fact, lead to real inner change. David Myers, the author of the most widely read textbooks in psychology, observes, "If social psychology has taught us anything during the last 25 years, it is that we are likely not only to think ourselves into a way of acting but also to act ourselves into a way of thinking."[9] We are masters at self-persuasion. Studies have shown, for example, that we come to like people we help. And we end up disliking those we hurt.[10] The more often people do or say something, the more they believe it to be true. As a matter of fact, isn't this how we learn about ourselves? As the writer E. M. Forster put it, "How do I know what I think until I see what I say?"[11]

Actors sometimes work this psychology on themselves. British performers, in particular, tend to be proponents of the "outside-in" theory of acting—the belief that it's best to start with the exterior and out of this emerges the inner person. "I have been trained in the English theater [and] I start work from the outside," Tony Award–winning actor Jim Dale explained. "You buy your shoes first. But the shoes for the character. Get used to that. Then, once you see the character in your mind's eye, you get inside him and start working there."[12] Sir Laurence Olivier took the same approach. He began with the costume and then developed the walk, voice, posture, gestures, and mannerisms. The internal character followed spontaneously, he said. "Fake it until you make it," as they say in Alcoholics Anonymous.

Many "performers" in the Stanford experiment sounded as if they had taken a workshop with Olivier. Guard Hellman, looking back at the Stanford experiment, observed: "Once you put a uniform on, and are given a role, I mean, a job, saying 'your job is to keep these people in line,' then you're certainly not the same person if you're in street clothes and in a different role. You really become that person. You put on the khaki uniform, you put on the glasses, you take the nightstick, and you act the part."[13]

In the end, how we act and what we think feed off each other. If you'll excuse the jargon, they fall into a mutually reinforcing feedback loop. We become the part we act and act the part we become, and, once the cycle begins, the two are inseparable. The twelfth-century definition of a self wasn't far off: person, mask, character in a drama—they are not easy to tell apart. Roles don't just trigger performances. They bring new selves to life. These "subselves" join the troupe of actors we call our self. And if this is true, it comes with a warning. As Kurt Vonnegut observed, "We are what we pretend to be, so we must be careful about what we pretend to be."[14]

***

We are remarkably talented performers. In a stage play, the actor gets training and a script. In real life, however, you are assigned a role—prisoner, guard, father, mother, student, college professor—and pushed onstage. There are no rehearsals. This is high-pressure improv. But, for better or worse, we almost always get the job done. We cast, direct, act, and write our own scripts. We're theatrical polymaths, Leonardos of the human stage.

The source of our genius is a profound mystery. There's a powerful team below the surface: the voices of our parents and teachers, the movies we've seen, the books we've read, and, not to be underestimated, the information inherited through our wiring. There are times when the character seems to arrive fully formed, as if uploaded from some secret library in our cortex. Other times it feels as if the script is being fed to us line-by-line, as if it was being created on the spot by an emergency writer. Who/where/what is this creative team that waits on-call 24/7 for new work orders? I like to imagine F. Scott Fitzgerald in his Hollywood years lingering in his MGM bungalow. Mostly, he waited. But at any moment a breathless messenger might burst in with an emergency assignment from David Selznick or some other big shot to fix anything from a sliver of dialogue to working up a whole new character.

How many selves does a person possess? The legendary psychologist William James observed that "a man has as many social selves as there are individuals who recognize him and carry an image of him in their mind . . . he has as many different social selves as there are distinct groups of persons about whose opinions he cares."[15] I like to envision the entirety of my potential cast—past, present, and future, in a room. Are there enough me to fill a lecture hall? Could little ol' me sell out Madison Square Garden?

Whatever the precise number, there are many more than we will meet in our lifetime. Perhaps this is the true meaning of "self-potential." After all, striving to become a better person requires striving to become a different person.

***

Looking back at that first day of teaching, I appreciate how well things worked out. I know plenty of colleagues who experienced less pleasant transformations. I recently conducted informal interviews with self-described burnt-out instructors I know. One colleague told me the role turns him into a control freak. He says he hates himself for it, but, even after years of struggle, he can't seem to turn it off. The feeling surprises him, he says, because he tends to be a welcoming, laid-back guy in most other situations. Another colleague told me she can't stand how critical she gets with students. Then she gets critical with herself for being so critical. Several reported they feel their confidence drain the moment they get in front of a class. A now-retired professor told me he would get so nervous before giving a lecture, every lecture, that he allowed a few extra minutes before class in case he had to throw up. He retired as soon as he could afford to. A very successful, well-respected colleague told me that no matter what he accomplishes, he always feels like a phony. "The more I accomplish," he says, "the more the impostor syndrome raises its dirty head." I, obviously, was very lucky.

Predicting success in my profession is a lot like something football scouts call "the quarterback problem," in reference to the historically consistent failure rates professional teams have had trying to draft good quarterbacks. They sometimes point to the 1999 college draft, for example, which appeared so rich in quarterback potential that five college quarterback stars were picked by teams in the first round. Four of the five, however, turned into very expensive busts: one fizzled out after a few decent games, and the other three never produced at all. One even ended up failing in the Canadian Football League after he lost his NFL job. Only one of the five (Donovan McNabb) went on to a successful career. In other words, some of the best scouts in America, armed with all their experience, data, and resources, had a grand hit rate of 20 percent. The problem, scouts explain, is that it is very difficult to know whether a quarterback who has dominated against less talented college opponents will be able to raise his game to the demands of professional competition.[16]

Like quarterbacks, the role of a professor is typically so novel that it necessitates not just a quantitative but a qualitative transformation.

What kind of teacher will the novice become? That, as I learned, is an awfully tough question to answer. The most we can say is that it will probably be someone very different from anything he or she was before. The same is true for any profession that requires a sudden transition.

Being an educator, I'm surrounded by students trying to decide what to do with their lives. I advise them that, whatever profession they're considering, to give it an early test run. Try the role on for size. If it's teaching, perhaps become a classroom volunteer. Ask to supervise a lesson or, even better, present a guest lecture. One thing I guarantee is that it will bring out a new facet of themselves. If they do their homework better than I did, they won't have to wait until their first day on the job to find out what that will turn out to be.

Most of all, however, I use the opportunity to teach them two of the most important lessons I've learned as a social psychologist: First, that social situations are enormously and deceivingly powerful and, second, that what we identify as our self is really a multiplicity of characters, any of which can be elicited by the particulars of a time and place.

***

There is a simple psychological test you might try. Write the question "Who am I?" across the top of a sheet of paper. Then list the first twenty answers that come to mind. Work quickly, answering in a word or phrase, with a minimum of self-censorship.[17] When you are done, read through the list. How well does it describe you? What is your impression of the person you have described? Now, ask two people who know you well to give their own twenty answers to the question about *you*. You might, for example, ask one of your parents and an intimate friend or lover to do this. Write the question "Who is (your name)?" across the top of a page and have them write out the first twenty answers that come to their minds. Compare the answers on the three (your and their two) lists. How many answers on the three lists overlap? Do you think an outsider would know the three were the same person? More important, however, where are the differences? Which descriptions appear on only some of the lists? Which of these contradict each other?

Next, cross out the differences that have less to do with you than the needs and expectations of the raters. Say, for example, your mother is the only one who wrote "brilliant" to describe you. Perhaps this has less to do with your actual brilliance than the fact that your mother wants to see you that way. Or, maybe your lover was the only one who described you as "overcontrolling" when, in truth, the real problem lies in his issues with women. This should leave the differences between the lists that are attributable to you. In other words, these are ways that you actually become a different person with different people. Think about this troupe of players—the versions of you that appear to your parents, to each of your friends, to your lover, your teachers, at work, at home, on first dates, at family gatherings. Imagine inviting this entire group to your house for dinner. Introduce them around. Would they recognize each other? Would they get along? What would they talk about?

And, finally, do you think you would like them? I can't think of a more important question.

14
A Geography of the Self

The squeaky wheel gets the grease.
—Popular saying in the United States

Deru kugi ha utareru.
(A nail that sticks out must be hammered down.)
—Popular saying in Japan

It is human to act differently in different situations. This the reality.[1] But it is a notion that not everyone embraces. Some people believe multiplicity and flexibility are virtues; others condemn these qualities as moral shortcomings. Are they weaknesses to be discouraged or skills to be honed? Is role playing disingenuous, or is it one's essential social obligation? The answers to questions like these profoundly affect the way people conceive of themselves and how they conduct their lives. And, it turns out, these differences are often less a matter of who you are than where you come from. They are, more than anything, about culture, which we turn to in this chapter.

***

Several years ago, I served as a visiting professor in Sapporo, Japan.[2] My primary host was a sweet, smart, and extremely capable young faculty member named Suguru Sato. Sato, in classic Japanese fashion, was absolutely dedicated to his job. Everyone in his department worked hard. But Sato, who was the most junior professor, took it to another level. He worked six days a week, frequently from early morning until midnight and took at most two or three vacation days a year. His work was his life, and his accomplishments were impressive.

There is nothing singularly Japanese about junior professors working harder than their big shot colleagues. Practically every one I've known in the United States also feels more pressure to publish, obtain grants, teach, and serve on committees that no one else wants to join. But Sato's chores didn't stop there. He was also expected to fulfill social obligations on a scale that a foreigner like me found hard to fathom. I came to see that the biggest difference between the work of professors in Japan and the United States were the social obligations. No matter how busy he was, Sato was expected not only to attend every scheduled social event but to be available to his colleagues 24/7 for any even the most informal of gatherings.

Not once, for example, did I see Sato leave lunch before his less-rushed seniors finished eating and chatting. Over the course of that semester, even on days when he was too busy to sleep more than a few hours a night, Sato would watch entire baseball games on television with his colleagues. Or he would play, or even just watch his colleagues play, two- to three-hour marathons of the board game *Goban* (Go). At least once a week, they all went bar-hopping into the early morning hours, and Sato never once left before anyone else. And, no matter what they did together, he always looked as if there was nothing he would rather be doing then spending this time with his friends. He seamlessly and enthusiastically transformed himself into whatever companion his colleagues wanted from him.

Sato didn't dislike these activities. But, he explained to me, whether he did or didn't wasn't the point. He understood that happily participating—more precisely, to appear to be happily participating—was a crucial part of his job. In my mind, these social activities were wasted time. Sato had real work to do. To him, however, playing the part—to become whatever person his colleagues needed him to be—was anything but wasted. The most important of all Japanese social values is *wa*, or harmony, and Sato's performances were essential to the *wa* of his department and, in turn, his university. It was, he believed, the most important aspect of his job—or, put another way, the component of his job where poor performance would be least excusable.

Once, for example, I noticed on Sato's résumé that his department colleagues—there were three senior professors in his small department—were listed as coauthors on most of his publications. I try to avoid judging my hosts when I'm a guest in their culture. But this got under my skin. "These are your ideas. You ran the studies. You analyzed the data. You wrote up the papers," I said. "Why won't you take all the credit? We both know it's what you deserve."

This, Sato said, would be bad for everyone concerned, above all for himself. He explained: from the earliest age, children in Japan are taught to devote themselves to the group. This doesn't mean that they themselves don't count. But they are taught that their own welfare is inexorably tied to that of the groups they are part of. Personal success is measured by the prosperity of the larger collective—your classmates, friends, eventual co-workers and, ultimately, your fellow Japanese citizens. Any hint of selfish individualism upsets the *wa*. That, in turn, leads the group to chastise or even reject the selfish offender—a wicked punishment in a culture where one's group counts more than anything.

Compare this with the United States, where children are taught to rise above the crowd. Kindergarteners—five-year-olds, for God's sake—compete to be "Student of the Month." If a student in Japan got singled out for an award like that, his or her parents would be mortified. In America, parents advertise the news on their car bumpers. In the United States, it is said that "the squeaky wheel gets the grease." In Japan, one is taught *Deru kugi ha utareru* (A nail that sticks out must be hammered down). In one national survey, "ordinary" (*heibon*) was cited by the majority of Japanese as the most desirable thing to be.

***

Our differences, I came to understand, reflected a profound cultural divide. Americans are individualists. We tend to believe that the welfare of the individual and one's nuclear family takes precedence over that of the extended group. The Japanese are collectivists. They believe one's own needs count less than what you contribute to the *wa*.

Individualists resonate with Shakespeare's observation: "To thine own self be true, and it must follow, as the night the day, thou canst not then be false to any man." Americans—the poster children for the individualist point of view—generally dislike thinking of ourselves as performers. It sounds so superficial. Worse yet, it seems devoid of a moral compass. How does one trust people who transform themselves to suit the audience of the moment? They are chameleons—pretty at the moment, perhaps, but who are they at the end of the day? This is the M.O. of hypocrites and manipulators, or even psychopaths.

Americans tend to regard self-consistency as a moral virtue. Our icons of integrity know who they are, remain true to themselves, and could care less what others think of them. Andy Warhol wouldn't add a little green to a painting to please a collector. Albert Einstein didn't modify his theory of relativity depending on the audience. Martin Luther King Jr. didn't water down his demands when confronted with a racist politician. Call it the "I'll do it my way" school of thought, in honor of that legendary Western social philosopher, Mr. Frank Sinatra.

The Japanese—seemingly always Exhibit A for the collectivist point of view—look at this very differently. If everyone does it his or her way, won't we be stepping all over each other? And, so, children are taught that they all must understand their place and play their part. Doing what is expected isn't simply acceptable in Japan. It is a moral virtue. If achieving *wa* requires a bit of performing, then so be it. The Japanese distinguish between *honne*—one's true feelings—and *tatemai*—the face one wears in public. When one's *honne* is at odds with the harmony of the group, mature people rise above their own selfish feelings. What Americans may perceive as phoniness and hypocritical behavior is not only tolerated in Japan but esteemed as good character.

***

Let us return to the topic of acting (see last chapter). In the West, actors try to appear informal and natural. A good actor makes the audience forget it is all fake. Think of method acting—Robert De Niro in *Raging Bull* or Meryl Streep in anything. In Japan, it is often the other way around. Traditional actors don't care about hiding the fake. "On the contrary," observes Ian Baruma, who has written extensively about Japanese arts and society, "artificiality is often appreciated for its own sake. Performers do not try to seem informal or real, for it is the form, the art of faking, if you like, that is the whole point of the exercise."[3] Perhaps the most blatant examples are the stylized patterns (known as *kata*) in traditional Japanese arts, such as Kabuki theater, which leave almost no room for personal expression.[4]

This tight choreography spills into real life in Japan, where a person of good character, like Sato, understands the importance of playing different roles. "Acting, that is, presenting oneself consciously in a certain prescribed way, is a part of social life everywhere" in Japan, says Baruma. "People in the West are so obsessed with appearing 'genuine' that they fool themselves they are not acting, that they are, well . . . real." In the extreme, even rudeness or hurting another person is seen as "a commendably honest way of 'being oneself'" in the West. In Japan, on the other hand, it's simply self-centered arrogance. The Japanese are remarkably polite people. And, being this way, they spend most of their time acting.

Then again, who is to say whether acting is any less honest than nonacting? As Oscar Wilde—a Westerner, of all things—observed: "Man is least himself when he talks in his own person. Give him a mask and he will tell you the truth."[5]

***

Let's return to the "Who am I?" test from the previous chapter. Americans generally come up with twenty answers fairly quickly. These answers tend to be in the form of sweeping psychological traits. For example, they might say "I am kind" or "I am outgoing."

Social psychologist Stephen Cousins, at the time a professor at a Japanese university, found that students there responded very differently to the same question. The Japanese, unlike Americans, had a hard time coming up with twenty answers. And the ones they gave weren't particularly informative. They tended to list narrowly defined roles (for example, "I am Yuko's mother"; "I am a professor at Keio University") or specific behaviors ("I play mah-jongg on Friday nights"; "I play tennis on the weekend") or they simply stated physical characteristics ("I am 167 cm. tall").[6] They rarely listed traits, however. To Americans, it might seem the Japanese had little to say about the person they are, their inner core.

Cousins then tried a different approach. He again posed the "Who am I?" question. This time, however, he attached specific contexts to the question: Who are you at home? Who are you at school? Who are you when you're with close friends? Contextualizing in this way made all the difference. The Japanese now described themselves with even more personality traits than Americans did. But these traits varied depending on the context.

In Japan, the person and the role are inseparable. Sato may create one version of himself for, say, his boss and a different version for his best friend. But, to him, there's nothing phony about this. Both of these are Sato's selves. Both have their own integrity. Selfness in Japan "is not a constant," the Japanese scholar Hamaguchi Esyun has observed.[7] Rather, it "denotes a fluid concept which changes through time and situations according to interpersonal relationships." It is the totality of these social selves that define a person's conception of who he or she is.

The notion that "A man's gotta be what a man's gotta be"—to quote that other great Western philosopher, Mr. John Wayne (aka The Duke)— is a recipe for trouble in Japan. Behaving true to one's *honne*, which by its very nature requires playing without a script, is best left for those water buffalo Americans and their individualist colleagues. Among the Japanese, it is expected that different you's will show up in different situations. One must answer to the *wa*.

***

The longer the time I spent with the Japanese, the more I came to admire their skill at reading situations. In the lingo of cross-cultural psychology, Japan is what is called a "high context" culture. When the Japanese enter a situation, they study the entire context. If, for example, the Japanese are shown a photo with a prominent person in the foreground and a group of lesser-known people in the background, they will, if questioned, tell you about the entire group. Americans, on the other hand, focus on the prominent person and will usually recall little or nothing about the people in the background. Needless to say, we Americans score low on lists of contextualist cultures.

When I am at home in the United States, I think of myself as a pretty sensitive guy. But in Japan I watched my hosts weave seamlessly from one gathering to another, reading the subtlest of cues with a grace and subtlety beyond my vision. Compared with them, I must have seemed empathy-challenged. I can't tell you how many times I apologized for saying the wrong thing or asking the wrong question. (The only reason my hosts never called me a pathetic boor, I figured, was because they were such polite people. It wouldn't be that way with my fellow Americans, I can assure you.)

The Japanese find it hard to conceive of a "me" outside a social context. The self is a social product. If you care about other people, they might ask, how could you believe otherwise?

***

The Japanese way of thinking is common in many countries.[8] In China, for example, there is a famous saying: "Cut toes, fit shoe." A person not only *can* be malleable but *should* be malleable. The Chinese "are situation-centered. They are obliged to be sensitive to their environment," observes the psychologist Chi-yue Chiu. "Americans are individual-centered. They expect their environment to cater to them."[9]

In China, as in Japan, parents place little importance on individual identity. A recent survey found only 8 percent of Chinese mothers, compared with 64 percent of European-American mothers, believe that building a "sense of themselves" should be an important goal of child rearing.[10] Westerners emphasize individualism and competition. Chinese parents teach about community, cooperation, and interrelatedness.[11]

India, the spiritual cradle of selflessness, also emphasizes context. One study found that Indians were three times as likely as Americans to specify a context when describing their peers. Where Americans might use generalizations like "He is cheap," Indians are more likely to say things like "He is hesitant to give money away to his family."[12]

***

My students Gary Hagy, Ruthie Lichtenstein, and Michelle Fabros, and I, with the assistance of a team of international researchers,[13] have compared these ways of thinking in a variety of nations. In one survey, we asked people what they thought of a person "who willingly changes his or her behavior to suit different people and different situations." We asked our question in three traditionally collectivistic Asian countries—China, India, and Nepal—and two individualistic countries in the Americas—the United States and Brazil.[14] There were clear differences. The collectivists tended to use words like "mature," "honest," "trustworthy," and "sincere" to describe the changeling. Individualists were more likely to use words like "dishonest," "untrustworthy," and "insincere." In some comparisons, the patterns of responses were mirror opposites. For example, the Indians were almost four times more likely than Brazilians (75.2 percent vs. 19.6 percent) to describe the changeling as a sincere person.

The notion of sincerity didn't mean much to anyone until recently. There is no evidence the word "sincerity" even existed in the English language until the fourteenth century, observes R. Jay Magill in his book *Sincerity*. Even then, it initially referred to physical objects—say, how much copper was in a coin or the purity of your water. It would be another two hundred years before the term took hold in the sense it does among individualists today—"the twin ideals that insist you say what you feel and be true to who you are."[15] The watershed was capitalist expansion. A new type of city emerged where, for the first time, people were encountering strangers on a regular basis and, as a result, it became fashionable to conceal one's true self. Ornaments like wigs, rouge, and fans became fashionable. There were strict rules for good manners. Social life, Magill observes, had become "an elaborated lie." This is when it became important to distinguish appearance from "truth."

"How can you become immediately the friend of a man whom you have never seen before?" Rousseau wrote. "The true human interest, the plain and noble effusion of an honest soul—these speak a language far different from the insincere demonstration of politeness (and the false appearance) which the custom of the great world demand."[16] Or, as Holden Caulfield put it years later in *The Catcher in the Rye*, "Grand. There's a word I really hate. It's a phony. I could puke everytime I hear it."[17]

In the United States, we mistrust people who waver too much.[18] Any political consultant in America will tell a candidate that it's better to be an inflexible dogmatist than too open-minded. Stay "on message," and, God forbid, don't be a "flip-flopper." In countries like China and Japan, it's the other way around. Cut toes, fit shoes. What is inconsistency and hypocrisy in one part of the world is morally esteemed in another. It's easy to see how these beliefs become self-perpetuating. The more a group of people value self-consistency, the greater the benefits of adhering to that norm. And the more people adhere, the more the norm is valued. As the cycle gathers steam, it feeds on itself.[19]

***

When push comes to shove, which is more important: The welfare of yourself and your nuclear family or that of your larger group and community? This is the essence of the individualism-collectivism question. Individualists are offended by a person who changes personae to fit the situation. They believe in consistency, sincerity, and singularity. Collectivists not only approve of bringing out multiple selves but believe that a person who insists on consistency, sincerity, and singularity no matter the situation is socially deficient. But there is a more basic division between individualists and collectivists that brings us back to the very meaning of "the self." Where does one draw the boundary between oneself and others, and how porous is the boundary between the two? We have tackled these questions from the biological and cognitive perspectives in earlier chapters. To these, we shall now add the impact of culture.

In another study, my students Ann-Marie Clayton and Arantes Armendariz and I asked people from different countries to illustrate their conceptions of the self. To ease the task, we gave them a series of cutout circles, each labeled with the name of one of eight characters: Self, Father, Mother, Sibling, Romantic partner, Friend, Co-worker, and Stranger. There were four different size circles (very small, small, medium, and large) for each of the eight people. All told, then, they began with thirty-two circles. The respondents were asked to think about each of the eight individuals as they existed in their social world. They were then instructed to, first, select the circle for each person that represented the relative "size" they imagined each of the eight people to be. And, second, they were instructed to arrange the eight circles they had chosen into a "picture" that described their image of how all of them fit together.

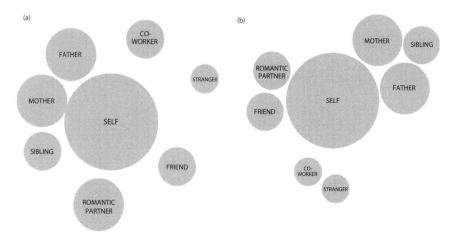

Fig. 1. Examples of drawings of an independent view of the self (United States).

We began our study with Anglo-Americans. Not surprisingly, no two pictures were exactly alike. But almost all reflected what psychologists call an "independent" view of the self.[20] Next, we asked a group of Americans of East Asian descent, most of whom were from Japan and China, to arrange the circles. Before we began, I showed some of the Anglo-Americans' drawings to my own university colleague Hong Ni, a psychology professor who grew up in Nanjing, China. Hong's first words were: "I can't believe this is what Americans think." I asked whether these pictures would make any sense in China. "No, no, no. It feels all wrong." Two problems jumped out at her: First, "The self is too big." Second: "Why are there spaces between the circles?"

The illustrations from our sample of East Asians underscored Ni's comments. There were, as with Americans, individual variations. Some, for example, used the biggest circle for their mother. This was often the case of Japanese respondents. Others chose the biggest circle for their father. This was more often true among the Chinese. But almost all the drawings described an "interdependent" view of the self. In the two typical examples shown, the assemblage labeled (a) was created by a Japanese woman and the one labeled (b) is by a Chinese woman.

Think about this. If you were raised in the United States, you will probably spend your life feeling that you are an independent human being at the center of your personal universe. But, if by a twist of fate you

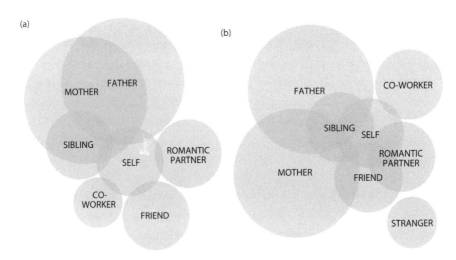

Fig. 2. Examples of an interdependent view of the self: (a) Japan, (b) China.

had been born in Japan or China, you would think of yourself as a subordinate player whose identity was inseparable from the people around you. It would be an entirely different sense of what it means to be a person.

∗∗∗

These values are communicated practically from day one. In America, parents like their babies to get used to sleeping in their own beds pretty much from the get-go. If possible, they get their own bedroom. It is very different in other cultures. In most of the world, babies sleep in the same bed as their siblings and/or their parents. Their own bedroom? In a survey of child-rearing practices in one hundred societies conducted several years ago, anthropologists Roger Burton and John Whiting found that American parents were the only ones who cared much about creating a separate room for their young one.[21]

It is not just an issue of available space. These preferences are driven by deeply rooted convictions about who we are. American parents strive for an ideal of autonomy. Our children, we believe, "are needy and fragile and should be encouraged to be alone at night so that they can learn to be self-reliant and independent and to care for themselves," observes

Roger Shweder, a cultural anthropologist at the University of Chicago. In most other cultures, however, children are seen as vulnerable beings who need to be protected and nurtured through increasingly interdependent relationships if they are to properly develop. Asking a baby to sleep alone would be considered child abuse, Schweder observes.[22]

This is certainly the case in Japan. When Japanese parents don't have a big enough bed to host their child, it is often the father who gets sent to sleep somewhere else.[23] Japanese mothers aren't just apathetic about independence. They try to shower their child with so much supportive and uncritical love that the psychological boundaries between the two of them become blurred—creating what's known in Japan as *amae*. Mothers see their children as extensions of themselves and, through *amae*, they establish a permanent, inescapable bond. This may sound overbearing to many Americans. But, from the Japanese viewpoint, it is the most important gift a mother can give a child: the irrevocable understanding that one will never be alone. The feeling of *amae* persists throughout life, spreading to other important people and groups in one's social and work worlds. Adults strive for a more mature form of dependence in these relationships. But what they don't strive for is independence.

A few years back, Japanese and American researchers at the University of Michigan's Institute for Social Research wanted to compare the closeness adults felt toward their mothers in their respective countries. The answers poured in practically before the study got started. One of the first tasks was to develop a set of questions. The Japanese researchers insisted the response scale should include the option "I want to be with my mother all the time." The Americans thought this would look so ridiculous that people wouldn't take the questions seriously.[24] The researchers eventually reached a compromise, but their differences were as informative as the subsequent data they collected. In America, we call him a "momma's boy." In Japan he's a well-adjusted son.

The differences appear at the neurological level as well. There is an area in the brain called the medial prefrontal cortex (MPFC) that lights up when we process self-referential information. But what if one is from a culture that blurs the boundary between you and another person? Psychologist Ying Zhu and his colleagues tested this question by hooking up groups of native Chinese and Westerners (American, English, Canadian, and Australian) to fMRIs and then asking them to describe both themselves and their mothers. Not surprisingly, both groups showed increased MPFC activity when they were describing themselves. After all, what could be a more self-referential activity? When describing their mothers, however, it was as if the two groups had been asked different questions. There were virtually no increases in MPFC activity when Westerners thought about their mothers. The interdependent Chinese, on the other hand, had as much MPFC activity when they were describing their mother as they did when they were describing themselves. Self and mother merged at the neural level.[25]

***

When you grow up believing that you and your mother are inseparable, it stays with you. For a dramatic example, consider the experience of Amy Chua. Chua is a first-generation Chinese-American who, at first glance, seems completely integrated into American culture. Professionally, she is a highly respected Yale Law School professor and, personally, she is married to a Jewish husband. But when it came time to raise children, her Chinese training took center stage.

In her bestselling book, *Battle Hymn of the Tiger Mom*, Chua describes how she raised her children the same way her immigrant parents tried to raise her: with an uncompromising program of nonstop, punishing labor. Her two daughters sat through relentless sessions of piano and violin practice and, when these were over, seemingly endless hours of homework. There were no sleepovers. No missed assignments. No grades below A. Ms. Chua supervised these activities with a dictatorial regimen of taunting, scolding, screaming, and intimidation.

In a typical example, she tells of an occasion when she had been arguing with her younger daughter, Lulu, who wanted to give up trying to learn a difficult piano piece. "I hauled Lulu's dollhouse to the car and told her I'd donate it to the Salvation Army piece by piece if she didn't have 'The Little White Donkey' perfect by the next day. I threatened her with no lunch, no dinner, no Christmas or Hanukkah presents, no birthday parties for two, three, four years. I told her to stop being lazy, cowardly, self-indulgent and pathetic."

Chua gives new meaning to the term "helicopter parent." She doesn't just hover above. She moves inside her children's heads. Chua recalls how once, during a practice session, Lulu screamed out:

"Stop it, Mommy. Just stop it."

"Lulu, I didn't say anything," I replied. "I didn't say one word."

"Your brain is annoying me," Lulu said. "I know what you're thinking."

"I'm not thinking anything," I said indignantly. Actually, I'd been thinking that Lulu's right elbow was too high, that her dynamics were all wrong, and that she needed to shape her phrases better.

"Just turn off your brain!" Lulu ordered. "I'm not going to play anymore unless you turn off your brain."

Chua accomplished her goals. Each of her daughters has achieved extraordinary success in both music and academics. They also feel very close to their mother and, for the most part we're told, grateful for where she has brought them. American mothers—who bought Chua's book in great numbers—yearn for successes like these in their own children. But they were repulsed by her methods. When an article about Chua's parenting practices appeared in the *Wall Street Journal*, nearly ten thousand readers sent in comments calling her everything from an obnoxious bully to dangerous and far worse.[26]

Chinese readers, however, both in the United States and China, mostly saw Chua as she saw herself: a tireless, loving mother who gave every ounce of herself for her daughters. There was considerable debate over the harshness of her discipline but not about her motives. It was generally understood that the relentless authoritarianism was evidence of a loving mother passionately dedicated to the betterment of her children in the traditional Chinese style.

"Here's a question I often get," says Chua: "'Who are you doing all this pushing for—your daughters'—and here always the cocked head, the knowing tone—'or yourself?'" Chua has a firm answer: "Everything I do is unequivocally 100% for my daughters." This, of course, is the same answer an American helicopter parent might give. But whereas the claim sounds like self-justification from a needy mother in the case of zealous Americans, it follows sensibly and logically from Chinese teachings in

Chua's case. "I find this a very Western question to ask," she says. "Because in Chinese thinking, the child is the extension of the self."[27]

Are you doing this for your child or for yourself? The question is meaningless when there's no boundary between the two.

***

It is even difficult to find a single word for an independent or individualistic self in many languages. In Japanese, for example, there are different terms for "I" depending on who is speaking, whom the person is addressing, and the particular situation. "When a man refers to himself in relation to his college chums he might say *Boku* or *Ore*," observes cross-cultural psychologist Richard Nisbett. "When a father talks to his child he says *Otosan* (Dad). A young girl might refer to herself by her nickname when talking to a family member: 'Tomo is going to school today.'"[28] The Japanese word for "self" is *jibun*, which literally translates as "one's share," the implication being the share of the social context in which one exists. Outside a context, there is no self.

There is no single word in the Chinese language for "individualism." The closest equivalent is a term that literally translates to "selfishness." The word "benevolence" is represented by the character *jên*, which means "two men." The same holds true when one speaks of another individual. "In Korean, the sentence 'Could you come to dinner?' requires different words for 'you,' which is common in many languages, but also for 'dinner,' depending on whether one was inviting a student or professor," Nisbett observes. This is more than simply politeness. It reflects an understanding that one is expected to become a different person in different situations and with different people.

***

Ethnocentrism is a universal myopia. Every culture believes its own ways of thinking—its shared values, beliefs, and practices—are the normal ones, that is, the norms. This is certainly the case when it comes to conceptions of the self. If you are raised to believe people are ultimately separate and individual, then it is difficult to accept a philosophy that sees otherwise; and, of course, the reverse is equally true.

Assume you could strip away everything you have been raised to believe. Would what is left more closely resemble the interdependent conception of the Japanese or the individualistic version I grew up with? I've thought about this question often since living in Japan. And I think I've finally figured out an answer. At the risk of insulting people from the East *and* the West, I believe that we're mostly like a colony of ants.[29] Allow me to explain.

Individual ants are simple creatures. They are capable of only a few basic actions, their memory is limited, and, when it comes to intelligence, they are not the brightest bulbs in the room. After all, their brains are about one-millionth the size of our own. Put them in a colony, however, and these modest creatures are something else entirely. Ant colonies are huge. A single colony of the *Atta sexdens* species, for example, may contain as many as eight million ants, just a little less than the population of Paris.[30] But unlike the people of Paris, or practically any other human collective I'm familiar with, the system works.

Ants are the only animal besides humans who appear to grow and process their own food. They also construct their own housing. When I lived in Brazil early in my career, I would routinely come across huge mounds of sculpted dirt, often ten or more feet across, with dozens of turrets protruding from its surface. They looked like fantastic sand castles. It turned out they were rooftops of a colony's living quarters. Below the surface was a vastly larger, multiunit apartment complex (that is, the ant nest), complete with networks of roads, tunnels, and bridges. The turrets were part of a ventilation system circulating air throughout the nest. It was a city built by ants.

How can so many stupid creatures, with no boss, add up to be so smart? How does such complexity emerge from a group where there is no leader and everyone in town is stupid? Scientists turn giddy when they speak about ant societies. They marvel at "the mind of the colony." Computer designers and brain scientists use them as models for their own designs. These are interdependent selves at their finest.

But there is another way of looking at them. Squint down, and you see rugged individualists. Think about the food gatherers, for example, who hike deep into the forest to bite off pieces of the right leaves, which they then toss over their backs and carry all the way home. These loads can be huge. An individual leafcutter can handle close to ten times its own weight, which is the equivalent of a two-hundred-pound human carrying five four-hundred-pound refrigerators.

Watch that tiny creature struggle with those five refrigerators on its shoulders, stopping and starting, shifting the weight back and forth, trudging forward no matter how formidable the obstacle in its path. Excuse the anthropomorphism, but I, for one, can't help but revering them as courageous athletes at these moments. I know they are programmed to be little socialists. But that is just the backstory. When they are flinging those barbells across their backs, I want to applaud their individual effort.

Are humans so different? I recently attended the annual conference of the American Psychological Association (APA) in Washington, D.C. More than thirteen thousand of my colleagues were scampering about, attending meetings, listening to lectures, flitting from one poster to another, catching up with old acquaintances, pitching their own stuff to people they wanted to impress. At one point, as I was looking down from a balcony, I couldn't help but thinking of a giant colony of ants moving in quirky unison, jutting closer then further apart from each other, bursts of communication followed by abrupt good-byes as they went back to doing their own thing. They might as well have been brushing each other's antennae. On Monday morning, we were mostly back at our own desks in our own offices working with all our might on our own projects. Perhaps some of us were thinking that if we worked extra hard it might be our turn to win a big APA award next year. Individualists to the core.

From a grander perspective, however, there is the anthill of psychology. The discipline doesn't care whether I or my colleague down the hall conducts the next great experiment; all that's important is that it gets conducted. Science is what matters, and scientists make science. I like to think of us as ants building an arch. We begin in separate places but meet up somewhere along the way to produce something bigger than any of us might have predicted. We march to the mind of the colony. Individualists just don't think of it this way. Collectivists do.

If you happen to have been raised as a full-blooded individualist, here's something to consider: numerically, you're the freak. The independent view is pretty much limited to the United States and parts of Europe. The interdependent view predominates to one degree or another almost everywhere else. "If we took a headcount around the world, we would surely find that most people participate in collectivistic cultures where interdependent selves are more common," observes cross-cultural psychologist Steven Heine. More than 80 percent of the world's cultures, Heine estimates, find it hard to conceive of a truly separate self.[31] In other words, if we define normal as "the norm," then the notion of an independent self is clearly abnormal. Whether this preference serves people best is another matter. But it is certainly how most of the world sees it.

***

Is it sincere or playacting? Are we hypocrites or team players? Independent or interdependent? These are the wrong questions. As they might say in quantum physics, we are sometimes particles and sometimes waves. It is a messy reality. But it also oozes with possibilities.

My own advice is to recognize the narrowness of one's cultural dogma. The actor-writer Peter Ustinov once described hell as "Italian punctuality, German humour, and English wine." These are stereotypes, to be sure, but they contain kernels of truth. Such is the danger of ethnocentrism. Why not pirate the best of other cultures? This doesn't mean discarding what we have been taught but simply opening oneself to other ways of thinking. There are times when it is best to swallow the hard "reality" that you are ultimately alone. If, say, you have an assignment due the next morning, and it's 2 a.m., and you've been staring out the window since dinner, it's probably wise to conclude that you're in this fix alone, so you'd better shut off your phone and just get to it. But there are also times when the "reality" that we are profoundly connected with each other gives us strength. It can be both comforting and productive to recognize that, in the most profound way, we're all in this together. If assuming people are independent and separate helps get you overcome a challenge, then I say, use it. If, on the other hand, you feel empowered by a belief in interdependence and inseparability from others, embrace that.

One thing is for sure: The more tools in your arsenal, the greater your options.

15
Finding the Schindler Button

All the lives we could live, all the people we will never know,
never will be, they are everywhere. That is what the world is.
—Aleksandar Hemon, *The Lazarus Project*

How odd to think of the versions of me I've known. There are memories of the first day of kindergarten, of graduating grammar school, getting into trouble in high school, being a young professor, having a young son. (The accuracy of these memories is another matter.) I somehow claim all these people as the person I call myself. But how can that be, when they are so different from one another? I'm more similar to practically every adult in my life than I am to that five-year-old in kindergarten. Really, what do I have in common with that little boy except some chromosomes? What would could we possibly talk about? Yet I am convinced the five-year-old is me and my closest friend is not.

I'm not denying that people have a core. Each of us brings our particular combination of physical and personality dispositions to any situation, and some of these dispositions remain stable throughout our lives. But that stability is oh, so relative.

My friend Miranda is a good example. In an informal study, I asked a group of acquaintances, Miranda included, to rate themselves from 0 to 10 on a series of personality traits. Their answers were within a couple of points of each other on most items. When it came to "extroversion," however, Miranda had far and away the highest score. It didn't surprise her. She told me she had thought of herself this way for as long as she could remember. It was, in fact, the first term she would use to describe herself.

I asked Miranda to keep an activity diary for one waking day. I gave her a portable electronic device that was programmed to "beep" at random intervals, on average three times each hour. This is referred to as the "experience sampling" technique. Each time she heard the signal, Miranda was to record (1) the activity she was currently engaged in, and (2) how extroverted she had been since this activity began. She made forty-five entries over the course of the day. And on how many of these forty-five did she rate herself as extroverted? A grand total of twelve—fewer than one out of three. But when we looked at what she was doing the other thirty-three times, it made perfect sense. Miranda recorded no signs of extroversion when she was

- with friends but felt exhausted (two entries)

- talking to an aggressive guy she was trying to discourage (two entries, both with the same guy)

- with a friend she described as exasperatingly hyperactive (one entry)

- trying to get her mom off the phone (one entry)

- alone (twenty-seven entries)

I rate myself closer to average (5) when it comes to extroversion, much lower than Miranda. This was confirmed when I chronicled my own activities for a day. I made forty-three entries. (I took a nap that afternoon, thus the fewer entries). Of those, I recorded only five occasions when I was extroverted—fewer than half as many as Miranda. So Miranda does score higher than me on extroversion. She is more likely to be extroverted than I am in certain social situations, and she is more likely to engage in these situations. But in the grander scheme of her life, the extrovert is one persona among many. And, like each of her personas, it is dormant much more than it is active. In other words, most of the time Miranda is no more extroverted than me or anyone else. "There is as much difference between us and ourselves as between us and others," as Montaigne observed many years ago.[1]

The characteristics we identify with are hit-and-miss affairs that come and go depending on the time and place. We are all dramatically more outgoing with some people, in some situations, and in particular stages of life. Turn the next corner, and who knows how extroverted you will be. It is practically our mantra in social psychology to never underestimate the power of the situation. Study after study has demonstrated that the characteristics of a time and place are often better predictors of how people will act than the type of person they supposedly are.[2] The situation creates the person.

These findings have mostly focused on the dark side of human nature. Research like that of the Stanford Prison Experiment has shown how easily good people can be corrupted. Other studies have demonstrated that subtle, even invisible social pressures can, for example, persuade typically independent thinking people to go along with obviously ridiculous group decisions; turn usually nonprejudiced children into blatant bigots; and create bullies out of former friends. And, in the most famous of all social psychology experiments, Stanley Milgram found that two-thirds of a sample of normal men were willing to administer potentially lethal shocks to a stranger when—in just the right context—an authority figure told them to do so.[3] These examples are just the tip of the iceberg. It is a disturbingly long list.[4]

But, as the Chinese saying goes, where there is danger, there is opportunity.[5] Herein lies the beauty: We are capable of transformations from bad to good that are every bit as dramatic as those from good to bad. Seemingly minor events can call forth tremendous compassion, sometimes from the people who seem least likely to be capable of it.

***

Consider the story of Mike McGarvin. Mike is *the* symbol of benevolence in Fresno, California, the city I have called home for most of my adult life. And for good reason. Mike and his new wife, Mary, moved here in 1973 with hardly a dime to their names. They started out living in a twelve by eighty-four–foot trailer in back of Mary's parents' house on a street that, Mike recalls, could have passed for a set for Tobacco Road. They were surrounded by cheap bars and single-room occupancy hotels with homeless people everywhere. Despite his own struggles, however, Mike wanted to do something for those less fortunate. One hot summer morning he went out and bought some loaves of bread at a day-old bakery, stocked up on peanut butter and jelly, went back to the trailer, and, with Mary, prepared a stack of sandwiches. He collected a jug of ice water and some disposable cups and started walking the streets of Chinatown handing out free lunches to anyone who wanted one. Within a few years he found a storefront for his operation, which he named The Poverello House, from the Italian word for "little poor man."

With time, Poverello House moved to larger quarters. Nowadays, staff and volunteers prepare and serve more than a thousand free meals each day. The diversity of services has also increased considerably. Today's Poverello House, in fact, resembles a small campus. There is an overnight facility for single women. There is the Village of Hope, a self-policing, self-governing community of homeless people who live in sheds in a fenced yard on Poverello House property. There are also a resident drug rehabilitation program, impressive medical and dental clinics, shower and laundry facilities, a free clothing distribution center, and a loosely run library. Mike has engaged many partners, contributors, and volunteers. He has connected with government officials and religious groups and to this day gives talks to any community group that asks. There are so many willing volunteers that, at holiday season, people need to sign up months in advance to get a spot.

But what still defines Mike to Fresno's homeless is his presence on the street. Practically every day, at 6:20 a.m., almost like clockwork, he steps out of his back door and makes his rounds. He still listens to every story and gives the impression there is nothing he would rather be doing than listening to the person he is with. He attends to every pitch, even those he has heard hundreds of times before. People turn to him when they need money for a bus ticket, or maybe a shirt for a job interview, or to arrange a ride to the motor vehicle department or the courthouse. His clients refer to him as "Papa Mike."

Mike has earned considerable recognition for his work. He has received awards from numerous religious, community, and social organizations; the California State Legislature; and even the White House.[6] Mike McGarvin is pretty much *the* symbol of goodness and altruism in this corner of California. In the eyes of many Fresnans, he is saintly.

***

Social scientists want to understand what creates a "humanitarian type" like Mike. We study his story for clues to his goodness. That story, however, opens up more questions than it answers. Mike's family life was dysfunctional by any standards. He grew up in a suburban, middle-class neighborhood in the town of Altadena, just outside of Pasadena in Southern California. But, Mike says, what looked like an Ozzie and Harriet sort of place was, for him, more like "Ozzie and Harriet on a bender." His parents' marriage was unstable and violent. They separated, divorced, and reunited several times. His father was an alcoholic.

Mike despised his father. He offers an example of what the man was like: "I had two pet chickens that I had raised from chicks. I was pretty wrapped up in these chickens, I guess because I felt like such a nothing in my family. I fed them, looked after them, and loved them as only a kid can do. One Sunday we sat down for dinner. We had chicken with all the fixings. Dad kept looking at me with a strange little smile, which made me nervous. I finished as quickly as I could, then went out to feed my pets. They weren't there. He'd killed them and dressed them out for dinner. I'd eaten my own pet chickens, and he thought it was funny."[7]

Worst of all was his father's chronic spousal abuse. The man's cruelty, Mike was convinced, drove his mother to several attempts at suicide. After one attempt, Mike decided they had all experienced enough of his father's toxicity. He stole one of his father's hunting rifles, aimed it point blank at the man, and started squeezing the trigger. The only reason he stopped, Mike says, was the realization that "if I killed him, it would be over quickly, and he'd feel no pain, but my Mom would."[8]

Not surprisingly, Mike was in constant trouble. His home life turned him "into a powder keg waiting for a lighted match," Mike recalls.[9] When he was seven, a playmate accidentally hurt him in a game of cops and robbers. The next day, Mike carved a spear out of a broom handle and cheerfully threw it into the friend's back. Fortunately, he recalls, the injury wasn't "too serious." On another occasion, Mike and a friend were tossing firecrackers at each other in a game of war. When the friend upped the attacks by throwing a whole string of them, Mike retaliated by shoving a cherry bomb in the friend's hand, lighting the cherry bomb and forcing the terrified friend's hand shut. The skin on his friend's hand, he recalls, was "blown wide open."[10]

He developed into a precocious and innovative criminal. Mike's father was a part-time photographer and had a studio in the basement of their house. Around the age of twelve or thirteen, Mike discovered that the man was using the studio to take pornographic pictures of live models. Mike stole some of the pictures and started selling them at school. Later he set up a peep show where he charged kids to peer at the models through a corner of the studio window, twenty-five cents for five minutes. By his senior year in high school, Mike had advanced to pimping for his girlfriend.

When his mother put Mike in the Boy Scouts, he used the opportunity to steal equipment from his troop leader's job site. When, exasperated, she sent Mike to church to get a moral education, he robbed it, too, this time by swiping the prizes awarded for learning Bible verses out of the church's display case. The only activity Mike seemed committed to was beating people up. Drinking and fighting became a routine. He would take on anyone who crossed his path. He could be just plain vicious. When he was seventeen, Mike spotted an older fellow who had once bullied him and his friends. Mike, who was now considerably bigger than the bully, happily took his time to allow the man to remember what he'd done to Mike and, then, watched the man register what Mike was now going to do to him. Then Mike started whaling on the guy, "really getting into it. When I had rearranged his face substantially, I decided to stomp his hands so that he couldn't do anything to little kids again. I left him in a pool of blood."[11]

***

What should a social scientist take away from this? Sigmund Freud forged nearly a century of psychology dogma with his assertion that our adult personalities are mostly cast by the age of five. This, we now know, is an overstatement, but there remains considerable evidence that personality traits observed in childhood are strong predictors of adult behavior.[12] But almost nothing in Mike's early years seems to predict the compassionate, generous adult he was to become. In fact, it wasn't until his mid-twenties that Mike showed any signs of hope. Clearly, something changed him. But if you are looking to build a humanitarian prototype, the story gets even more puzzling at this point.

The roots of transformation began when he moved to a new environment. It wasn't his choice, mind you. The decision came after the Southern California police got fed up dealing with Mike and confronted him with a choice: "Leave town or go to jail." Mike chose to go to San Francisco. The move, however, happened to take place in the summer of 1965, the cusp of the infamous summer of love. And, of more relevance, the summer of drugs. At first, it was a wild and wonderful candy store for Mike. He describes a two-year binge of alcohol and drugs. Over time, however, the substances took their toll. The lows began to outweigh the highs. Life became progressively less satisfying. He felt "empty, hopeless and depressed."

One morning Mike was riding his motorcycle around San Francisco's Tenderloin district, one of the seediest areas in the city, notorious for poverty, prostitution, violence, and extremely high crime rates. He stopped at a bohemian-looking coffee shop that looked like his kind of hangout. Maybe, he thought, a place to score a new type of drug. The café turned out to be even grimier on the inside. Down-and-out-looking street people were scattered around tables. Mike noticed this smiling, enthusiastic old guy serving coffee. The man turned out to be Father Simon, a former businessman turned minister. Father Simon, Mike later learned, had created the coffeehouse as a safe refuge for the local needy. It was a place for them to find "acceptance, hot coffee, and a few smiles." He named it the "Poverello Coffeehouse."

Father Simon discovered early on that his customers could be difficult, and he was always on the lookout for helping hands. As Mike was talking to Father Simon that morning, one of the patrons began beating up another guy. Mike never liked bullying. He moved right in and ably broke up the fight. Father Simon didn't know a thing about Mike's moral fiber. But Mike's physical toughness, he recognized, was a skill that would come in plenty handy. He told Mike he could really use his help and asked if he would be willing to volunteer a little of his time at the café. Mike was concerned this would cut into his partying, "smoking weed and dropping acid," but he also recalled that "it felt good when I broke up that fight. For the first time in quite a while, I felt useful, and I kind of liked it." Mike agreed to give it a try and, has he put it, "Thus began my career as a 'Bouncer for Jesus.'"[13]

Over time, Mike gradually upped his volunteer hours and became increasingly engaged in the welfare of the clients in the café. His role expanded from bouncer to something of a social worker-at-large. His substance abuse and violent habits became less and less problematic. Five years later, he and Mary moved to Fresno. Soon after, he began handing out the peanut butter sandwiches that led to the creation of his own Poverello House.

***

It is an inspiring story that people love to hear. Mike is asked to repeat it often to parent, community, and religious groups. It suggests that goodness is always just around the corner. In a sense, this perception is correct. Good did triumph over evil in Mike's case. But here's the thing: Neither the magnitude of Mike's transformation nor the direction it took were at all preordained. The morning Mike dropped by the Poverello Coffeehouse, he was clearly primed for change. What transpired, however, was just one of many possibilities. It was, in fact, a highly unlikely one. Let's consider the details.

To begin with, the timing had to be just right. If Mike had wandered into the coffeehouse a few months earlier, the only thing he probably would have left with, he says, were some new drugs. If it were a few months later, he probably would have been too burnt-out to rise above his own problems. Father Simon was precisely the right person for the moment. If a less street-smart version of a saint was running the coffeehouse, Mike would have been greeted with a lecture about love and compassion that would have turned him off from the get-go. Father Simon, however, grasped right off that Mike had to be brought around slowly and on Mike's terms. Even breaking up fights frightened Mike at first, not because he was afraid of getting hurt but, rather, because he was terrified of getting involved in anyone else's welfare. "I was in my middle twenties, and I'd never volunteered for anything before," Mike said. Volunteering left him with a "wonderful, warm feeling." But "it was also scary. My life had been all about me to that point," Mike recalled.[14]

Father Simon wisely let Mike advance at his own pace. "I took it easy," Mike said. "First, I volunteered one day a week. Then I built it up to two days. I wanted to ease my way into it. Little by little I built up to two to three days and, only after several years, up to a full week." It was almost a year before he expanded his duties beyond troubleshooting. If Mike had been pressed to move any faster—say, if he had fallen in with a less patient or perceptive mentor or assigned a rigid, heavy schedule of community service by the courts—he probably would have been frightened off.

The single most powerful catalyst in Mike's transformation was his success in breaking up the fight that erupted that first morning in the coffeehouse. To begin with, it is what led Father Simon to take special notice of Mike. Without the fight, Father Simon would have probably written Mike off as just another troubled guy passing through. This street brawling motorcyclist certainly couldn't have shown much promise of becoming a great humanitarian. If Father Simon was on the lookout for a social worker, it is doubtful Mike would have been his first choice.

Even more important, the event led Mike to take the critical next step of returning to the coffeehouse. And this led him to make progressively larger commitments. It was crucially fortuitous, however, that Father Simon's most pressing need at that moment was for someone to break up fights. "I became the designated brawl-buster," Mike said. "My size, coupled with the bar-fighting experience on my résumé, made me the perfect candidate for maintaining calm among the guests." In fact, there is little else in the way of volunteering that Mike probably would have agreed to. I asked Mike what he would have done if Father Simon had, say, asked him to read stories to sick children. "That's something I'd have had trouble getting into," he said.

Consider another of Mike's experiences around the same time. After his success at the coffeehouse, Mike wanted to try volunteering somewhere else. He started spending Sunday mornings talking to elderly patients in a large nursing home in San Francisco. "There were hundreds and hundreds of folks in often very bad physical shape," he recalled, " in bed after bed after bed. Sadly, many had been dumped there by their families, who never came to visit. Some people can handle this. I couldn't." Mike lasted a year, but it was a very unpleasant experience. The more he tried to cheer the clients up, the more depressed he got. Worse yet, he upped his alcohol consumption. He and a friend "would take the folks to mass and then go out to lunch," Mike said. "At the beginning, we'd cap off lunch with a drink. After a while, it was to heck with lunch and we were having maybe eight drinks. We'd be depressed and get absolutely smashed. It's the only way I could choke down what I'd seen. I knew this just wasn't working. I realized I just couldn't do this. It brought out a dark part of me."

In other words, traditional social worker–type altruism brought out the worst in Mike at that moment in his life. But breaking up brawls brought out his best. "I'd finally found a place that needed me, and moreover, needed the particular talents I had developed during my hell-raising years," Mike explains.[15]

***

When you tell people how something turned out, they have a tendency to overestimate their ability to have foreseen that outcome. Psychologists call this the "hindsight bias," also known as the "I-knew-it-all-along" phenomenon. McGarvin is a case in point. You look at this smiling, gentle, kind man and think, of course, this is just the type of person who would dedicate his life to helping the less fortunate. From there, it's all too easy to look back and connect the dots. It all makes sense. The problem is, if you start at the beginning, there's almost no chance you would have predicted the ending.

We're easily seduced by the hindsight bias. The late evolutionary biologist Stephen Jay Gould provides a vivid example. He argues that we make the same mistake when explaining the history of all human life. Think about the classic illustrations of the evolution of man. It typically begins with an image of a primitive ancestor, perhaps a hairy apelike creature dragging along the ground, and then progresses to a Neanderthal and Cro-Magnons and, eventually, to a glorious human standing fully erect. The changes are linear and positive at every step. In truth, however, an endless number of paths might have sprouted at any point along the way. Invertebrates could have evolved into endlessly possible creatures that, in turn, could have evolved into endlessly possible other creatures. The history of life isn't linear, progressive, or predictable. "Humans arose," Gould points out, "as a fortuitous and contingent outcome of thousands of linked events, any one of which could have occurred differently and sent history on an alternative pathway that would not have led to consciousness."[16] Evolution is not ruled by progress but by quick and quirky responses to minute, ever-changing conditions.

The same holds true for the lives of individuals. We, like evolution itself, experience more false starts and unconstructive turns than sustainable successes. How might Mike McGarvin's life have progressed if any of the events had played out differently? It doesn't take much to imagine a scenario in which one unfortunate event leads to another and Mike ends up a chronic alcoholic or drug addict, in and out of prison, and/or depressed and on the street. The fact is, given what we know of Mike's past, any of these outcomes would have been considerably more likely than what actually evolved. And, in retrospect, people would have said it made sense that he had turned out *that* way.

***

The precariousness of heroism is underscored by another tale of transformation, one of the best-known of our times. Let's turn next to the story of Oskar Schindler, whose famous list saved some 1,300 Jewish prisoners from almost certain death during the Holocaust.

The basics of Schindler's story have become legendary through Thomas Keneally's book and Steven Spielberg's subsequent Academy Award–winning film. Shortly after the German invasion of Poland, Schindler took over an enamelware factory near the city of Kraków. His motives were purely capitalistic. He quickly recognized a lucrative opportunity to employ hundreds of Jews as a source of cheap labor and built a work camp to house them at his complex. Menachem Stern, whose late uncle Yizhad (played in the film by Ben Kingsley) served as Schindler's business manager and a key confidant, observed, "Schindler built the factory up to make money. He did not employ Jews in order to save them."[17] Schindler enjoyed the good life his business success brought. He rode pure-blooded racehorses around the factory, caroused with the Nazis, and enjoyed their dinners and their women. He was a frequent drinking buddy of Amon Goeth, the psychopathic SS commander of the Nazi labor camp in nearby Płaszów.

It wasn't until later, when the Nazi atrocities escalated, that Schindler's interest in "his Jews" turned to their welfare. There is considerable controversy over what converted him to a savior. Some believe it was a day when he was out on his horse and saw what was being done to the Jews in the camp; others speculate he was just angry about the stupidity and arrogance of the Nazis for telling him how to run his business and his Jews. Whatever the hot button, it had historic consequences. Schindler spent the next six years obsessed with saving Jewish lives. When the Nazis ordered him to dismantle the enamelware factory, he devised a scheme to keep his Jewish workers from being sent to death camps. He built a new factory, a supposed munitions plant, near his hometown in German-speaking Czechoslovakia. He then drew up a list of Jews— *Schindler's List*—who allegedly had to be transported to his factory because they were essential to the war effort.

The facade of a productive factory was used to rescue entire families. Records were falsified to prove that children were doing critical jobs. At one point, Schindler explained to Nazi officials that only children's tiny hands were capable of polishing the insides of shells. In reality, his factory never manufactured a single bullet. Schindler would instead purchase small supplies from another factory when weapons inspectors came around. On a number of occasions, he deflected the furious complaints of inspectors that he was producing defective munitions by giving them massive gifts of liquor and cash bribes. He was arrested and interrogated on at least two occasions but exerted a combination of smooth talk and name dropping to save his life. His wealth and power were completely gone by the end of the war, but the 1,300 Jews on his list were saved. It is estimated that more than six thousand people—including children and grandchildren of those on the list—would not be alive today had it not been for Schindler's efforts.

***

Schindler's is one of the great episodes of altruism of our time. Like Papa Mike, however, little in Schindler's past would have predicted his greatness. In both cases, we see how the situation made the man, more so than the other way around. Their transformations were elicited by an unusual, complex, and specific set of circumstances. They became the right person at the right time in the right place. The people we think of as the humanitarian-types would, in fact, have been hopeless failures in either of these situations. Can you imagine Gandhi or Mother Theresa breaking up fights in Father Simon's café? And how do you think they would have fared in Płaszów?

Schindler's biggest problem was Goeth, the sadistic commandant of the Płaszów concentration camp. Mietek Pemper, a Jewish prisoner in the Płaszów camp, worked more closely with Schindler and Goeth than anyone. He served 540 days—from March 17, 1943, to September 13, 1944—as Goeth's personal stenographer, during which time he had unparalleled access to Goeth's day-to-day communications, comings and goings, and other Nazi operations. During this period he also began collaborating with Schindler, secretly feeding him information that became key to the survival of his Jews. Pemper was so intimately involved with the workings of the camp that, after the war, he was a prime witness in the war crime trials against Goeth and other Nazis.

Pemper, in his autobiographical account of his concentration camp experience, *The Road to Rescue*, described how capricious and terrifying Goeth could be. He recalled how Goeth liked to sit and watch a mirror outside his office window that gave him a clear view of the area in front of the barracks. Often, while Pemper was in the office taking dictation, Goeth would suddenly "stand up, take one of the rifles from the rack on the wall, and open the window. I would hear a few shots and then nothing but screams. As if he had interrupted the dictation only to take a telephone call, Goeth would come back to his desk and say, 'Where were we?'"

Schindler was precisely the man to handle Goeth. "Schindler was tall, powerfully built, and could hold his liquor," Pemper observes. He pushed one hot button after another. Schindler "visited Goeth in the camp, supplied him with expensive cognac, partied with the SS men, and treated them to schnapps and cigarettes.... We were lucky that Schindler was the way he was: devil-may-care, plucky gutsy, fearless, and able to hold his liquor," Pemper says.[18] The situation required something of a con man, a partyer, reckless, without a plan, even a bit of a psychopath. In his book, Thomas Keneally observes, "It was Oskar's nature to believe that you could drink with the devil to adjust the balance of evil over a snifter of cognac." One of the reasons Schindler succeeded, Keneally argues, is that "like few others, he was capable of staying canny while drinking, of keeping his head."[19] Do you think Mother Theresa could have done that?

Yad Vashem, the Holocaust memorial in Jerusalem, has recognized Schindler as a Righteous Gentile, its highest honor. When Schindler died in 1974, Dr. Mordecai Paldiel, who directs Yad Vashem's Department for the Righteous among the Nations, summed up the fortuitous blend of social and psychological forces that spawned the man's heroism. If Schindler had been a straitlaced, honest businessman, Paldiel observed, "He might have been able to help a few people, to save one or two Jews, but he never would have been able to pull something like this." The worst aspects of Schindler's character, Paldiel maintains, were precisely what enabled him to "play the greatest role."[20]

Schindler's cohorts underwent their own transformations. Mietek Pemper perceptively observes, "After being forced to work for Amon Goeth and after having had the privilege of working with Oskar Schindler, I've often wondered what would have happened if there had been no war and no Nazi ideology with its racist mania. Goeth would probably not have become a mass murderer, nor Schindler a saver of lives. It was only the extraordinary circumstances of war and the immense power granted to individual men that revealed the nature of these men to such an impressive and terrifying degree."[21]

***

The stories of Oskar Schindler and Mike McGarvin demonstrate how radically a person can be transformed by the forces of a situation. But, as in Steven Jay Gould's explanation of evolution, it is important to recognize that change is an ongoing process and, as with evolution, change does not necessarily equate with progress.

This brings us to the final, less discussed chapter of Schindler's life. When the war ended, Schindler was suddenly, literally, estranged from the world that produced his greatness. He had to move on. The results were unimpressive. Even his greatest admirers describe postwar Schindler with terms like "thief," "smuggler," "drinker," "liar," and "adulterer." When his long-suffering wife, Emilie, whom he left in Argentina after the war, was asked to comment about her late husband after Spielberg's film came out, she remarked: "I was taught that if you have nothing good to say about a person you shouldn't say anything. So I won't say anything."

On a more talkative occasion, she commented: "He was stupid. Useless. Half crazy. To hell with him."[22]

Schindler's postwar life consisted of a series of personal and business failures. In a poignant reversal of the master and servant roles, he was often supported by the grateful Jews whom he had saved. Toward the end, he was out of work, living in a shabby furnished room overlooking the Frankfurt railroad station, drowning his sorrows in schnapps and nostalgia, having lost or gambled away $100,000 in German government compensation for the loss of his factory. He had even sold the gold ring inscribed with a line from the Talmud, "Whoever saves one life saves the entire world," that his Jews had made from a prisoner's tooth and presented to him as he was fleeing the camp to avoid capture at the end of the war. "The six war years were his glory years. Neither before 1939 nor after 1945 did he particularly distinguish himself," Pemper recalls.

It is interesting to contrast Schindler's arc with that of McGarvin. Why did Schindler's life deteriorate while McGarvin has continued along the productive path that began all those years ago? The explanation, I would argue, comes back to the power of the situation. In McGarvin's case, the circumstances that brought out his finest qualities remained. The war on poverty did not end. The circumstances that elicited Schindler's heroism—the atrocities of Nazism—did end. The qualities he inhabited so successfully in defeating the Nazis didn't transfer outside that situation, at least not to sustaining the role of a great humanitarian. His new, postwar circumstances triggered a different side of Schindler, and, unfortunately, it was not his most attractive.

***

Are any of these Schindlers—the opportunist, the bon vivant, the savior, the disappointing husband—any more *real* than the others? Are any of the Mike McGarvins—the escapist, the violent street fighter, the peacemaker, the volunteer—more *real* than his others? Was one or another of these roles their destiny? The fact is that Schindler and McGarvin, like all of us, contain the potential for all of these selves and endless others.

To be sure, there exists a scattering of pure psychopaths who are incapable of altruism, and there are probably an even tinier number of people who are incapable of acting badly. These, however, are the outliers, the mutants. As for the rest of us, we are merely more or less likely to act better or worse in a given situation. But these are just probabilities. A situation that draws out my finest side may bring out the worst of yours, and vice versa. If you are scouting for future heroes, it can be a waste of time to dwell on types of people. The more informative question focuses on context: What situations draw out the best in a person?

I've told the stories of Mike McGarvin and Oskar Schindler in some detail, not only because they demonstrate our essential malleability but, even more important, because they underscore the necessity of understanding the quirkiness of the process. Malleability creates possibilities. But the devil—you should excuse the term—is in the details. Every step of the way.

16
Heroes in Waiting

I always wanted to be somebody, but now
I realize I should have been more specific.
—Lily Tomlin

The physicist Stephen Hawking tells the story of a famous scholar (rumored to have been Bertrand Russell) who had just given a public lecture on astronomy. The man was describing how the moon orbits Earth, that Earth goes around the sun, and the sun orbits the center of a huge mass of stars we call our galaxy. When he was finished, a little old lady in back stood up and said: "What you have told us is rubbish. The world is really a flat plate supported on the back of a giant tortoise." The scientist smiled and asked her, "What is the tortoise standing on?" To which the old lady shot back: "You're very clever, young man, very clever. But it's turtles all the way down!"[1]

The same could be said about our inner identities. We speak of our self as if it were an object. I imagine a *my*self and a *your*self, a *you* and a *me*, as if they were items I could line up on a table. But look closely and the only things you'll see are neurons. The actual self? It is a trace. A ghost. "When I enter most intimately into what I call myself, I always stumble on some particular perception or other, of heat or cold, light or shade, love or hatred, pain or pleasure. I never can catch myself at any time without a perception, and never can observe any thing but the perception," the philosopher David Hume famously observed.[2] In other words, turtles all the way down.

***

Our pursuit of the elusive entity has covered a wide range of perspectives. We have crossed multiple disciplines—from the physical to the social sciences—at multiple levels—from the microscopic to the macroscopic, from our bodies to our minds. Given the vast differences in these approaches, it shouldn't be surprising that what we have come across, seen in isolation, sometimes appears anecdotal and idiosyncratic. After all, if you're a hammer, everything looks like the head of a nail, to paraphrase the great psychologist Abraham Maslow. But the broader approach has allowed us to step back and see connections between the narrower foci that might not otherwise be clear. I have argued that four overlapping themes weave through the chapters.

First, the boundaries that separate self from non-self are vague, quirky, and fickle. Look inward and we are confronted by a body that is part us, part other. Looking outward, the line that separates where we end and other begins is arbitrary and often defies logic. The boundaries of a self may be experienced as anywhere from the confines of one's body to an entire village, depending on who you are and how you were educated.

Second, we contain multitudes. We are a collection of the many and diverse from our genetic underpinnings, to the voices in our heads, to the persona we present to the world. And these multitudes often treat each other like strangers, even adversaries. Seen as a whole, we are more like a republic than an individual.

Third, the entity we call our self is ever-changing at multiple levels. Banal as it may sound, change truly is the only thing about us that stays the same. It is our human condition. We have seen this from many perspectives in the previous chapters. Bodily speaking, our very cells are unrecognizable from one point in time to another. Our perceptions of our bodies are just as changeable: a single glitch, for example, can make us lose track of a body part, or of our entire body, or to confuse our own bodies with someone else's. Psychologically speaking, we switch back and forth like quicksilver between incongruent, sometimes adversarial subselves, more than we can keep track of. Socially speaking we appear to be little more than an ever-changing troupe of actors.

Our *real* self? It is just a story we tell ourselves. We weave a narrative that does its best to make sense of—well, of . . . ourselves. It is an enormous creative challenge. There is such a mass of data to confront—everything we have experienced, each word we have spoken and action we have taken, all the people we have been, our endlessly changing minds and bodies past, present, and future—that there's no end to the connections that can be hacked out of the mess. A well-crafted narrative gives our life meaning. But good storytelling shouldn't be confused with factual reporting. It is simply a way of connecting the dots, a self-serving selection of the most convenient dots, that is. The goal is to create an identity we can live with, and we select, filter, and organize as much as necessary to achieve this goal. The story is a work of art. And, like all good art, it is subject to the whims of its creator.

The narrator in Richard Ford's novel *Canada*, captures it nicely when describing his personal history: "When I think of those times . . . it's all of a piece, like a musical score with movements, or a puzzle, wherein I am seeking to restore and maintain my life in a whole and acceptable state, regardless of the frontiers I've crossed. I know it's only me who makes these connections. But not to try to make them is to commit yourself to the waves that toss you and dash you against the rocks of despair."[3] The self we conceive is a fiction. The realities are vague, arbitrary, and utterly intangible. Does this mean we should all pack up and go to the beach? Not at all. Our changeability, in fact, is where the possibilities begin. This brings us to my fourth theme. Fluidity creates malleability, and this malleability unleashes a wealth of potential. The self is what we make of it. It is an act of creation. As the great Eastern philosopher Lao Tzu observed, "When I let go of what I am, I become what I might be."[4]

This is not to say our powers are unlimited. There is no denying we haven't nearly as much control over ourselves as we might like. Our conscious self is not—in the lexicon of a former U.S. president—the main "decider." We don't even become aware of our decisions until after they are made. But consciousness has a weapon that supersedes these limitations. It has the capacity to accept, reject, polish, and/or revise what we are handed. We have been granted editorial powers. But actualizing these powers requires work. There is an old saying: "The mind is an excellent servant but a terrible master." Our fallback state is to mindlessly play out the scripts our inner voices dictate. It is easy and comfortable. But there are times when these scripts lead to unfortunate endings. It doesn't have to be this way, however. We, that executive editor, have the capacity to improve upon our default settings.

***

The science we have reviewed is instructive in this process. To begin with, it underscores the need for a counterintuitive way of thinking about ourselves if we want to circumvent our factory defaults. The intuitive, "right" path to self-governance is through intentional will or "self-discipline." Perhaps we make a resolution—say, to work harder, or to be nicer to waitresses, or quit smoking, or stay out of the casino. If this succeeds, congratulations. If you are like most people, however, this brand of discipline will only take you so far. In the phrase of the late political activist Abbie Hoffman, it can be like telling a depressed person to "just cheer up." The problem, as we have seen, is that the self of awareness is an editor, not the creator.

This reality, however, runs counter to the "self-will" way of thinking. How, then, do we convince ourselves to become something we would not necessarily become if left to our factory defaults? Permit me to suggest an editorial approach that I, for one, have found helpful. It begins by thinking of oneself as another person. Envision a stranger in the mirror, a disobedient stranger who will require clever persuasion to do your bidding. Direct orders are not an option. Indirect strategies are, however. The key to these lies in another lesson from the research: the power of the situation to determine how a person acts and thinks. Our task as self-editors is to identify the influences that bring out our best and to then devise strategies that exploit their potential.

The process requires self-reflection. We need to step back, to step *outside* ourselves, and gather data with an objective eye. The word "objective" is critical. We reflect all day long. It is a never-ending monologue ("That was a nice thing I did." "I ate too much." "I think I'm shouting."). But we need to systematize the process so it rises above background noise. There are many ways to approach this. Some people meditate. Others keep a journal. Or hire a psychotherapist. Whatever the chosen technique, it should objectively articulate your reflections. You need to think about yourself thinking about yourself. I know this sounds peculiar. But don't forget we're talking about the self here.

You can then design strategies for change. Look for ways to rise above kneejerk reactions that, in the past, have either served you badly or obstructed opportunities for growth. Think about ways to maximize the time you spend in situations that bring out your best and minimize the time you spend in those that bring out your worst. Search for nuances within those situations. As we have seen in the cases of Mike McGarvin, Oskar Schindler, and throughout this book, even the most dramatic transformations may be triggered by ostensibly trivial features in one's environment.

There is no single formula. It might be a simple engineering problem. It could, for example, call for scheduling ten minutes of non-negotiable quiet time each day, or going on that lunch date you keep postponing, or just saying "How are you?" to a particular person. Or it may require more creative psychology. I still want to stand up and applaud how the (flesh-and-blood) editor of my first book got me to completely change its ending without my realizing she had anything to do with it.[5] "The trick," she confessed later, "is to assure your client that they are in charge. You're simply going to help them tweak their masterpiece. What you don't tell them is how much difference those tweaks are going to make."

If all else fails, you may need to trade carrots for sticks. Victor Hugo threatened himself with embarrassment. Zelda Gamson used blackmail. The procrastinators from MIT put their careers in jeopardy. Set up a Ulysses contract. Make yourself a deal you can't refuse.

***

Social psychologists have begun to develop educational programs that cultivate self-enhancement. The goal of these programs is to understand the psychology that draws our worst traits forward and to then learn to use this same psychology to bring out our best.

One promising example is the Heroic Imagination Project (HIP), an ambitious educational program developed by Philip Zimbardo. Forty years ago, his Stanford Prison Experiment demonstrated how the power of a situation could so easily transform everyday college students into despicable prison guards. HIP has now flipped the equation 180 degrees by applying the same social psychological principles to cultivate the positive in people.[6]

The program, with which I collaborate, offers an expansive definition of heroism that reflects contemporary realities. Today's heroes, HIP argues, are people who attempt to address injustice or create positive change in the world, especially in those situations when they face pressure, personal risks, and costs to do otherwise. It is about standing up for what is right when everyone around you remains silent. This includes on-the-spot reactions to emergency situations as well as mindfully initiating prosocial behavior over the long run.[7] The project's former educational director, Clint Wilkins, and his colleague Bryan Dickerson have developed a series of workshops that address the kneejerk responses that can obstruct our heroic potential.

One lesson, for example, targets bystander apathy. It begins with the problem: The silence of good people has been responsible for as many of history's evils as the actions of bad people. Yet, when confronted with the suffering of others, even the best of us may feel drawn to toward silence. It is normal to feel safer not to get involved even when, in reality, it is anything but.

Imagine, for example, that you are sitting in a quiet waiting room filling out forms along with a dozen strangers. There is no supervisor in the room. After a few minutes, you get a whiff of smoke. Soon the smoke is pouring under the door. The others occasionally glance at the smoke but no one appears concerned. The smoke eventually fills the room. Still, none of the others seems alarmed. What would you do? If you are like most people, you probably think you would take action. If you actually did, however, you would be in the minority. A classic experiment by John Darley and Bibb Latané found that, when people were surrounded by as few as two passive bystanders in a similar situation, only about a third of them reported the smoke; and these numbers diminish as the number of bystanders increases.[8] The tendency to overestimate our willingness to take action in situations like this is an important lesson. It is a comforting illusion in the short run, but it leaves you unprepared when the problem occurs. We create a psychological blind spot.

The problem—the reason most people act so inadequately in these instances—begins with the invisibility of the forces at work. If an enemy threatens me, I know what I am fighting against. Bystander apathy, however, is rooted in conformity, and conformity is a stealth attacker. It operates covertly. Nobody tells us to conform. To overcome these forces, we need to reveal their faces. We need to recognize their workings in real-life situations in order to develop strategies to overcome them.

I'm a good case study. Public disapproval makes me cringe even when I know I'm right. You certainly wouldn't want to depend on me to be the guy who goes out on a limb in the fire-in-the-room scenario. But as wussy as I am when it comes to standing up to a group, I have no qualms about taking the lead with a stranger sitting next to me. It's easy for me to lean over and quietly ask, "Is it just me, or do you think we should check what that smoke is about?" And if I do this, and that person has been thinking the same thing, I've made an ally. Both of us now repeat the exchange with others. They, in turn draw out other allies-in-waiting, who draw out others. The forces of conformity remain, but they have shifted direction. There it is: One simple question to the person in the next chair and I'm a hero. With a little social psychology, it can be as easy as that.[9]

"Heroes," Zimbardo observes, "have a good sense of when people are in trouble. [They] sense that things are a little bit out of place or don't fit." They are people who are quick to recognize when, for example, teasing has crossed into racism or a well-liked professor should be confronted for an inappropriate rant. This conception of heroism has less to do with the type of person you are than the one you are capable of becoming. It is founded on habits and scripts that prepare an individual to act with intelligence, compassion, and courage in challenging situations and moments of decision making. The aim is to create a "hero in waiting"—a welcome addition to anyone's cast of performers.

And there is a bonus. One of the most provocative findings to come out of recent happiness research is that people get greater and more sustained pleasure when they do something for another person than when they do things for themselves.[10] By cultivating your inner hero, it not only benefits the people you are serving. It also enhances the quality of your own life. It is—pardon the cliché—a win-win situation.

***

It may not seem surprising that people can transform themselves at the levels of social behavior and psychological experience. I have argued throughout this book, however, that change and multiplicity characterize virtually every aspect of the self, clear down to the purely physical. And, in one of the most startling discoveries to emerge out of the new science of the self, it is becoming increasingly evident that we have the potential to improve upon our default settings at the heart of this physical core—the genome itself. Our genetic inheritance, like everything else about ourselves, contains fonts of possibility beyond what we once imagined. This brings us to the cutting-edge discipline of epigenetics.

Almost every cell in our body contains each of the approximately twenty-two thousand genes we are born with. And, true, short of a mutation, these are the genes we will carry pretty much unchanged the rest of our lives. But the behavior of this genome is another story. Only a tiny percentage of a cell's genes are actively expressed at any moment. And this ever-changing "gene expression," not our genetic makeup, is what lays the foundation for who we are and who we can become.

The epigenome, which literally means "above the genome," decides which genes need to be turned on and to what intensity at any given time. It can be thought of as an on-off switch, or a dimmer switch, or simply the software that controls the cell's hardware, the genome. It tells each of those genes when, how, and how much to work. It essentially decides what kind of cell a cell should be.[11] This is why your skin looks like skin and your hair looks like hair even though your skin cells and hair cells have exactly the same DNA. It is also the key to biological adaptation. It is, for example, how certain genes are activated when we go into a growth spurt at puberty and how they are deactivated when puberty comes to an end; or how genes turn on when we are fighting an infection or healing a broken bone.

The fact that genetic expression is changeable at the biological level has been understood for some time. In the past two decades, however, we have begun to understand how closely it intertwines with our social experiences. Although most of this research has been confined to animal studies, provocative findings are now beginning to emerge at the human level. In one notable program of research, UCLA geneticist Steve Cole and his colleagues have discovered an unexpectedly strong relationship between social stress and specific patterns of gene expression. They monitored the genetic profiles of a variety of people who feel trapped in stressful conditions, ranging from self-reported chronically lonely people to psychologically depressed individuals suffering from cancer. In each case, they have discovered virtually the same unusual pattern of expression in a specific subset of genes—a pattern that turned out to put these individuals at risk for immune-related health disorders such as hypertension, type 2 diabetes, atherosclerosis, heart failure, and stroke.[12] In one study, they watched the gene profile develop in real time when young women they were observing became enmeshed in difficult social problems with people close to them.[13]

Studies like these show that our DNA isn't a non-negotiable blueprint so much as a set of possibilities. The people and events in our lives don't just change the way we feel; they change our genes.[14] The revised epigenome, in turn, changes the person we become, and that person goes on to impact his or her surroundings in new ways. Our minds, our social surroundings, and our epigenome are joined in an ongoing dance.

Cole often ends his lectures with a bit of advice "Your experiences today will influence the molecular composition of your body for the next two to three months or, perhaps, for the rest of your life. Plan your day accordingly."[15] Impressive as this is, it may be an understatement. There is intriguing new evidence coming out of animal studies that epigenetic changes may not only persist over the animal's lifetime but that they can be passed on to their offspring. If this turns out to be true in humans, it would mean that the life we live, and perhaps even the lives our mother and grandmother lived, can alter the gene activity of future generations.[16]

***

When a rich kid at my high school showed too much swagger, we liked to put him down with the saying: "The guy was born on third base and thought he hit a triple." But don't we all share this delusion? The lights of consciousness turn on one day, and there we be, staring at our own third base. I was assigned my mind and you were given yours. How much credit do either of us deserve for the person we are? I suggest two answers: Not much and everything. The architecture—that mind and body we woke up to on the base path—was pretty much a gift. That's the "not much" answer. But there is that sliver of light: our editorial powers. This is the "everything."

I once asked a prolific story writer I know how he managed to produce so much good work so quickly. He actually works very slowly, he explained. Most pieces took him months to finish; sometimes years. His "trick," he said, is to plant lots of seedlings and let them mature at their own pace. When he gets an idea for an interesting character, for example, he mentally scribbles a few notes and imagines he is storing them in his unconscious. "I conjure an image of the character hanging on a stick. It looks something like a fishing pole. Then I dip it into this bubble-world in the back of my mind. I leave it there to germinate next to the other characters I've already planted." Every so often, he'll dip his stick into the bubble-world to pull up a character and check its progress. "If it doesn't look fully developed, I might scribble out a few mental changes. Then I lower it back down. Or I might toss it in the trash. But if I like what I see, and if it fits the story I'm writing, I polish it up and put it to work."

It is an approach worth considering for one's life. Illusion or not, we recall our past as *our* past, project our future as *our* future, and recognize in our present awareness that these *we*'s converge on a single thread. These mental acrobatics allow us to develop, design, and improve on who we are and have been. We can nurture the best of our selves, weed out the worst, and cultivate new additions. Each time you ask yourself "How should I act?" you are also asking "Who is the person I want to become?" Every brushstroke reinvents every future.

And so, after forty years as a psychologist, I offer this humble advice: Cultivate your backstage characters. Learn to cast the right ones for the right parts. Edit and re-edit their scripts. And, while you're at it, try not to beat yourself up too often. Face it. You're all in this together.

Notes

Chapter 1. Introduction: Theseus's Paradox

1. This is not her real name.
2. In fact, our "relationship" lasted less than a month, if you must know.
3. It is believed that a few cell types, notably some or all of those associated with the cerebral cortex, endure from birth to death.
4. See, e.g., Nicholas Wade, "Your Body Is Younger Than You Think," *New York Times*, August 2, 2005, http://www.nytimes.com/2005/08/02/science/your-body-is-younger-than-you-think.html.
5. Roderick Chisholm, *Person and Object: A Metaphysical Study* (New York: Taylor and Francis, 2004), 89.
6. This thought experiment is based on one developed by Derek Parfit in his brilliant book *Reasons and Persons* (New York: Oxford University Press, 1986), 202.
7. Walt Whitman, *Song of Myself*. BrainyQuote.com, http://www.brainyquote.com/quotes/quotes/w/waltwhitma132584.html, accessed November 10, 2015. The full verse reads:

   Do I contradict myself?
   Very well, then I contradict myself.
   (I am large, I contain multitudes.)

8. Rebecca Goldstein, *36 Arguments for the Existence of God* (New York: Pantheon, 2010), 17.

Chapter 2. The Brain

1. Francis Crick, *The Astonishing Hypothesis: The Scientific Search for the Soul* (New York: Scribner, 1994).
2. Milan Kundera, *Immortality* (New York: Harper Perennial, 1999), 12.
3. Paul Broks, *Into the Silent Land* (New York: Grove Press, 2003), 63.
4. Gilbert Ryle, *The Concept of Mind* (Chicago: University of Chicago Press, 1949), 22.
5. Associated Press, "Two-Fifths in Poll Would Take a New Brain," *Fresno Bee*, March 4, 1990, B5.
6. "Frankenstein Fears after Head Transplant," BBC News, April 6, 2001, http://news.bbc.co.uk/2/hi/health/1263758.stm.
7. Derek Parfit, *Reasons and Persons* (New York: Oxford University Press, 1986), 204. See also Larissa MacFarquhar, "How to Be Good," *New Yorker*, September 5, 2011, 47–53.

8. Benedict Carey, "Brain Researchers Open Door to Editing Memory," *New York Times*, April 6, 2009, A1, A10.

9. Michael Frayn, *Copenhagen* (New York: Anchor Books, 1998), 74.

10. Carl Zimmer, *Soul Made Flesh: The Discovery of the Brain and How It Changed the World* (New York: Free Press, 2004), 9.

11. Henry More, *An Antidote against Atheisme, or, An Appeal to the Natural Faculties of the Mind of Man, Whether There Be Not a God* (London, 1653); quoted in Zimmer, *Soul Made Flesh*, 5.

12. Todd Feinberg, *From Axons to Identity* (New York: W.W. Norton, 2009), 132–58 (chap. 5); and Benedict Carey, "After Injury, Fighting to Regain a Sense of Self," *New York Times*, August 9, 2009, A1, A15.

13. Broks, *Into the Silent Land*, 48.

14. David Eagleman, *Incognito: The Secret Lives of the Brain* (New York: Pantheon, 2011), 1.

15. V. S. Ramachandran, "Secrets of the Mind," *NOVA* (PBS), October 23, 2001.

16. Katrina Firlik, *Another Day in the Frontal Lobe* (New York: Random House, 2006), 194.

17. Daniel Drubach, *The Brain Explained* (Englewood Cliffs, NJ: Prentice Hall, 2000).

18. Norman Doidge, *The Brain That Changes Itself* (New York: Penguin, 2007).

19. Ibid.

20. Steven Johnson, *Mind Wide Open: Your Brain and the Neuroscience of Everyday Life* (New York: Simon and Schuster, 2004), 10.

Chapter 3. Two Brains, One Person

1. Kimon Nicolaides, *The Natural Way to Draw* (Boston: Houghton-Mifflin, 1941), 159.

2. L. Wechsler, *Seeing Is Forgetting the Name of the Thing One Sees: A Life of Contemporary Artist Robert Irwin* (Berkeley: University of California Press, 1982). The title is taken from Paul Valery's observation: "To see is to forget the name of the thing one sees."

3. Betty Edwards, *Drawing on the Right Side of the Brain: A Course in Enhancing Creativity and Artistic Confidence* (Los Angeles: J. P. Tarcher, 1979).

4. Michael S. Gazzaniga, "The Split Brain in Man," *Scientific American* 217 (August 1, 1967): 24–29.

5. Ibid.

6. For further descriptions of these and other experiments by Sperry's group, see, e.g., Michael S. Gazzaniga, *The Bisected Brain* (New York: Appleton-Century-Crofts, 1970). An excellent secondary source is Robert E. Ornstein, *The Psychology of Consciousness*, 2nd ed. (New York: Harcourt, Brace Jovanovich, 1977).

7. K. Goldstein, "Zur Lehre vonder motorisschen Apraxie," *Journal fur Psychologie und Neurologie* 9 (1908): 169–87; cited by Todd Feinberg, *From Axons to Identity* (New York: W.W. Norton, 2009), 191.

8. R. Leiguarda, S. Starkstein, and M. Berthier, "Anterior Callosal Haemorrhage: A Partial Interhemispheric Disconnection Syndrome," *Brain* 112 (1989): 1019–37.

9. D. Geschwind, M. Iacobini, M. Mega, D. Zaidel, T. Cloughesy, and E. Zaidel, "Alien Hand Syndrome: Interhemispheric Motor Disconnection Due to a Lesion in the Midbody of the Corpus Callosum," *Neurology* 45 (4) (1995): 802–8.

10. Ibid.

11. Feinberg, *From Axons to Identity*, 193.

12. Melissa Dahl, "When One Hand Develops a Mind of Its Own," MSNBC, October 29, 2010, http://bodyodd.msnbc.msn.com/_news/2010/10/29/5354143-when-one-hand-develops-a-mind-of-its-own, accessed January 14, 2011.

13. Leiguarda et al., "Anterior Callosal Haemorrhage."

14. Dahl, "When One Hand Develops a Mind of Its Own."

15. Feinberg, *From Axons to Identity*, 194.

16. Geschwind et al., "Alien Hand Syndrome."

17. Leiguarda et al., "Anterior Callosal Haemorrhage."

18. R. Leiguarda, S. Starkstein, M. Nogues, M. Berthier, and R. Arbelaiz, (1993). "Paroxysmal Alien Hand Syndrome," *Journal of Neurology, Neurosurgery, and Psychiatry* 56 (1993): 788–92.

19. S. J. Dimond, *Neuropsychology* (Boston: Buttersworths, 1980), 434.

20. Leiguarda et al., "Paroxysmal Alien Hand Syndrome."

21. Michael S. Gazzaniga, "One Brain—Two Minds?," *American Scientist* 60 (1972): 311–17; quoted in Michael S. Gazzaniga, *Who's in Charge? Free Will and the Science of the Brain* (New York: Harper's, 2011), 59.

22. Gazzaniga, "The Split Brain in Man."

Chapter 4. Bodies without Borders: Or, Pardon Me, Is This My Arm or Yours?

1. First described by M. Botvinick and J. Cohen, "Rubber Hands 'Feel' Touch That Eyes See," *Nature* 391 (1998): 756.

2. Good descriptions of several variations on this illusion can be found in G. Lawton, "Whose Body Is It Anyway?," *New Scientist*, March 21, 2009, 36–37.

3. T. Metzinger, *The Ego Tunnel* (New York: Basic Books, 2009), 75–114 (chap. 3).

4. M. Slater, D. Perez-Marcos, H. Ehrsson, and M. Sanchez-Vives, "Introducing Illusory Ownership of a Virtual Body," *Frontiers in Neuroscience* 3 (2009): 214–20.

5. S. Milgram, "The Experience of Living in Cities," *Science* 167 (1970): 1461–68.

6. Natalie Angier, "Primal, Acute and Easily Duped: Our Sense of Touch," *New York Times*, December 9, 2008, Science Times sec., D2.

7. Brain facts and figures have been gathered from several textbooks, reported on a University of Washington website, http://faculty.washington.edu/chudler/facts.html.

8. V. I. Petkova and H. H. Ehrsson, "If I Were You: Perceptual Illusion of Body Swapping," *PLOS ONE* 3 (12) (2008): doi:10.1371/journal.pone.0003832.

9. Ibid.

10. For a good review of these studies, see L. Maister, M. Slater, M. Sanchez-Vias, and M. Tsakiris, "Changing Bodies Changes Minds: Owning Another Body Affects Social Cognition," *Trends in Cognitive Sciences* 19 (1) (2015): 6–12.

11. Harry Farmer, Ana Tajadura-Jiménez, and Manos Tsakiris, "Beyond the Colour of My Skin: How Skin Colour Affects the Sense of Body-Ownership," *Consciousness and Cognition* 21 (3) (2012): 1242–56.

12. Maister et al., "Changing Bodies Changes Minds."

13. V. S. Ramachandran and W. Hirstein, "The Perception of Phantom Limbs: The D. O. Hebb Lecture," *Brain* 121 (1998): 1603–30.

14. S. W. Mitchell, "Phantom Limbs," *Lippincott's Magazine of Popular Literature & Science* 8 (1871): 563–69.

15. R. Sherman, C. Sherman, and L. Parker, "Chronic Phantom and Stump Pain among American Veterans: Results of a Survey," *Pain* 18 (1984): 83–95.

16. Unless otherwise noted, quotes from Ramachandran concerning his phantom limb surgery are from the following sources: J. Colapinto, "Brain Games: The Marco Polo of Neuroscience," *New Yorker*, May 11, 2009, 76–87; Metzinger, *The Ego Tunnel*; Ramachandran and Hirstein, "The Perception of Phantom Limbs"; V. S. Ramachandran (2007, March). "On your Mind," video podcast, March 2007, TED.com, http://www.ted.com/talks/vilayanur_ramachandran_on_your_mind.html; and V. S. Ramachandran, "Secrets of the Mind," *NOVA* (PBS), October 23, 2001.

17. Ramachandran referred to the patient as Philip in early reports but now calls him by his real name, Derek.

18. Colapinto, "Brain Games."

19. D. Harvie, M. Broecker, R. Smith, A. Meulders, V. Madden, and G. Moseley, "Bogus Visual Feedback Alters Onset of Movement-Evoked Pain in People with Neck Pain," *Psychological Science* 26 (4) (2015): 385–92.

20. L. Schmalzl, C. Ragnö, and H. H. Ehrsson, "An Alternative Version of Mirror Therapy: Illusory Touch Can Reduce Phantom Pain When Illusory Movement Does Not," *Clinical Journal of Pain* 29 (2013): E10–E18.

21. Composite Tissue Allotransplantation, http://www.handtransplant.com. Statistics are from March 2011.

22. J. Dubernard, E. Owen, M. Lanzetta, and N. Hakim, "What Is Happening with Hand Transplants?," *Lancet* 357 (9269) (May 26, 2001): 1711–12. This alien feeling is an issue for any transplant involving a body part the patient can see. Perhaps the most memorable case concerned the first successful penis transplant on a man in China who had lost his original organ in what was described as "an unfortunate traumatic accident." Two weeks after the surgery, both the man and his wife changed their minds, saying they were repulsed by the new penis. It was surgically removed.

23. Quoted in Claudia Dreifus, "A Blank Canvas to Create Smart Limbs: A Conversation with Hugh Herr," *New York Times*, April 30, 2013, D3.

24. Hugh Herr, interview by Terry Gross, "The Double Amputee Who Designs Better

Limbs," *Fresh Air* (NPR), August 10, 2011, http://www.npr.org/templates/tran
script/transcript.php?storyId=137552538.

25. B. Rosén, H. Ehrsson, C. Antfolk, C. Cipriani, F. Sebelius, and G. Lundborg, "Re-
ferral of Sensation to an Advanced Humanoid Robotic Hand Prosthesis," *Scandi-
navian Journal of Plastic Reconstructive Hand Surgery* 43 (5) (2009): 260–66.

26. Herr quoted in Neal Everson, "Biomechatronics," http://ffden-2.phys.uaf.edu/212
_spring2007.web.dir/neal_everson/neal_everson_004.htm.

27. Quoted in Anil Ananthaswamy, *Do No Harm: The People Who Amputate Their Perfectly Healthy Limbs, and the Doctors Who Help Them* (2012), Kindle edition, location
182.

28. Ibid., location 52.

29. Ibid., location 136.

30. Patrick is now a respected gatekeeper for surgeries in the BIID community. He
evaluates candidates and, if qualified, supervises arrangements for the operation
with a trusted surgeon in Asia.

31. Quoted in Sabine Mueller, "Amputee Envy," *Scientific American Mind* 18 (2007–8):
60–65.

32. Quotation is from BIID surgeon Michael First, reported in Robin Henig, "At War
with Their Bodies, They Seek to Sever Limbs," *New York Times*, March 22, 2005,
http://www.nytimes.com/2005/03/22/health/psychology/22ampu.html?_r=0&
pagewanted=print&position=.

33. Ananthaswamy, *Do No Harm*.

34. Quoted in Henig, "At War with Their Bodies."

35. Paul Rozin and April Fallon, "A Perspective on Disgust," *Psychological Review* 94
(1987): 23–41. See also Paul Broks, *Into the Silent Land* (New York: Grove Press,
2003), 108.

36. Falkow and other researcher quoted in Michael Pollan, "Some of My Best Friends
Are Bacteria," *New York Times Magazine*, May 19, 2013.

37. Michael Pollan, "Some of My Best Friends Are Germs," *New York Times*, May 15,
2013, http://www.nytimes.com/2013/05/19/magazine/say-hello-to-the-100-trillion
-bacteria-that-make-up-your-microbiome.html?pagewanted=all&_r=0.

38. Pam Belluck, "A Promising Pill, Not So Hard to Swallow," *New York Times*, October 11, 2014, http://www.nytimes.com/2014/10/12/us/a-promising-pill-not-so
-hard-to-swallow.html?_r=0.

39. E.g., J. F. Cryan and T. G. Dinan, "Mind-Altering Microorganisms: The Impact of
the Gut Microbiota on Brain and Behavior," *Nature Reviews: Neuroscience* 13
(2012): 701–12.

40. For a good overview of these and other studies, see, e.g., Charles Schimidt, "Mental Health May Depend on Creatures in the Gut," *Scientific American* 312 (3) (February 17, 2015): http://www.scientificamerican.com/article/mental-health-may
-depend-on-creatures-in-the-gut.

41. Mayer quoted in David Kohn, "When Gut Bacteria Changes [*sic*] Brain Function,"

Atlantic, June 24, 2015, http://www.theatlantic.com/health/archive/2015/06/gut -bacteria-on-the-brain/395918.

42. Pollan, "Some of My Best Friends Are Germs."

Chapter 5. Parasites 'R Us

1. N. R. Hanson, "From *Patterns of Discovery*," in *Perception*, ed. Robert Schwartz (Malden, MA: Blackwell, 2004), 294.

2. Coyne quoted in Adrian Forsyth and Kenneth Miyata, *Tropical Nature* (New York: Charles Scribner's, 1984), 153.

3. Jerry Coyne, interview by Robert Krulwich and Jad Abumrad, producers and co-hosts, *Radiolab* (WNYC/NPR), December 12, 2008.

4. Jerry Coyne, personal communication, February 16, 2010.

5. Coyne, interview by Krulwich.

6. Ibid.

7. Ibid.

8. Ibid.

9. Jerry Coyne, personal communication, February 16, 2010.

10. Coyne, interview by Krulwich.

11. Ibid.

12. Ibid.

13. Jerry Coyne, personal communication, February 16, 2010.

14. Coyne, interview by Krulwich.

15. Jerry Coyne, personal communication, February 16, 2010.

16. Paul Crosbie, personal communication, February 26, 2010.

17. Darwin quoted in Carl Zimmer, *Parasite Rex* (New York: Free Press, 2001), 14.

18. Zimmer, *Parasite Rex*.

19. Ibid.

20. R. Brusca and M. Gilligan, M. (1983). "Tongue Replacement in a Marine Fish (*Lutjanus guttatus*) by a Parasitic Isopod (Crustacea: *Isopoda*)," *Copeia* 3 (1983): 813–16.

21. You can see a photo of this unappetizing creature at WordPress.com, http://weird imals.wordpress.com/2009/11.

22. Nick Lane, *Power, Sex, Suicide: Mitochondria and the Meaning of Life* (New York: Oxford University Press, 2005). See also T. Saey, "Repairing a Cell's Faulty Batteries," *Science News* 177 (May 8, 2010): 16.

23. Lewis Thomas, "Organelles as Organisms" (1974), reprinted in Thomas, *The Lives of a Cell* (New York: Viking, 1974), 81–87.

24. Haplogroups are families of chromosome types that trace back to significant events in human prehistory. They are described in more detail on the 23andMe website: https://www.23andme.com/you/haplogroup/paternal.

25. In case anyone cares, I descend from the maternal haplogroup V, a subgroup of R0.

26. Mitochondrial DNA also recombines. But it recombines with copies of itself that exist within the same mitochondrion. As a result (aside from mutations) the virtually same DNA is passed down from parent to offspring. See, e.g., W. Brown, M. George, and A. Wilson, "Rapid evolution of mitochondrial DNA," *Proceedings of the National Academy of Sciences USA* 76 (4) (1979): 1967–71.

27. This time estimate, more precisely, describes *Homo sapiens sapiens*, which refers to the *sapiens* variety of the species *Homo sapiens*.

28. David Schardt, "Manipulating Mitochondria: Playing in the Fountain of Youth," *Nutrition Action Healthletter*, December 2008, at FindArticles.com., http://findarticles.com/p/articles/mi_m0813/is_10_35/ai_n31043591, accessed April 28, 2010.

29. The estimate that 10 percent of our body weight is mitochondria is from Lane, *Power, Sex, Suicide*, 1–18. Lewis Thomas, "Organelles as Organisms," on the other hand, estimates as much as 50 percent of our body weight is mitochondria.

30. Lane, *Power, Sex, Suicide*, 111–14.

31. Thomas, "Organelles as Organisms."

32. Adam Liptak, "Justices, 9–0, Bar Patenting Human Genes," *New York Times*, June 13, 2013, http://www.nytimes.com/2013/06/14/us/supreme-court-rules-human-genes-may-not-be-patented.html?_r=0.

33. Lynn Margulis and Dorian Sagan, "Rethinking Life on Earth: The Parts; Power to the Protoctists," *Earthwatch* 11 (1992): 25–29.

34. Jerry Coyne, personal communication, February 16, 2010.

35. It turns out, in fact, that not only do we have cellular DNA and mitochondrial DNA under our skin, but at least a few of us actually have two sets of mitochondrial DNA, a chimera within a chimera. This is where paternal DNA comes in. The argument goes something like this: Biologists used to think no mitochondria were passed down from fathers. Paternal mitochondria, we have long known, play a vital role in fertilization. Basically, a pack of them attach to the tail of the sperm where, at the right moment, they provide a jolt of energy that propels the sperm toward the egg. This, however, is usually the end of the line for the paternal mitochondria, which now break off with the rest of the tail as the front of the sperm continues onward. They are like the first stage of a NASA rocket, whose only job is to power the main ship to the edge of the earth's atmosphere; once there, the unit detaches from the ship never to be seen again. It was believed all paternal mitochondria suffered such a fate. But then, in 2002, a *New England Journal of Medicine* article by two Danish physicians, Marianne Schwartz and John Vissing, reported a patient with two distinct sets of mDNA, one matching his mother's and the other his father's. This was the first unequivocal evidence that paternal mitochondrial DNA can be inherited in humans. The two DNAs were arranged as a mosaic. Actually a variety of mosaics: The mDNA in the patient's muscle cells, for example, was 10 percent paternal and 90 percent maternal, while the mDNA in his blood cells was close to 100 percent maternal. He was a mitochondrial chimera. See M. Schwartz and J. Vissing, "Paternal Inheritance of Mitochondrial DNA," *New England Journal of Medicine* 347 (2002): 576–80.

Chapter 6. Multiple Personalities, Multiple People

1. Except as otherwise noted, all quotations in this chapter from Karen Keegan and her doctors are taken from an interview by Robert Krulwich and Jad Abumrad, producers and co-hosts, "(So-Called) Life," *Radiolab* (WNYC/NPR), March 14, 2008, http://www.radiolab.org/story/91596-so-called-life.

2. Kruskall quoted in Claire Ainsworth, "The Stranger Within," *New Scientist* 180 (2421) (November 15, 2003): 34.

3. Ibid.

4. See also L. Strain, J. Dean, M. Hamilton, and D. Bonthron, "A True Hermaphrodite Chimera Resulting from Embryo Amalgamation after In Vitro Fertilization," *New England Journal of Medicine* 338 (1998): 166–69.

5. Catherine Arcabascio, "Chimeras: Double the DNA—Double the Fun for Crime Scene Investigators, Prosecutors, and Defense Attorneys?," *Akron Law Review* 40 (3) (2007): 435–63.

6. Carl Zimmer, "DNA Double Take," *New York Times*, September 17, 2013, D1.

7. J. L. Nelson, "Your Cells Are My Cells," *Scientific American* 298 (2) (February 2008): 72–79.

8. Ibid.

9. Randolph quoted in Zimmer, "DNA Double Take." The chimera review article is K. Chen, R. H. Chmait, D. Vanderbilt, S. Wu, and L. Randolph, "Chimerism in Monochorionic Dizygotic Twins: Case Study and Review," *American Journal of Medical Genetics Part A* 161 (7) (2013): 1817–24.

10. Ainsworth, "The Stranger Within," 34.

11. There is increasing evidence that these migrant cells can also be detrimental to the health of the host. They may be especially problematic in causing autoimmune diseases in adults. See, e.g., Nelson, "Your Cells Are My Cells"; and Ainsworth, "The Stranger Within."

12. Nelson, "Your Cells Are My Cells."

13. Ainsworth, "The Stranger Within."

14. W. F. N. Chan, C. Gurnot, T. J. Montine, J. A. Sonnen, K. A. Guthrie, et al., "Male Microchimerism in the Human Female Brain," *PLOS ONE* 7 (9) (2012): doi:10.1371/journal.pone.0045592.

15. Nelson, "Your Cells Are My Cells."

16. N. G. Waller, F. W. Putnam, and E. B. Carlson, "Types of Dissociation and Dissociative Types: A Taxometric Analysis of Dissociative Experiences," *Psychological Methods* 1 (3) (1996): 300–321.

17. Zoe Farris, interview by Natasha Mitchell, narrator/producer, "Many Selves, One Body: Dissociation and Early Trauma," *All in the Mind*, August 22, 2009, ABC Radio National (Australian Broadcasting Corporation). All subsequent quotations of Farris are from this source.

18. American Psychiatric Association, *Diagnostic and Statistical Manual of Mental Disorders*, 4th ed. (Washington, DC: American Psychiatric Association, 1994).

19. C. H. Thigpen and H. Cleckley, "A Case of Multiple Personality," *Journal of Abnormal and Social Psychology* 49 (1954): 135–51.

20. Erving Goffman, *The Presentation of Self in Everyday Life* (New York: Anchor Books, 1959).

21. Coons quoted in Robert Todd Carroll, The Skeptic's Dictionary, s.v. Multiple personality disorder [dissociative identity disorder], http://skepdic.com/mpd.html.

Chapter 7. Stranger in the Mirror

1. G. G. Gallup, "Self-Awareness in Primates," *American Scientist* 67 (1979): 417–21.

2. M. Lewis, M. W. Sullivan, C. Stanger, and M. Weiss, "Self-Development and Self-Conscious Emotions," *Child Development* 60 (1989): 146–56.

3. Shari Cookson and Nick Doob, directors and producers, *The Alzheimer's Project, Part 1: The Memory Loss Tapes* (HBO Documentaries, 2009).

4. N. Breen, D. Caine, and M. Coltheart, "Mirrored-Self Misidentification: Two Cases of Focal Onset Dementia," *Neurocase* 7 (3) (2001): 239–54.

5. M. Mendez, R. Martin, K. Smyth, and P. Whitehouse, "Disturbances of Person Identification in Alzheimer's Disease," *Journal of Nervous and Mental Disease* 180 (1992): 94–96.

6. Oliver Sacks, "Face-Blind," *New Yorker*, August 30, 2010, 36–40.

7. L. K. Gluckman, "A Case of Capgras Syndrome," *Australian and New Zealand Journal of Psychiatry* 2 (1968): 39–43. All subsequent quotations about this patient are from this source.

8. Todd Feinberg, *From Axons to Identity* (New York: W. W. Norton, 2009), 46.

9. A. Barnier, R. Cox, A. O'Connor, M. Coltheart, R. Langdon, N. Breen, and M. Turner, "Developing Hypnotic Analogues of Clinical Delusions: Mirrored-Self Misidentification," *Cognitive Neuropsychiatry* 13 (5) (2008): 406–30.

10. There was also a third condition, the mirror-as-a-window group, in which subjects were told: "When you look to your left, you will see a window to another room."

11. M. Nash, "The Truth and the Hype of Hypnosis," *Scientific American*, 285 (1) (July 2001): 48–54.

12. Søren Kierkegaard, *The Sickness unto Death*, ed. and trans. Howard V. Hong and Edna H. Hong (Princeton, NJ: Princeton University Press, 1985), 32–33.

13. Breen et al., "Mirrored-Self Misidentification."

Chapter 8. Two Bodies, One Self: Or, What if You Met Your Identical Twin?

Chapter epigraph is from *On the Black Hill* by Bruce Chatwin, copyright © 1982 by Bruce Chatwin. Used by permission of Viking Books, an imprint of Penguin Publishing Group, a division of Penguin Random House LLC.

1. Quotations and details about Barbara and Daphne and other twin pairs in this chapter, except where otherwise noted, are from Elyse Schein and Paula Bernstein,

Identical Strangers (New York: Random House, 2007); William Wright, *Born That Way: Genes, Behavior, Personality* (New York: Knopf, 1998); and Peter Watson, *Twins: An Uncanny Relationship* (Chicago: Contemporary Books, 1981).

2. Lawrence Wright, *Twins: And What They Tell Us about Who We Are* (Hoboken, NJ: Wiley, 1997).
3. From a 1979 article in the *Minnesota Tribune*, quoted in ibid., 44.
4. Jims quoted in Watson, *Twins: An Uncanny Relationship*, 10.
5. Ibid.
6. Bouchard quoted in Schein and Bernstein, *Identical Strangers*, 112.
7. Watson, *Twins: An Uncanny Relationship*, 10–11.
8. Bouchard quoted in Wright, *Twins: And What They Tell Us about Who We Are*, 53.
9. Watson, *Twins: An Uncanny Relationship*, 9–13.
10. Abigail Pogrebin, *One and the Same* (New York: Doubleday, 2009), 239.
11. Ibid., 52.
12. Nancy Segal, *Entwined Lives: Twins and What They Tell Us about Human Behavior* (New York: Penguin, 1999), 52.
13. Quotations from Tiki Barber, Sam Zarante, and Sandy Miller are from Pogrebin, *One and the Same*, 26.
14. Paul quoted in Pogrebin, *One and the Same*, 95.
15. Caroline Paul, *Fighting Fire* (New York: St. Martin's Press, 1998).
16. Schein and Bernstein, *Identical Strangers*, vii.
17. Pogrebin, *One and the Same*, 238.
18. Wright, *Twins: And What They Tell Us about Who We Are*, 157–58.

Chapter 9. The Art of Self-Cloning

1. All references are from G. N. Christodoulou, "Syndrome of Subjective Doubles," *American Journal of Psychiatry* 135 (1978): 249–51.
2. J. Kamanitz, R. El-Mallakh, and A. Tasman, "Delusional Misidentification Involving the Self," *Journal of Nervous and Mental Disease* 177 (1989): 695–98.
3. Edgar Allan Poe, "William Wilson," *Burton's Gentleman's Magazine*, October 1839.
4. Fyodor Dostoevsky, *The Double: Two Versions*, trans. Evelyn Harden (Ann Arbor, MI: Ardis, 1985), 177.
5. Ibid., 71.
6. These percentages are based on the combined number of subjects who rated each option as mildly, moderately, or extremely likable versus the total of those who expressed mild, moderate, or extreme dislike. Those who rated the option as "neutral" ($N = 23$ for the first scenario; $N = 15$ for the second scenario) are not included in the percentages. Complete data are available from the author.
7. For scenario one, thirteen said they absolutely hated the idea, and five said they absolutely loved it. For scenario two, twenty absolutely hated it, and five absolutely loved it.

8. Jim Blascovich and Jeremy Bailenson, *Infinite Reality* (New York: William Morrow, 2011), 83–94 (chap. 5).

9. Reported in ibid.

10. Byron Reeves and Clifford Nass, *The Media Equation: How People Treat Computers, Televisions and New Media like Real People and Places* (Cambridge: Cambridge University Press, 1996).

11. N. Yee, J. N. Bailenson, and N. Ducheneaut, "The Proteus Effect: Implications of Transformed Digital Self-Representation on Online and Offline Behavior," *Communication Research* 36 (2009): 285–312. See also N. Yee and J. Bailenson, "The Proteus Effect: The Effect of Transformed Self-Representation on Behavior," *Human Communication Research*, in press.

12. Yee, Bailenson, and Ducheneaut, "The Proteus Effect: Implications of Transformed Digital Self-Representation on Online and Offline Behavior."

13. This and the remainder of the findings on this list are reported in Blascovich and Bailenson, *Infinite Reality*, 109–21.

14. You will soon be able to experience sex through your avatar. Engineers in an emerging industry known as "teledildonics" are developing systems that can digitally transmit the sexual actions of your avatar to vibrating devices that attach to your sexual organs. The male model is connected to an artificial hand and the female model is connected to a vibrator. See, e.g., IGN.com, http://gear.ign.com/articles/112/1123976p1.html.

15. Blascovich and Bailenson, *Infinite Reality*, 144.

16. See, e.g., the website for the company Virtual Eternity, https://www.virtualeternity.com.

17. Blascovich and Bailenson, *Infinite Reality*, 145.

Chapter 10. Who Thinks the Thoughts?

1. Eric Klinger, "Daydreaming and Fantasizing: Thought Flow and Emotion," in K. Markman, W. Klein, and J. Sahr, eds., *Handbook of Imagination and Mental Stimulation* (New York: Psychology Press, 2009), 225–40.

2. B. Libet, C. A. Gleason, E. W. Wright, and D. K. Pearl, "Time of Conscious Intention to Act in Relation to Onset of Cerebral Activity (Readiness-Potential): The Unconscious Initiation of a Freely Voluntary Act," *Brain: A Journal of Neurology* 106 (3) (1983): 623–42.

3. C. Soon, M. Brass, H. Heinze, and J. Haynes, "Unconscious Determinants of Free Decisions in the Human Brain," *Nature Neuroscience* 11 (2008): 544–45.

4. Haynes quoted in "Brain Scans Can Reveal Your Decisions 7 Seconds before You 'Decide,'" Exploring the Mind!, http://exploringthemind.com/the-mind/brain-scans-can-reveal-your-decisions-7-seconds-before-you-decide, accessed August 25, 2015.

5. Wegbreit quoted in Jonah Lehrer, "The Eureka Hunt," *New Yorker*, July 28, 2008, 40–45.

6. J. Kounios and M. Beeman, "The Aha! Moment: The Cognitive Neuroscience of Insight," *Current Directions in Psychological Science* 18 (2009): 210–16.

7. E.g., Thomas Huxley, "On the Hypothesis That Animals Are Automata, and Its History," *Nature* 10 (1874): 362–66.

8. J. A. Bargh, "Reply to the Commentaries," in R. S. Wyer, ed., *The Automaticity of Everyday Life: Advances in Social Cognition* (Mahwah, NJ: Erlbaum, 1997), 231–46.

9. Quoted in Lehrer, "The Eureka Hunt."

10. Henri Poincaré, "Mathematical Creation," in James R. Newman, ed., *The World of Mathematics* (New York: Simon and Schuster, 1958), 2041–50.

11. Blake quoted in Celine Mansanti, "William Blake in *transition* Magazine (Paris, 1927–38): The Modalities of a Blake Revival in France during the 1920s and 1930s," *Blake: An Illustrated Quarterly*, 43 (2) (Fall 2009): 52.

12. John Forster, *The Life of Charles Dickens* (London: Cecil Palmer, 1872–74), 3:61.

13. Van der Beek quoted in B. Stoney, *Enid Blyton: A Biography* (London: Hodder and Stoughton, 1974), 197.

14. Harold Pinter, interview by Larry Bensky, "Harold Pinter: The Art of Theater No. 3," *Paris Review* 39 (Fall 1966): http://www.theparisreview.org/interviews/4351/the-art-of-theater-no-3-harold-pinter.

15. John Lahr, "Demolition Man: Harold Pinter and 'The Homecoming,'" *New Yorker*, December 24, 2007, 54–69.

16. As recalled by writer Liz Gilbert, interview by Jad Abumrad and Robert Krulwich, producers and co-hosts, "Help!? Narrators," *Radiolab* (WNYC/NPR), March 8, 2011.

17. Robertson Davies, interview by Elisabeth Sifton, "The Art of Fiction," *Paris Review* 110 (Spring 1989): http://www.theparisreview.org/interviews/2441/the-art-of-fiction-no-107-robertson-davies.

18. Emma Letley's introduction to the Oxford World Classic's edition of *The Strange Case of Dr. Jekyll and Mr. Hyde*, quoted in Paul Broks, *Into the Silent Land* (New York: Grove Press, 2003), 171–80. I have drawn liberally from Broks's excellent chapter, "The Dreams of Robert Louis Stevenson," in this discussion of Stevenson.

19. Robert Louis Stevenson, "A Chapter on Dreams (Annotated)," Musings of Historically Significant Authors, Kindle edition, location 62.

20. Ibid., location 81.

21. Ibid., location 79.

22. Ibid., location 121.

23. Jad Abumrad and Robert Krulwich, narrators, "Who Am I?," *Radiolab* (WNYC/NPR), February 4, 2005.

24. Quoted in Claire Harman, *Myself and the Other Fellow: A Life of Robert Louis Stevenson* (New York: HarperCollins, 2005).

25. Graham Balfour, *The Life of Robert Louis Stevenson* (London: Methuen, 1901), 2:17.

26. Nash quoted in Deidre Barrett, "Answers in Your Dreams," *Scientific American Mind* (November/December 2011): 27–35.

27. "A Brilliant Madness," *PBS American Experience*, 2002; transcript at PBS.org, http://www.pbs.org/wgbh/amex/nash/filmmore/pt.html, accessed October 20, 2014.

28. Interview with Robert Louis Stevenson, *New York Herald*, September 8, 1887, in Christopher Silvester, ed., *The Penguin Book of Interviews* (New York: Penguin Books, 1993).

29. For an excellent review of the evolution of the concept of "genius," see Darrin McMahon, *Divine Fury: A History of Genius* (New York: Basic Books, 2013).

30. The name for the iPhone's Siri was coined by Dag Kittalaus, the Norwegian cocreator of the iPhone 4S. Siri means "beautiful woman who leads you to victory" in Norwegian.

31. Stevenson, "A Chapter on Dreams," location 193.

32. Jorge Luis Borges, "Borges and I," in *Labyrinths*, trans. James E. Irby (New York: New Directions, 1962), 246.

Chapter 11. The Voices

1. See, e.g., Robert K. Ressler and Tom Schachiman, *Whoever Fights Monsters: My Twenty Years Hunting Serial Killers for the FBI* (New York: St. Martin's Press, 1992), 145–51.

2. T. N. Nayani and A. S. David, "The Auditory Hallucination: A Phenomenological Survey," *Psychological Medicine* 26 (1996): 177–89.

3. M. K. Looi, producer, "Voices in the Dark: The People Who Hear Voices," *Mosaic: The Science of Life*, December 9, 2014, audio podcast, http://mosaicscience.com/story/hearing-voices.

4. Ibid.

5. Gromov quoted in Sylvia Nasar, *A Beautiful Mind: The Life of Mathematical Genius and Nobel Laureate John Nash* (New York: Touchstone, 1998).

6. Nasar, *A Beautiful Mind*, 1.

7. D. L. Rosenhan, "Being Sane in Insane Places," *Science* 179 (1973): 250–58. For another interesting description of the study and its consequences, see Malcolm Gladwell, "Connecting the Dots," *New Yorker*, March 10, 2003, 83–88.

8. Julian Jaynes, *The Origin of Consciousness in the Breakdown of the Bicameral Mind* (Boston: Houghton Mifflin, 1976), 1–64.

9. Ivan Leudar and Philip Thomas, *Voices of Reason, Voices of Madness: Studies of Verbal Hallucinations* (London: Routledge, 2000), 7–27.

10. The modern definition of the term "hallucination" traces to the writings of a Frenchman named Jean-Etienne Esquirol in 1835.

11. Oliver Sacks, *Hallucinations* (New York: Knopf, 2012), 60.

12. L. C. Johns, J. Y. Nazroo, P. Bebbington, and E. Kuipers, "Occurrence of Hallucinatory Experiences in a Community Sample and Ethnic Variations," *British Journal of Psychiatry* 180 (2002): 174–78.

13. Eugene Raikhel, "The Culture, Mind and Brain Conference and Tanya Luhrmann

on 'Hearing Voices in Accra and Chennai,'" Somatosphere, http://somatosphere .net/?p=4232, accessed October 22, 2012.

14. Kim T. Mueser and Susan Gingerich, *The Complete Family Guide to Schizophrenia* (New York: Guilford Press, 2006), 22.

15. T. B. Posey and M. R. Losch, "Auditory Hallucinations of Hearing Voices in 375 Normal Subjects," *Imagination, Cognition and Personality* 2 (1983): 99–113.

16. Quoted in C. Green and C. McCreery, *Apparitions* (London: Hamish Hamilton, 1975), 85.

17. T. R. Barrett and J. B. Etheridge, "Verbal Hallucinations in Normals, I: People Who Hear 'Voices,'" *Applied Cognitive Psychology* 6 (1992): S379–S387.

18. T. X. Barber and D. S. Calverey, "An Experimental Study of Hypnotic (Auditory and Visual) Hallucinations," *Journal of Abnormal and Social Psychology* 68 (1964): 13–20.

19. D. M. Wegner and S. Zanakos, "Chronic Thought Suppression," *Journal of Personality* 62 (1994): 615–40.

20. Its website is http://www.intervoiceonline.org.

21. Hearing Voices of Denver, http://www.denvervoices.org/about.htm.

22. J. Glicksohn and T. R. Barrett, "Absorption and Hallucinatory Experience," *Applied Cognitive Psychology* 17 (2003): 833–49.

23. A. Woods, N. Jones, B. Alderson-Day, and C. Fernyhough, "Experiences of Hearing Voices: Analysis of a Novel Phenomenological Survey," *Lancet Psychiatry* 2 (2015): 323–31. (Of the 153 respondents, 26 had no history of mental illness.)

24. B. Gordon, "Why Is It Impossible to Stop Thinking, to Render the Mind a Complete Blank?," *Scientific American Mind* (November/December 2012): 78.

25. Mark Leary, *The Curse of the Self: Self-Awareness, Egotism, and the Quality of Human Life* (Oxford: Oxford University Press, 2004), 45.

26. Sacks, *Hallucinations*, 58.

27. Joe Simpson, *Touching the Void* (New York: HarperCollins, 1988), 116.

28. Eleanor Longden, "Listening to Voices," *Scientific American Mind* (September/October 2013): 34–39.

29. Leudar and Thomas, *Voices of Reason, Voices of Madness*.

30. Sacks, *Hallucinations*, 68.

31. Charles Fernyhough, *A Thousand Days of Wonder: A Scientist's Chronicle of His Daughter's Developing Mind* (New York: Avery, 2008), 93.

32. L. Magrassi, G. Aromataris, A. Cabrini, V. Annovazzi-Lodi, and A. Moro, "Sound Representation in Higher Language Areas during Language Generation," *PNAS* 112 (6) (2015): 1868–73.

33. L. S. Vygotsky, *Mind and Society: The Development of Higher Mental Processes* (Cambridge, MA: Harvard University Press, 1978), 57.

34. Parts of this discussion are taken from Jad Abumrad and Robert Krulwich, narrators, "Voices in Your Head," *Radiolab* (WNYC/NPR), September 7, 2010.

35. Fernyhough, *A Thousand Days of Wonder*, 97.

36. Mikhail Bakhtin, *Speech Genres and Other Late Essays*, trans. Vern W. McGee (Austin: University of Texas Press, 1986), 88.

Chapter 12. Herding the Cats

1. E.g., L. Cosmides and J. Tooby, "Evolutionary Psychology and the Generation of Culture, Part II: Case Study; A Computational Theory of Social Exchange," *Ethology and Sociobiology* 10 (1989): 1–97.
2. The children waited an average of six minutes.
3. W. Mischel, Y. Shoda, and M. L. Rodriguez, "Delay of Gratification in Children," *Science* 244 (1989): 933–38.
4. M. K. Rothbart, S. A. Ahadi, and D. E. Evans, "Temperament and Personality: Origins and Outcomes," *Journal of Personality and Social Psychology* 78 (2000): 122–35.
5. S. Frederick, G. Loewenstein, and T. O'Donoghue, "Time Discounting and Time Preference: A Critical Review," *Journal of Economic Literature* 40 (2) (2000): 351–401.
6. An excellent source of information about procrastination can be found at the website of the Procrastination Research Group at Carleton University (Timothy Pychyl, director), http://http-server.carleton.ca/~tpychyl.
7. Christine Tappolet, "Procrastination and Personal Identity," in Chrisoula Andreou and Mark White, eds., *The Thief of Time: Philosophical Essays on Procrastination* (New York: Oxford University Press, 2010), 115–29.
8. Ainslie quoted in James Surowiecki, "What Does Procrastination Tell Us about Ourselves?," *New Yorker*, October 11, 2010, 110–13.
9. D. Ariely and K. Wertenbroch, "Procrastination, Deadlines, and Performance: Self-Control and Precommitment," *Psychological Science* 13 (2002): 219–24.
10. Surowiecki, "What Does Procrastination Tell Us about Ourselves?"
11. John Perry, "How to Procrastinate and Still Get Things Done," *Chronicle of Higher Education* (February 23, 1996): http://chronicle.com/article/How-to-Procrastinate-Still/93959.
12. Reported in Surowiecki, "What Does Procrastination Tell Us about Ourselves?"
13. Schelling quoted in Ian Ayres, *Carrots and Sticks: Unlock the Power of Incentives to Get Things Done* (New York: Bantam, 2010), 87.
14. Interview with Zelda Gamson, interview by Jad Abumrad and Robert Krulwich, producers and co-hosts, "Help!? Narrators," *Radiolab* (WNYC/NPR), March 8, 2011.
15. Ayres, *Carrots and Sticks*. Also, Ayres and his colleagues have set up a website called StickK, which guides you through the process of setting up personal contracts and allows you to monitor and enhance your progress, http://www.stickk.com.
16. Ayres, *Carrots and Sticks*, 90.
17. See http://www.chabad.org/holidays/jewishnewyear/resolutions_cdo/aid/1943153/jewish/New-Years-Resolution-Solution.htm.

18. Seligson quoted in Rachel Hirshfeld, "E-Mail 'Nagger' Helps You Keep Rosh Ha-shannah Vows," September 19, 2012, Israelnationalnews.com, http://www.israel nationalnews.com/News/News.aspx/160078, accessed November 1, 2014.

19. Described in Ayres, *Carrots and Sticks*, 90–96

20. Joseph Heath and Joel Anderson, "Procrastination and the Extended Will," in An-dreou and White, *The Thief of Time*, 233–52.

21. Jay McInerney, "It's Six A.M.: Do You Know Where You Are?," in *How It Ended: New and Collected Stories* (New York: Knopf, 2009), 3–11.

Chapter 13. A Troupe of Performers

1. *Pisher* is a Yiddish term defined variously as "a small child," "a young and inexperi-enced person," "a little squirt," and "a nobody"; see, e.g., Michael Wex, *Born to Kvetch: Yiddish Language and Culture in All of Its Moods* (New York: Harper, 2005.)

2. Robert Sapolsky, *The Trouble with Testosterone* (New York: Scribner, 1998), 204.

3. Personal communication, May 29, 2009.

4. Except where otherwise noted, quotations concerning the Stanford Prison Study are from Philip Zimbardo, "The Mind Is a Formidable Jailer: A Pirandellian Prison," *New York Times Magazine*, April 8, 1973, 38–57; and Zimbardo, *The Lucifer Effect* (New York: Random House, 2007).

5. From an interview in *Quiet Rage: The Stanford Prison Experiment*, videotape pro-duced by Philip Zimbardo (Stanford, CA: Stanford Instructional Television Net-work, 1992).

6. Quoted in Zimbardo, "The Mind Is a Formidable Jailer."

7. Quotations in this paragraph are from Philip Zimbardo, "The Psychology of Evil: A Situationist Perspective on Recruiting Good People to Engage in Antisocial Acts," unpublished manuscript, Stanford, CA.

8. Philip Roth, *The Counterlife* (New York: Vintage, 1996), 300–301.

9. David Myers, *Social Psychology*, 5th ed. (New York: McGraw-Hill, 1996), 131. There is considerable research concerning the degree to which our beliefs and attitudes are consistent with our actions, as well as the conditions when consistency is more or less likely. For a summary, see, e.g., Myers, *Social Psychology*, 11th ed. (New York: McGraw-Hill, 2013), 118–49.

10. F. A. Blanchard and S. W. Cook, "Effects of Helping a Less Competent Member of a Cooperating Interracial Group on the Development of Interpersonal Attraction," *Journal of Personality and Social Psychology* 34 (1976): 1245–55; and D. Glass, "Changes in Liking as a Means of Reducing Cognitive Discrepancies between Self-Esteem and Aggression," *Journal of Personality* 32 (1964): 491–549.

11. Forester quoted in Terry Blackhawk, *To Light a Fire: 20 Years with the InsideOut Literary Arts Project* (Detroit: Wayne State University Press, 2015), 10.

12. Jim Dale quotation is taken from David Black, *The Magic of Theater* (New York: Macmillan, 1993).

13. Quoted in Zimbardo, *The Lucifer Effect*, 191.
14. Kurt Vonnegut, *Mother Night* (New York: Random House, 2009), v.
15. William James, *Psychology: The Briefer Course*, ed. G. Allport (1892; Notre Dame, IN: University of Notre Dame Press, 1985), 46.
16. Malcolm Gladwell, "Most Likely to Succeed," *New Yorker*, December 15, 2008, 36–42.
17. This exercise is adapted from A. Pines and C. Maslach, *Experiencing Social Psychology: Readings and Projects*, 2nd ed. (New York: McGraw-Hill, 1984), 73–88 (chap. 4).

Chapter 14. A Geography of the Self

1. There are, of course, individual differences. Some people are relatively consistent from one encounter to another, while others are Zelig-like change artists. At the clinical extreme are sociopaths, one of whose defining characteristics is a compulsion is to manipulate people by playing any part they think will get what they want.

   There is a psychological test called the Self-Monitoring Scale that appraises the tendency to alter one's behavior to fit the situation. Typical questions include: "I tend to show different sides of myself to different people," and "Different people tend to have different impressions about the type of person I am." See, e.g., M. Snyder, "Self-Monitoring of Expressive Behavior," *Journal of Personality and Social Psychology* 30 (1974): 526–37.
2. At Sapporo Medical University, to which I am immensely grateful for its hospitality and my education in Japanese culture.
3. Ian Baruma, *Behind the Mask: On Sexual Demons, Sacred Mothers, Transvestites, Gangsters and Other Japanese Cultural Heroes* (New York: New American Library, 1984), 69.
4. A few personal touches, visible only to connoisseurs of the art, have been added by some famous actors over the years.
5. Oscar Wilde, "The Critic as an Artist," in Josephine M. Guy, ed., *The Complete Works of Oscar Wilde* (1891; New York: Oxford University Press, 2007), 6:183.
6. S. Cousins, "Culture and Self-Perception in Japan and the United States," *Journal of Personality and Social Psychology* 56 (1989): 124–31.
7. Cited in H. Markus and S. Kitayama, "Culture and the Self: Implications for Cognition, Emotion, and Motivation," *Psychological Review* 98 (1991): 224–51.
8. The uses of nationalistic categories (e.g., "Americans," "Japanese," "Chinese," etc.) are understood to be overgeneralizations. I use them here in the "scholarly" sense—as heuristic categories to denote cultural traits, not strict rules of conduct or biological inevitabilities or such.
9. Quoted in I. Choi, R. Nisbett, and A. Norenzayan, "Causal Attribution East and West: Asian Contextualism and Universal Dispositionism," unpublished manuscript, University of Michigan.

10. R. K. Chao, "East and West: Concepts of the Self Expressed in Mothers' Reports of Their Child Rearing," unpublished manuscript, 1993; cited in H. Markus and S. Kitayama, "A Collective Fear of the Collective: Implications for Selves and Theories of Selves," *Personality and Social Psychology Bulletin* 20 (1994): 568–79.

11. E.g., J. Gonzalez-Mena, *Multicultural Issues in Child Care* (Mountain View, CA: Mayfield Publishing, 1993).

12. J. G. Miller, "Culture and the Development of Everyday Social Explanation," *Journal of Personality and Social Psychology* 46 (1984): 961–78. See also P. Smith and M. Bond, *Social Psychology across Cultures*, 2nd ed. (Needham Heights, MA: Allyn and Bacon, 1999).

13. Our international collaborators include Jyoti Verma (India), Virginia O'Leary (Nepal), Suguru Sato (Japan), Fabio Iglesias and Valdiney Gouveia (Brazil), and Zhongquan Li (China).

14. We also gave the survey in Japan but later discovered problems in translation of key items.

15. The first recorded use of the word in today's sense was in 1533, when the Protestant reformer John Frith described a former religious outcast as a person who had led a "very sincere life." The outcast, unfortunately, was despised by the religious authorities as a dangerous heretic. They became so enraged when Frith equated morality with sincerity that they ended up burning him at the stake. R. Jay Magill, *Sincerity: How a Moral Ideal Born Five Hundred Years Ago Inspired Religious Wars, Modern Art, Hipster Chic, and the Curious Notion That We All Have Something to Say (No Matter How Dull)* (New York: W. W. Norton, 2012).

16. Jean-Jacques Rousseau quoted in Richard Sennett, *The Fall of Public Man* (New York: W. W. Norton, 1992), 119.

17. J. D. Salinger, *The Catcher in the Rye* (1951; New York: Little, Brown, 1991), 12.

18. Eunook Suh, "Culture, Identity Consistency, and Subjective Well-Being," *Journal of Personality and Social Psychology* 83 (2000): 1378–91.

19. R. Lichtenstein and R. Levine, "Differences in Evaluations of Self-Concept Consistency across Five Cultures," poster presented at the annual meeting of the Western Psychological Association, San Francisco, April 2012; and G. Hagy, M. Fabros, R. Levine, S. Sato, J. Verma, and F. Iglesias, "Consistency of Self from Kin versus Non-kin Perspectives," poster presented at the annual meeting of the Western Psychological Association, San Francisco, April 2012.

20. H. Markus and S. Kitayama, "Culture and the Self: Implications for Cognition, Emotion, and Motivation," *Psychological Review* 98 (1991): 224–51.

21. Roger V. Burton and John M. Whiting, "The Absent Father and Cross-Sex Identity," *Merrill-Palmer Quarterly* 7 (1961): 85–95; and M. J. Suzuki, "Child-Rearing and Educational Practices in the United States and Japan: Comparative Perspectives," *Hyogo Kyoiku Daigaku Kenkyu Kiyo* [*Hyogo University of Teacher Education Journal*] 20 (2000): 177–86.

22. R. A. Shweder, L. A. Jensen, and W. Goldstein, "Who Sleeps by Whom Revisited:

A Method for Extracting the Moral Goods Implicit in Practice," in J. J. Goodnow, P. J. Miller, and F. Kessel, eds., *Cultural Practices as Contexts for Development*, New Directions for Child Development, no. 67 (San Francisco: Jossey Bass, 1995), 21–39.

23. Burton and Whiting, "The Absent Father and Cross-Sex Identity"; and Suzuki, "Child-Rearing and Educational Practices in the United States and Japan."

24. Richard Nisbett, *The Geography of Thought* (New York: Free Press, 2003), 57–58.

25. Y. Zhu, L. Zhang, J. Fan, and S. Han, "Neural Basis of Cultural Influence on Self-Representation," *NeuroImage* 34 (2007): 1310–16.

26. Amy Chua, "Tiger Mom's Long-Distance Cub," *Wall Street Journal*, December 24, 2011, http://www.wsj.com/articles/SB10001424052970204791104577110870328419222.

27. Amy Chua, *Battle Hymn of the Tiger Mother* (New York: Penguin, 2011).

28. Nisbett, *The Geography of Thought*, 52–53.

29. See, e.g., "The Lurker's Guide to Leafcutter Ants," Blueboard.com, http://www.blueboard.com/leafcutters/what.htm. Or, practically anything written by Edward O. Wilson.

30. The estimated population of Paris in 2012 was 9,638,000, according to *The Times Atlas of the World*.

31. Steven J. Heine, *Cultural Psychology*, 2nd ed. (New York: W. W. Norton, 2011), 206.

Chapter 15. Finding the Schindler Button

Chapter epigraph is from *The Lazaruz Project* by Aleksander Hemon, copyright © 2008 by Aleksander Hemon. Used by permission of Riverhead, an imprint of Penguin Publishing Group, a division of Penguin Random House; and ARAGI, Inc.

1. Michel de Montaigne, "On the Inconstancy of Our Actions," in *The Complete Essays*, trans. M. A. Screech (New York: Penguin, 1991), 380.

2. The question of the extent to which traits remain stable over time and across situations is a matter of considerable debate in psychology. For two good reviews of the evidence, see D. Y. Kenrick and D. C. Funder, "Profiting from Controversy: Lessons from the Person-Situation Debate," *American Psychologist* 43 (1988): 23–24; and W. Mischel, "Personality Dispositions Revisited and Revised: A View after Three Decades," in A. Pervin, ed., *Handbook of Personality: Theory and Research* (New York: Guilford Press, 1990), 111–34.

3. Milgram actually conducted a series of variations on his obedience paradigm in which he investigated how obedience was affected by such factors as the proximity of the experimenter to the subject, the proximity of the subject to the victim, using women as subjects, and surrounding the subject with peers. Obedience varied from one condition to another but, in almost every case, was frighteningly high. For a detailed description of the studies, see Stanley Milgram, *Obedience to Authority: An Experimental View* (New York: Harper and Row, 1974).

4. See, e.g., Carl Horowitz, "Jane Elliott and Her Blue-Eyed Devil Children," FrontPageMagazine.com, January 1, 2007, http://www.frontpagemag.com/Articles /Read.aspx?GUID={0448677C-CFCC-45FB-B50C-A1B8881BAE69}. For a good overview of research demonstrating how subtle features of the environment can bring out the worst in people, see, e.g., D. G. Myers, "How Nice People Get Corrupted (Module 14)," in Myers, *Exploring Social Psychology*, 6th ed. (New York: McGraw-Hill, 2011).

5. The accuracy of this English translation has been criticized. The character *wēi* (危), which supposedly means "opportunity," is more accurately translated as "critical point."

6. In 1989, for example, Temple Beth Israel presented Mike with its first Social Action Award. In 1990, Helene Curtis and *People* magazine gave Mike their "People Who Make a Difference Award." In 1991, President Bush gave Mike's organization the nation's "Daily Point of Light Award." In 2005, the national Italian Catholic Federation presented Mike with its Pope John XXIII award for his humanitarian achievements.

7. Mike McGarvin, *Papa Mike* (Fresno, CA: Poverello House, 2003), 10.

8. Ibid., 28.

9. Ibid., 13.

10. Ibid., 15.

11. Ibid., 18.

12. E.g., C. Nave, R. Sherman, D. Funder, S. Hampson, and L. Goldberg, "On the Contextual Independence of Personality: Teachers' Assessments Predict Directly Observed Behavior after Four Decades," *Social Psychological and Personality Science*, published online before print (July 8, 2010): doi:10.1177/1948550610370717.

13. McGarvin, *Papa Mike*, 47.

14. Mike McGarvin, interview by author, Poverello House, Fresno, CA, December 8, 2007. Unless otherwise indicated, subsequent quotations are from this interview.

15. McGarvin, *Papa Mike*, 47.

16. S. J. Gould, "The Evolution of Life on the Earth," *Scientific American* 271 (44) (1994): 85–91.

17. Stern quoted in C. Schrag, "His Jews Recall Liar-Rescuer," *St. Louis Post-Dispatch*, March 23, 1994, 5b.

18. Mietek Pemper, *The Road to Rescue: The Untold Story of Schindler's List* (New York: Other Press, 2005), 131.

19. Thomas Keneally, *Schindler's List* (New York: Touchstone, 1982), 14.

20. Paldiel quoted in Schrag, "His Jews Recall Liar-Rescuer."

21. Pemper, *The Road to Rescue*, xii.

22. Emilie Schindler quoted in David Crowe, *Oskar Schindler: The Untold Account of His Life, Wartime Activities, and the True Story Behind the List* (New York: Basic Books, 2007), 605.

Chapter 16. Heroes in Waiting

1. Stephen Hawking, *A Brief History of Time: From the Big Bang to Black Holes* (New York: Bantam, 1990), 1.

2. David Hume, *A Treatise of Human Nature*, ed. L. A. Selby Bigge (1739; reprint, Oxford: Clarendon Press, 1896), 254.

3. Richard Ford, *Canada* (New York: HarperCollins, 2012), 384.

4. Lao Tzu, BrainyQuote.com, http://www.brainyquote.com/quotes/quotes/l/laotzu 379182.html, accessed November 11, 2015.

5. The wonderful Gail Winston.

6. Heroic Imagination Project: Transforming Compassion into Heroic Action, November 2012, http://www.heroicimagination.org, accessed October 9, 2015.

7. Philip Zimbardo, personal communication, May 12, 2013.

8. J. M. Darley and B. Latané, "Bystander 'Apathy,'" *American Scientist* 57 (1969): 244–68. The bystanders were actually confederates of the experimenter.

9. Other HIP trainings focus on people's vulnerability to an array of social-psychological forces, including "automatic attributions," "stereotype threat," "labeling and prejudice," "the fixed mindset" and "change blindness." Workshop participants have ranged from elementary school students, to college undergraduates, to leaders in corporate organizations. Successes include the reduction of bullying in schools, helping former gang members come to grips with their past behavior so as to move forward with their lives, and enabling individuals to see that they have the power to create lasting positive change in their own lives and the lives of the people around them.

10. E.g., L. Aknin, E. Dunn, and M. Norton, "Happiness Runs in a Circular Motion: Evidence for a Positive Feedback Loop between Prosocial Spending and Happiness," *Journal of Happiness Studies* 13 (2012): 347–55.

11. Much of this discussion of epigenetics comes from the following sources: T. Powledge, "Behavioral Epigenetics: How Nurture Shapes Nature," *BioScience* 61 (8) (2011): 588–92; G. Miller, "Epigenetics: The Seductive Allure of Behavioral Epigenetics," *Science* 329 (5987) (July 2010): 24–27, doi:10.1126/science.329.5987.24; and "Epigenetics," PBS/NOVA scienceNOW, July 24, 2007, http://www.pbs.org/wgbh/nova/body/epigenetics.html. And special thanks to my biology colleague Jason Bush for his crash course in epigenetics.

12. Cole et al.'s research reported in David Dobbs, "The Social Life of Genes," *Pacific Standard Magazine*, September 3, 2013, http://www.psmag.com/navigation/health-and-behavior/the-social-life-of-genes-64616. This article also offers an excellent overview of the way our social lives impact our genetic activity.

13. G. Miller, N. Rohleder, and S. W. Cole, "Chronic Interpersonal Stress Predicts Activation of Pro- and Anti-Inflammatory Signaling Pathways Six Months Later," *Psychosomatic Medicine* 71 (1) (2009): 57–62, doi:10.1097/PSY.0b013e318190d7de.

14. To put it more precisely, it is the genome that changes itself.

15. Quoted in Dobbs, "The Social Life of Genes."
16. The connection between social experience and epigenetic experience in humans is only beginning to be understood, and, as such, any conclusions need to be considered with caution. See, e.g. Miller, "Epigenetics: The Seductive Allure of Behavioral Epigenetics."

Index